EMOTIONAL EXPERIENCE AND RELIGIOUS UNDERSTANDING

In this book Mark Wynn argues that the landscape of philosophical theology looks rather different from the perspective of a reconceived theory of emotion. In matters of religion, we do not need to opt for objective content over emotional form or vice versa. On the contrary, these strategies are mistaken at root, since form and content are not properly separable here – because 'inwardness' may contribute to 'thought-content', or because (to use the vocabulary of the book) emotional feelings can themselves constitute thoughts; or because, to put the point another way, in religious contexts, perception and conception are often infused by feeling. Wynn uses this perspective to forge a distinctive approach to a range of established topics in philosophy of religion, notably: religious experience; the problem of evil; the relationship of religion and ethics, and religion and art; and in general, the connection of 'feeling' to doctrine and tradition.

DR MARK WYNN teaches philosophy of religion and ethics in the Department of Theology, University of Exeter. He is the author of *God and Goodness: A Natural Theological Perspective* (Routledge, 1999).

EMOTIONAL EXPERIENCE AND RELIGIOUS UNDERSTANDING: INTEGRATING PERCEPTION, CONCEPTION AND FEELING

MARK WYNN

University of Exeter

CAMBRIDGE UNIVERSITY PRESS

CAMBRIDGE UNIVERSITY PRESS

Cambridge, New York, Melbourne, Madrid, Cape Town, Singapore, São Paulo

Cambridge University Press
The Edinburgh Building, Cambridge CB2 2RU, UK

Published in the United States of America by Cambridge University Press, New York

www.cambridge.org
Information on this title: www.cambridge.org/9780521840569

© Mark Wynn 2005

First published 2005

Printed in the United Kingdom at the University Press, Cambridge

A catalogue record for this book is available from the British Library

ISBN-13 978-0-521-84056-9   - hardback
ISBN-10 0-521-84056-2   - hardback
ISBN-13 978-0-521-54089-9   - paperback
ISBN-10 0-521-54989-2   - paperback

For Kate

First, therefore, I invite the reader
to the groans of prayer
   . . . so that he not believe
that reading is sufficient without unction,
speculation without devotion,
investigation without wonder,
observation without joy,
work without piety,
knowledge without love,
understanding without humility,
endeavor without divine grace,
reflection as a mirror without divinely inspired wisdom.

                    Bonaventure, *The Soul's Journey into God*

Contents

Preface

> *The objective accent falls on WHAT is said, the subjective accent on HOW it is said . . .* Objectively the interest is focussed merely on the thought-content, subjectively on the inwardness. At its maximum this inward 'how' is the passion of the infinite, and the passion of the infinite is the truth. But the passion of the infinite is precisely subjectivity, and thus subjectivity becomes the truth.[1]

Why consider the significance of the emotions in religious contexts? In the course of this book, I hope to provide quite a number of reasons for doing so, by showing how the landscape of philosophical theology and philosophy of religion looks rather different from the perspective of a reconceived theory of emotion. But even casual reflection will reveal that arguments about the cognitive status of religious belief often turn on some understanding of the significance of the emotions. Here, for example, is John Macquarrie's summing up of a central strand of the naturalistic critique of religious belief in the nineteenth century and later: 'In the nineteenth century the drift of philosophy had been increasingly in the direction of a mechanistic and materialistic world view, and in England this was powerfully advocated by such thinkers as Bertrand Russell, and, later, Alfred Ayer. The natural sciences were taken to furnish the only basis for assured knowledge, and anything that smacked of religion or mysticism was treated as non-cognitive and banished to the region of "mere emotion".'[2] One might try to evade this critique by keeping emotion out of religion, or at any rate by separating the cognitive bit of religion from the emotional bit – but any serious examination of the psychology of religious belief formation will reveal, will it not, the shaping influence of various kinds of emotional commitment? On this

1 Søren Kierkegaard, in *Kierkegaard's Concluding Unscientific Postscript*, tr. David Swenson and Walter Lowrie (Princeton, NJ: Princeton University Press, 1968), p. 181, Kierkegaard's italics.
2 John Macquarrie, review of Ralph McInerny, *The Very Rich Hours of Jacques Maritain: A Spiritual Life* (University of Notre Dame Press), *Times Literary Supplement*, 27 February 2004 (No. 5265), p. 28.

point, Ayer and other critics of religion are surely right. The quotation at the beginning of this preface suggests a second response, one that does acknowledge the close connection between emotional and religious commitment: let us allow that truth in religion is not after all 'objective' (a matter of 'thought-content' or 'what' is said) but has to do rather with a quality of relationship (with 'how' we rehearse that 'thought-content', and whether we commit ourselves to it with the requisite passionate inwardness).[3] The proposal of this book offers another response again, one which privileges neither the 'what' (as the first response) nor the 'how' (as the second): in matters of religion, we do not need to opt for (emotional) form over (objective) content, the 'how' over the 'what'; nor do we need to rid ourselves of the 'how' to retain the 'what'. On the contrary, these strategies are mistaken at root, since form and content are not properly separable here – because 'inwardness' may contribute to 'thought-content', or because (to use the vocabulary of this book) emotional feelings are intrinsically intentional (themselves constitute thoughts). Or because, to put the point in yet another way, in matters of religion, perception and conception are often infused by feeling. So in response to the question of why we should study the significance of the emotions in religious contexts, we might say: such a study offers the prospect of an account which is at once sensitive to the psychology of religious belief formation, germane to the key assumption of one central tradition of religious scepticism, and attentive to the possibility that the 'how' and the 'what' of religious thought are not always separable.

This book is also animated by the thought that a discussion of these questions is especially opportune just now. In recent years, there has been an explosion of interest in the emotions in a variety of fields, and most notably, for our purposes, in philosophy, neuroscience, and psychology. The central theme of this book is that these developments are potentially of far-reaching importance for our understanding of the significance of the emotions in religious contexts. Of course, there are a number of recent monographs in the philosophy of religion which consider the epistemic importance of the emotions. The outstanding example is perhaps William Wainwright's *Reason and the Heart*. However, this work was published before the most recent developments in philosophical treatments of the emotions to which I have just alluded.[4] Petri Järveläinen's *A Study on*

---

3 Of course, Kierkegaard himself did not deny the 'objective' truth of Christian doctrinal claims.

4 William Wainwright, *Reason and the Heart: A Prolegomenon to a Critique of Passional Reason* (Ithaca, NY: Cornell University Press, 1995). My reading of various historical figures, notably Newman, Edwards, and James, is much indebted to this discussion.

Religious Emotions is a helpful discussion which does engage with these
developments, but his interests are rather different from mine.[5] There are
also various texts which seek to integrate affective experience within a
larger account of the epistemology of religious belief without placing the
emotions at the centre of their analysis. A good example of this strategy is
William Abraham's defence of 'soft rationalism'. This is a stance which
retains a role for evidence and argument (unlike 'fideism') while also
assigning cognitive significance to personal, affectively toned experience
(unlike 'hard rationalism').[6] The discussion of this book could be read as a
filling out of the 'soft rationalist' option in ways that give particular
weight to the epistemic contribution of emotional experience.

As I have suggested, the book can also be read as a reworking of various
established topics in philosophical theology and philosophy of religion in
the light of recent developments in the philosophy (and psychology and
neuroscience) of the emotions. The key themes of the book are these:
emotional feelings can function as modes of value perception – in relation
to God, the world, and individual human beings (Chapters 1–3); they can
also function as 'paradigms', and can therefore properly direct the development of our discursive understanding, in religious and other contexts
(Chapters 4–5); and finally, representations of 'the gods' can be understood by analogy with representation in the arts (Chapter 6). Using these
themes, I seek to re-examine the topics of: religious experience, the
relationship of religion and ethics, and the 'problem of evil' (Chapters
1–3 respectively); the relationship of religion and art and the working
of religious language (Chapter 6); the idea that 'feeling' may run ahead
of 'doctrine' in the way suggested by William James and others (Chapters
4–5), and the idea that feelings, conceptions, and perceptions may contribute to complex wholes which cannot be understood reductively as
simply the sum of their parts (a recurring theme). The discussion is
underpinned throughout by a single presiding idea: that emotional feelings can themselves carry intellectual content. I also argue that in some
cases, this content may not be otherwise available, in which case feeling's
role may be not just constructive, but indispensable. Finally, in Chapter 7,
I consider some religiously motivated objections to the idea that affects

5 Petri Järveläinen, *A Study on Religious Emotions* (Helsinki: Luther-Agricola-Society, 2000). The
 primary differences are these: I shall focus on the role of 'feelings' in constituting (rather than just
 being caused by) thoughts, and I shall give more attention to the idea that religiously significant
 affects need not be evoked by any religiously explicit subject matter. I shall also order my discussion
 around various standard themes in the philosophy of religion.
6 William Abraham, *An Introduction to the Philosophy of Religion* (Englewood Cliffs, NJ: Prentice-
 Hall, 1985), Chapter 9.

can be assigned this sort of significance, and here I argue that my approach is in sympathy with at least one influential tradition of spiritual formation. The central proposals of the book are presented in summary form in Chapters 4-5, where I offer a more comprehensive examination of the developments in philosophy and psychology which provide the immediate rationale for my discussion (Chapter 4) and use this material to formulate four models of the relationship between emotional experience and religious understanding (Chapter 5). The upshot of the discussion is that we need to see religious understanding as a commitment of the person in their intellectual-behavioural-affective integrity.

In writing this book I have of course read with profit the various authors whose works are acknowledged in the text, but I have also benefited from conversations and written exchanges with many friends and colleagues. I would like to thank especially Peter Byrne, John Cottingham, and Peter Goldie, who very generously read and commented upon the typescript in its entirety, and discussed some of the key issues with me in person – thanks to them, the argument is better integrated with the wider literature, and has a much clearer overall focus. I would also like to thank two readers for Cambridge University Press, who offered both encouragement and detailed comment on early drafts of some parts of the book, which proved of great assistance in expanding and reworking the text for publication. I am also grateful to Brian Davies and Richard Swinburne, who first introduced me to philosophical reflection on religion, for their continued interest in my work. I have been fortunate too to have the opportunity to rehearse many of the themes in the book in presentations at the Universities of Durham, Exeter, Glasgow, London (King's College), and Oxford, and the College of St Mark and St John, Plymouth. I have also learnt much from conversations with my colleagues in the field, especially Tim Bartel, Douglas Hedley, Dave Leal, and Tim Mawson. I offer warm thanks too to my colleagues and research students in the Department of Theology at the University of Exeter for their intellectual companionship and hard work on my behalf, and also to my former colleagues, now simply my friends, in the School of Philosophy and the School of Theology of the Australian Catholic University, where my thoughts on these issues first began to take shape. My thanks too to my undergraduate students at Exeter for their vigorous and constructive participation in my 'Emotions, reasons, and faith' class. The text could not have been written without the generous assistance of the University of Exeter and the Arts and Humanities Research Board, which provided for a period of leave from my usual duties during the 2003–4 academic year; and I offer thanks too to Kate Brett and Gillian Dadd of Cambridge University Press and to Pauline Marsh for their energetic, and good-humoured, support, which has made possible the transition from electronic text to the book that is now in your hands. Most importantly, I owe a great debt of gratitude to my family, especially Kate and Rowan, Mum and Dad, Rob and Sarah, Gerard and Vania, and Mark and Sue, together with John and Margaret and the Australian wing of the family: I have not broached these topics much with them, but what I understand of the emotions I owe mostly to their nurture and concern. The book is dedicated to my wife, Kate – friend, guide, and luminous example (in a sense to be expounded in Chapter 2).

Acknowledgements

I am grateful to the Arts and Humanities Research Board for a period of study leave from 1 February to 31 May 2004, and also to the University of Exeter for a period of leave from 1 October 2003 to 31 January 2004.

I am grateful to the publisher for permission to quote from the following articles I have written: 'Representing "the Gods": The Role of Art and Feeling', *Religious Studies* 36 (2000), pp. 315–31 (the editor and Cambridge University Press); 'Valuing the World: The Emotions as Data for the Philosophy of Religion', *International Journal for Philosophy of Religion* 52 (2002), pp. 97–113 (with kind permission of Kluwer Academic Publishers); 'Religion and the Revelation of Value: The Emotions as Sources for Religious Understanding', in T. W. Bartel (ed.), *Comparative Theology: Essays for Keith Ward* (London: SPCK, 2003), pp. 44–54 (the editor and SPCK); 'Saintliness and the Moral Life: Gaita as a Source for Christian Ethics', *Journal of Religious Ethics* 31 (2003), pp. 463–85 (Blackwell Publishing); 'McDowell, Value Recognition and Affectively Toned Theistic Experience', *Ars Disputandi* 4 (2004) [http://www.arsdisputandi.org/] (the editors).

CHAPTER I

Religious experience and the perception of value

John and Joan are riding on a subway train, seated. There are no
empty seats and some people are standing; yet the subway car is not
packed so tightly as to be uncomfortable for everyone. One of the
passengers standing is a woman in her thirties holding two relatively
full shopping bags. John is not particularly paying attention to the
woman, but he is cognizant of her. Joan, by contrast, is distinctly
aware that the woman is uncomfortable . . . John, let us say, often
fails to take in people's discomfort, whereas Joan is characteristically
sensitive to such discomfort. It is thus in character for the discomfort
to be salient for Joan but not for John. That is to say, a morally
significant aspect of situations facing John characteristically fails to
be salient for him, and this is a defect of his character – not a very
serious moral defect, but a defect nevertheless. John misses
something of the moral reality confronting him . . . John's failure
to act stems from his failure to *see* (with the appropriate salience),
not from callousness about other people's discomfort. His deficiency
is a situational self-absorption or attentional laziness.[1]

In these remarks, Lawrence Blum describes a familiar set of circumstances.
Some human beings are habitually more sensitive than others to the needs
of their fellows; and in keeping with this passage we could think of this
sensitivity as involving, on occasions, a kind of 'seeing', one which
requires not just grasping the individual elements of a situation (here is
a woman, carrying some bags, in some discomfort, and so on), but
understanding their relative importance, or seeing them with proper
'salience'. On this account, while John may at some level recognise the
woman's discomfort, this recognition fails to weigh with him appropriately: he is not focally aware of her discomfort, or aware in a way which
involves a grasp of the proper significance of this fact, or aware in a

---

1 Lawrence Blum, *Moral Perception and Particularity* (Cambridge: Cambridge University Press,
1994), pp. 31–3, Blum's italics.

I

fashion that will stir him to action. In this passage, Blum makes no reference to the part that the emotions might play in helping a person to realise the sort of sensitivity that Joan exhibits and John fails to exhibit. But it is natural to think that emotional experience is importantly involved in the kind of capacity that he is describing. Often, it is through our felt responses to others that we grasp their needs at all, and grasp them (so far as we do) with appropriate seriousness. And we ought therefore to acknowledge, in Blum's own terms, 'the necessarily affective dimension to the empathic understanding often (though by no means always) required for fully adequate perception'.[2] So Joan's livelier sense of the woman's needs in Blum's example may be realised in her felt response to the woman's predicament, so that it is in virtue of what she feels for the woman that the woman's predicament assumes due salience in her awareness of the situation; while she is also cognisant of other features of the situation (what colour of coat the woman is wearing, the gestures of a further passenger, and so on), these further features do not weigh with her in the same fashion, because they do not elicit a felt response. To put the point in Nancy Sherman's terms, we could say that: 'Without emotions, we do not fully register the facts or record them with the sort of resonance or importance that only emotional involvement can sustain.'[3] In summary, then, Joan's capacity to recognise the needs of others may well take the form of certain habitual kinds of 'seeing', whereby those needs are acknowledged feelingly.

Blum's example suggests how, in ordinary, everyday contexts, we human beings are capable of a habitual, affectively toned, action-guiding taking stock of a situation, one which turns upon seeing the various elements of the situation in proper proportion, or with due salience. These various themes (of feeling as taking stock, guiding action, grounded in character, and enabling the elements of a situation to be seen with due salience) will all be central to the discussion of this book. In the first three chapters, we shall consider in turn how feelings may play some such role in relationship to 'perception' of God, of other human beings, and of the world as a whole. I shall begin, in this chapter, with a discussion of the contribution of feeling to experience which purports to be of God. This is, I appreciate, a contested starting point. The very idea of experience of God will strike many (believers as well as unbelievers) as conceptually problematic – compare Frederick Copleston's comment that 'the God of Christianity, Judaism, and Islam is not perceptible in

---

2 *Ibid.*, p. 35.
3 *The Fabric of Character: Aristotle's Theory of Virtue* (Oxford: Clarendon Press, 1989), p. 47.

principle'.[4] However, notwithstanding this difficulty, this starting point offers certain advantages. The question of the epistemic status of purported experience of God has been a central topic in recent philosophy of religion. So this issue offers a potentially helpful way of illustrating a larger claim of this book: that the landscape of philosophy of religion looks rather different when considered from the vantage point of a reconceived account of the significance of the emotions. Moreover, Copleston's target is, I take it, the thought that we can identify God as a spatio-temporal particular, in rather the way that we identify physical objects; and that is not the model of experience of God that will figure in our discussion. And a reconceived account of the nature of the emotions will itself make a difference to our understanding of what is involved in an affectively toned experience of God; so even if the notion of such an experience does seem initially problematic (for reasons that we shall examine), it may come to seem less so. Even so, some readers may wish to skip this chapter, or to read it in the spirit of a move being made within a debate whose foundational assumptions are wrong-headed. Readers who take this view will find other, quite different accounts of religious experience in later chapters, accounts which do not take such experience to involve encounter with God considered as a particular object of experience (let alone a spatio-temporally located object of experience).[5] I add one further caution: in this chapter, I am setting myself a relatively modest objective – I am not trying to provide a comprehensive treatment of the epistemic significance of theistic experience, but just to consider how certain standard objections to such experience may be seen in a new light given a reconceived account of the nature of the emotions.

MCDOWELL AND AFFECTIVELY TONED VALUE EXPERIENCE

Blum's remarks cited at the beginning of this chapter broach the possibility that our affective responses provide a mode of sensitivity to interpersonal values. I want to consider next whether this understanding of the

---

4 The comment is cited in Kai Nielsen, *Naturalism and Religion* (New York: Prometheus Books, 2001), p. 245. The comment is made in a review in the *Heythrop Journal*; I have not been able to trace the original source. In this book, Nielsen appeals for a shift in philosophy of religion away from discussion of the traditional arguments for and against the existence of God, and towards the question of 'whether we need a belief . . . in a Jewish, Christian or Islamic God to make sense of our lives and to live really human lives' (p. 21). Nielsen's own position is naturalistic, of course, but I hope that the present book constitutes a kind of response to his appeal to focus upon the connection of religious belief to larger questions of human agency and identity.

5 To name just one example, see the discussion of Chapter 6, where religious experience is understood in terms of recognising patterns in the sensory world.

role of affectively informed experience in disclosing values may be extended to the case of experience of God. I shall be interested in particular in the models of experience of God that have been developed in the work of William Alston and John Henry Newman. But before setting out their views, I am going to sketch another account (to set alongside Blum's) of the idea that affectively toned experience can involve something like a 'perception' of 'moral reality' or values 'in the world' (so that in some cases anyway things affect us favourably because they are of value, rather than their being of value being simply reducible to the fact that they affect us favourably). I shall be concerned specifically with John McDowell's defence of this stance in his paper 'Non-Cognitivism and Rule-Following'.[6] My aim is to show how McDowell's case may help to buttress the understanding of theistic experience that is defended in the work of Alston and Newman.

McDowell's argument takes the form of a response to an objection to a cognitivist reading of moral 'perception'. The objection runs as follows. Just as we can explain our colour experience by reference to qualities in the world which are themselves colourless (the 'primary qualities' of things), so we can explain our value experience by reference to qualities in the world which are themselves value-free. The conclusion to draw, so the argument goes, is that values, like colours, are not part of the fabric of things; they reflect not so much the character of the world as the character of the mind, and its way of apprehending the world. In general outline, the position that is articulated here is very familiar; it is of a piece with (though it does not require) the view that a thing counts as real if it features in the explanations of fundamental physics (or a perfected fundamental physics), and that things which lack an explanatory role in fundamental physics (be they colours, values, or whatever) are not fully real, but have rather to do with the way in which the mind represents to itself what is fundamentally real.

McDowell opposes this line of argument by challenging the distinction it seeks to draw between the element of value experience that can be attributed to value-free qualities 'in the world' and the element that reflects the human subject's contribution, its glossing of the world in the light of its needs and concerns. Perhaps it is possible to draw such a distinction in the case of colour experience, as when we suppose that light of a certain wavelength (where wavelength is understood in quantitative,

6 The paper appears in Steven Holtzmann and Christopher Leich (eds.), *Wittgenstein: To Follow a Rule* (London: Routledge & Kegan Paul, 1981), pp. 141–62.

colour-independent terms) gives rise to a certain kind of colour experience (seeing red, say). But, McDowell suggests, there should be no presumption that we can match up in the same sort of way value-neutral qualities in the world and various kinds of value experience. And in that case, this particular argument for 'non-cognitivism' about values (for the idea that values are simply projected) will fail, since the argument depends on the idea that because some such pairing off is possible, we can trace our value experience to qualities in the world which are value-neutral (and should therefore infer that value experience, so far as it is of anything, is really of these value-neutral qualities which are its source).[7]

McDowell's discussion is of interest to us because although he does not say much explicitly on the point, it is clear that he is thinking of value experience as affectively informed. For instance, he writes of the possibility that 'we can learn to see the world in terms of some specific set of evaluative classifications, aesthetic or moral, only because our affective and attitudinative propensities are such that we can be brought to care in appropriate ways about the things we learn to see as collected together by the classifications' (p. 142). So our question is this: if such affectively toned experience proves relevant to the identification of values in aesthetic and moral contexts, as McDowell proposes, then will it perhaps prove relevant to the identification of values in the case of religious experience? For example, perhaps theistic experience can be understood (in some cases anyway) as a kind of affectively toned sensitivity to the values that 'make up' God's reality? If this sort of case is to be made, it is important to show that an experience may be affectively toned and yet afford access to a value that is not simply the product of the mind's glossing of facts which in themselves are value-free (for on any standard view, God's goodness is not reducible to human responsiveness to a set of facts which in themselves are value-free). And this is the proposal that lies at the heart of McDowell's case.

McDowell does not present a simple knock-down argument for the claim that we cannot match up value-free qualities in the world and kinds of value experience in the way required by his hypothetical interlocutor. The main thread of his case runs as follows:

Consider, for instance, a specific conception of some moral virtue: the conception current in some reasonably cohesive moral community. If the

---

7 In fact, elsewhere McDowell has challenged the idea that this explaining away strategy works even for colours: see 'Values and Secondary Qualities', in J. Rachels (ed.), *Ethical Theory* (Oxford: Oxford University Press, 1998), pp. 228–44, especially pp. 237–8.

disentangling manoeuvre is always possible [i.e., in my terms, disentangling the contribution made to value experience by some value-free quality in the world and the contribution made by the mind], that implies that the extension of the associated term, as it would be used by someone who belonged to the community, could be mastered independently of the special concerns which, in the community, would show themselves in admiration or emulation of actions seen as falling under the concept. That is: one could know which actions the term would be applied to, so that one would be able to predict applications and withholdings of it in new cases – not merely without sharing the community's admiration (there need be no difficulty about that), but without even embarking on an attempt to make sense of their admiration. That would be an attempt to comprehend their special perspective; whereas, according to the position I am considering, the genuine feature to which the term is applied should be graspable without benefit of understanding the special perspective, since sensitivity to it is singled out as an independent ingredient in a purported explanation of why occupants of the perspective see things as they do. But is it at all plausible that this singling out can always be brought off?[8]

McDowell is suggesting, I take it, that the burden of proof in this debate rests on those who subscribe to the possibility of the 'disentangling manoeuvre'. For if such disentangling were possible, then we would be able to grasp the extension of value terms independently of any appreciation of the very 'concerns' which give rise to the use of those terms, and why think that is at all likely? The thesis of the paper is then that arguments for non-cognitivism about values which depend on appeal to the disentangling manoeuvre fail to assume the requisite burden of proof.

To bring out the sense and force of McDowell's remarks, it may help to consider a particular example. Take the quality of being funny or amusing. This quality seems to differ from qualities such as being in motion or being hot in so far as it cannot be specified independently of human reactions.[9] Moreover, it also seems to differ from colour properties, such as the property of being red, even if we suppose that such properties cannot be specified independently of human subjective experience; for we do not have a ready way of grouping all the things that are funny independently of their tendency to provoke amusement, whereas we do have a ready way of grouping all the things that appear red

---

8 McDowell, 'Non-Cognitivism and Rule-Following', p. 144.

9 Compare David Wiggins's discussion of 'the funny' in 'A Sensible Subjectivism', in Stephen Darwall, Allan Gibbard, and Peter Railton (eds.), *Moral Discourse and Practice: Some Philosophical Approaches* (Oxford: Oxford University Press, 1997), p. 232. See also Simon Blackburn on the range of things which we find comic, in his response to McDowell: 'Reply: Rule-Following and Moral Realism', in Holtzmann and Leich (eds.), *Wittgenstein*, p. 167. His remarks are cited below on pp. 26–7.

independently of their tendency to evoke this response (we can appeal to the fact that these things all reflect light of a certain wavelength). So to put the matter in McDowell's terms, whereas the term 'red' has an extension which can be picked out in colour-neutral terms, the extension of the term 'funny' cannot be given without reference to our responses of being amused. To turn to the case that interests us, we might say similarly that the class of morally wrong actions does not constitute a natural set when characterised in the language of physics, because the property of being morally wrong (unlike properties of an empirical kind) has a normative dimension, and its extension is therefore only visible in the light of a normative perspective, rather than the perspective of empirical science.

To summarise, on the view McDowell is challenging, we should 'explain away' value experience in rather the way that we can explain away colour experience: in each case, we should trace the experience to qualities which are themselves value- or colour-free, and therefore read the experience in so far as it involves value or colour as the mind's work (and not the product of a mind-independent reality which really is coloured or valuable). Against this view, McDowell urges that we cannot trace value experience to qualities in the world which are value-free, and the foundational assumption of the argument therefore cannot be sustained.

McDowell's proposal calls for further elucidation and assessment; and I shall return to these matters shortly. But first I want to consider how such an account might in principle be relevant to the case of religiously informed, affectively resonant value experience. Specifically, I want to consider the treatment of such experience in the work of John Henry Newman and William Alston; my aim is to show how the case that they present in support of the possibility of affectively toned theistic experience can be significantly strengthened at points if McDowell's arguments hold good.

ALSTON, AFFECTIVE EXPERIENCE, AND 'PERCEIVING GOD'

In his book *Perceiving God*, William Alston examines what he calls 'mystical perception' or (equivalently) 'direct perception of God'. In general, if one directly perceives X, then 'one is aware of X through a state of consciousness that is distinguishable from X, and can be made an object of absolutely immediate awareness, but is not perceived'.[10] (So my

10 *Perceiving God: The Epistemology of Religious Experience* (Ithaca, NY: Cornell University Press, 1991), p. 22.

awareness of the keyboard before me now will count as a case of direct perception on this account.) Alston goes on to consider the possibility that the state of consciousness through which we perceive God is purely affective in terms of its phenomenal content, and in this connection he writes:

One nagging worry is the possibility that the phenomenal content of mystical perception wholly consists of affective qualities, various ways the subject is feeling in reaction to what the subject takes to be the presence of God. No doubt such experiences are strongly affectively toned; my sample is entirely typical in this respect. The subjects speak of ecstasy, sweetness, love, delight, joy, contentment, peace, repose, bliss, awe, and wonder. Our inability to specify any other sort of non-sensory phenomenal qualities leads naturally to the suspicion that the experience is confined to affective reactions to a believed presence, leaving room for no experiential presentation of God or any other objective reality.[11]

Alston's remarks bring out the importance of our topic: a great deal of religious experience is indeed affectively toned. So an argument that purports to show that affects bear positively or negatively on the question of whether an experience can be taken to be veridical will be, potentially, of considerable importance for any assessment of the epistemic standing of theistic (and other kinds of religious) experience.

In the passage, Alston seems to allow that the phenomenal content of a genuine perception of God might be purely affective, but he regards this possibility as a source of 'nagging worry'. Why should he think of the possibility in these terms? At the beginning of the passage, he characterises the affective component of such an experience as 'various ways the subject is feeling in reaction to what the subject takes to be the presence of God'. It is striking that this formulation assumes that the element of feeling in a mystical perception is a 'reaction' to (what is presumably) a feeling-neutral thought. On this view, it seems that feelings are being construed as rather like sensations (such as the sensation of being bruised), in so far as they do not themselves bear any intentional content (they are not about anything), albeit that they differ from sensations in so far as they are occasioned by a thought, rather than by the impact of an object upon the sense organs. And this does indeed suggest that a theistic experience whose phenomenal content is purely affective will be epistemically dubious. For on this picture, it seems that the feeling component of the experience is not targeted at anything – or if it is, it is directed at the

11 *Ibid.*, pp. 49–50.

thought that God is present, rather than at God qua perceptual object. And that makes it difficult to see how such an experience could count as a case of perception. However, McDowell's discussion invites a rather different characterisation of the role of feeling, as I shall now argue.

We have seen that on McDowell's view, value experience should not be disaggregated into a value-neutral element that derives from 'the world' and a phenomenal element that reflects the mind's contribution to the experience. Instead, we should understand the source of such an experience in value-indexed terms, and accordingly think of values as 'in the world'. Moreover, as we have seen, on McDowell's account, it is by way of our affective responses that we come to recognise these values. As Simon Blackburn puts the matter, on McDowell's view, 'our affective natures expand our sensitivity to how things are, on the lines of any mode of perception'.[12] This suggests a model according to which feelings are ways of taking stock of (evaluative) features of the world, and to that extent, are themselves forms of thought. Indeed, it may be that our felt responses offer our only mode of access to certain values (just as in certain cases, our amused responses may offer our only mode of access to the quality of being funny).

If this is the right way to read McDowell, then his account does indeed pose a challenge to the model of affect that is implied in Alston's remarks. For on McDowell's picture, feelings are being represented as thoughts or perceptions (in the sense of having intentional content, or being about something) in their own right, and not simply by virtue of their association with some thought by which they are caused. By contrast, as we have seen, on Alston's account, feelings seem to be represented as in themselves thought-less, and as occasioned by feeling-less thoughts. It is, I suggest, this rather impoverished account of affect that leads Alston to remark (in the passage just cited) that: 'Our inability to specify any other sort [i.e., some non-affective sort] of non-sensory phenomenal qualities leads naturally to the suspicion that the experience is confined to affective reactions to a believed presence.' This suspicion is only 'natural', I suggest, given the assumption that affectively informed experiences can be (and in general ought to be) disaggregated into a thought component (which is of cognitive significance) and a feeling component (which is of no inherent cognitive significance); given that distinction, but not otherwise, it is natural to analyse an affectively toned experience which appears to be of God as simply an 'affective reaction' to a 'believed presence'. But if

12 'Reply', p. 164.

McDowell is right, then this distinction is open to challenge. So here is a first point where McDowell's discussion proves to be relevant to Alston's account of religious experience. If we adopt McDowell's conception of affective experience (rather than Alston's), it will be easier to see how a religious experience whose phenomenal content is purely affective may, even so, be veridical. Again, this is a matter of some significance, given that religious experience is so often infused by feeling.

In the passage we have been discussing, Alston seems to concede that there is rightly some initial scepticism about the trustworthiness of a mystical perception whose phenomenal content is purely affective. However, he goes on to give an account of how such an experience could be veridical even so, and here he cites an analogy with sense perception: 'even if, as seems possible, sensory phenomenal qualities are as subjective as affective qualities, that does not prevent them serving as a phenomenal vehicle of the perception of objective external realities'.[13] And in that case, Alston asks, could we not suppose similarly that affects may serve as the 'phenomenal vehicle' for the recognition of mind-independent realities? Does this proposal suggest a more generous assessment of the role of affects in theistic experience? Here Alston does seem to allow that feelings may have intentional content: a recognition of the character of 'objective reality' can be realised in affective experience. However, a McDowell-inspired view might still be wary of Alston's analogy, on the grounds that it assimilates sensory and value experience too quickly: unless certain distinctions are noted (concerning the possibility of the 'disentangling manoeuvre'), we might find ourselves allowing that affects have intentional content (just as our phenomenal-colour-informed experience of colour has intentional content), while failing to allow that the 'real' source of that experience is a set of 'objective' value properties. However, in fairness to Alston, he does indicate that he intends the analogy to apply with reference to the 'perception of objective external realities'. Even so, while he admits the possibility of affects playing this sort of role, it is striking that he persists in trying to downplay them (as we shall see again shortly). This suggests to me that while Alston sees no objection of principle to this reading of the significance of affects, he thinks that in practice the model of affects as occasioned by thoughts and as themselves thought-less is truer to our experience (or preferable for some other reason). In that case, we might take McDowell's account as a helpful corrective to the idea that while the affective dimension of an experience

---

13 *Perceiving God*, p. 50.

may bear some cognitive significance in its own right, nonetheless, in standard cases, our evaluative experience should be disaggregated into a thought component and a further, affective component which derives from the thought component and of itself carries no epistemic merit.

There is one other important strand in Alston's account that comes into new focus, I think, when viewed through the lens afforded by McDowell's discussion. Once again, Alston's observations at this point have as their target a perceived difficulty in the notion of 'mystical perception':

> It must be confessed that we are quite incapable of enumerating the basic phenomenal qualities of which 'divine phenomena' are configurations. That's the bad news. But the good news is that we can understand why this should be the case. To see this let's reflect on why it is that we are able to carry off this job for sense perception. The basic point is this. We know quite a bit about the ways in which sensory experience depends in a regular way on its physical, physiological, and psychological conditions. We have discovered quite a bit about the stimulus conditions of various sensory qualities, and we have been able to subject the experience of those qualities to a considerable degree of stimulus control. The more rudimentary forms of these accomplishments predate recorded history; this is why we have had an intersubjectively shared language for sensory qualities since time immemorial . . . But nothing like this has happened with respect to the perception of God, nor is it at all likely to. We know nothing of the mechanisms of such perception, if indeed it is proper to talk of mechanisms here; nor can we grasp any useful regularities in the conditions under which God will appear in one or another qualitatively distinctive way to one's experience. Perhaps such conditions have to do with God's purposes and intentions, and if so that gives us absolutely no handle on prediction and control.[14]

In this passage, Alston is responding to an implied objection to the trustworthiness of mystical perception. The objection maintains that there is a significant disanalogy between mystical and sensory perception, because only in the second case do we have a language for recording the phenomenal content (or more exactly, 'the basic phenomenal qualities') of the experience. This disanalogy poses a threat to Alston's project, I take it, in so far as it implies that religious experience may lack any (coherent) phenomenal content; for if that is so, then we might doubt whether such experience is really experience at all (or at any rate, experience which relates us to a coherent, objective reality). Interestingly, on this point, Alston's reply takes the form of allowing the disanalogy and seeking to explain it. (Contrast the strategy he uses in response to the thought that

14 *Ibid.*, p. 49.

the phenomenal content of mystical perception may be purely affective: here he appeals to a point of similarity between mystical and sense perception.[15])

In the passage just cited, Alston comments: 'We have discovered quite a bit about the stimulus conditions of various sensory qualities, and we have been able to subject the experience of those qualities to a considerable degree of stimulus control.' Now, if McDowell's account is on the right lines, then we might suppose that value and sensory experience are dissimilar in this respect. For while we can construct lawlike correlations between states of the physical world and the sensory experiences to which those states are likely to give rise, we cannot so easily correlate states of the physical world (picked out in scientific or value-neutral terms) and the value experiences to which they are likely to give rise. For example, we can relatively easily correlate the experience of red with various states of the physical world, and thereby we can relatively easily control the stimulus conditions for experience of red; but on McDowell's account, we cannot so readily pick out the stimulus conditions for value qualities, because these qualities cannot be mapped onto states of the physical world with the same neatness of fit – and accordingly, we cannot so easily control the stimulus conditions for value experiences. So if Alston is right to say that the difficulty in constructing a language for divine phenomena has to do with the difficulty in identifying and manipulating stimulus conditions for those phenomena, then McDowell's view seems to offer a further perspective on why such a language may be difficult to construct, by providing a further account of why it should be difficult to control the stimulus conditions of such experiences.

Does the McDowell-style explanation add much to Alston's? In the passage just cited, Alston envisages this possibility: perhaps the stimulus conditions for mystical perception 'have to do with God's purposes and

15 This two-pronged strategy corresponds to the book's appeal to 'double standards' and 'epistemic imperialism' when dealing with objections to religious experience: see *ibid.*, Chapter 6. To expect mystical perception to have a describable phenomenal content, like sensory perception, would be to fall into the error of epistemic imperialism (the error of applying the standards appropriate to sensory experience to experience in general); and to find fault with a mystical perception whose phenomenal content is purely affective while supposing that there is nothing problematic about sensory perception (despite its reliance upon phenomenal colours etc.) would be to fall into the error of applying double standards. Naturally, these approaches point in rather different directions (sometimes Alston is insisting on observing a distinction between sensory and mystical perception, sometimes he is asking for them to be treated similarly), but there is no contradiction here, providing that the two approaches are applied to different aspects of the relationship between sensory and mystical perception.

intentions, and if so that gives us absolutely no handle on prediction and control'. Here Alston may be implying that at least on occasion, God brings about mystical perceptions miraculously, so that there is no possibility even in principle of pairing off such perceptions with stimulus conditions characterised in physical terms. That would give us one account of the difficulty in identifying stimulus conditions for mystical perceptions. But suppose we drop this assumption, and allow that if God brings about a mystical perception in state of the world A, then God will bring about such a perception in a qualitatively indistinguishable state of the world B.[16] Now, on McDowell's account, we have reason to think that, even under these conditions, it will still be relatively difficult to construct a language to record the phenomenology of religious experience. This is because even given this relationship of supervenience (whereby sameness of physical state implies sameness of mystical perception), there will still be no simple way of mapping mystical perceptions onto stimulus conditions, where these stimulus conditions are seen to constitute a natural class when identified in purely physical terms. And in that case, it will be difficult to move from one example of a (partial) stimulus condition for mystical perception (for example, suppose someone has such a perception while watching the sun set) to some more general class of conditions, knowledge of which would enable us to pin down the phenomenal character of mystical perception by replication of those conditions.

So an appeal to the evaluative character of theistic experience seems to constitute a different kind of consideration from that cited by Alston and can therefore play a distinct, though potentially complementary, role within an account of the indescribability of the phenomenal content of theistic experience. This McDowell-inspired approach also constitutes at least a partial response to another, more standard objection to religious experience (an objection pressed by Anthony O'Hear and others).[17] This is the objection that such experiences are epistemically unreliable because they cannot be predicted. But the unpredictability of religious experiences, on the McDowell-style view, may reflect not so much the fact that they are 'merely subjective' (O'Hear's conclusion) as the fact that they

---

16 McDowell is explicit that he is not denying the supervenience of value properties upon non-evaluative properties: see 'Non-Cognitivism and Rule-Following', p. 145.
17 Anthony O'Hear, *Experience, Explanation and Faith* (London: Routledge & Kegan Paul, 1984), Chapter 2. O'Hear also defends here the idea that if theistic experiences were predictable, that would invite a naturalistic account of their origins: so such experiences seem to be discounted in either event.

cannot be correlated with a set of easily circumscribed physical stimulus conditions. And anyone who wishes to be a (McDowell-style) cognitivist about, say, moral experience may be hard-pressed to explain why this fact alone should call into question the reliability of religious experience.

We might wonder whether these reflections throw any light on the comparative difficulty of providing a language to record the phenomenology of religious experience as compared with, say, moral or aesthetic experience. After all, these are all cases of value experience, so on the hypothesis under consideration, shouldn't we expect the phenomenology of each to be equally difficult to capture linguistically? I do not think this does follow, for there is some reason to suppose that the kind of value experience that is relevant in religious contexts makes it especially difficult to undertake the mapping of experiences onto value-neutral stimulus conditions.[18] After all, it is relatively easy to specify, in physical, value-neutral terms, at least some of the conditions that are relevant to classifying an action as kind or cruel. But it is much more difficult to specify, in such terms, the circumstances which present proper stimulus conditions for a mystical perception. Even if the supervenience thesis holds for such experiences, it is very difficult for us to see how to move from one or two examples of acknowledged stimulus conditions to a larger class of stimulus conditions; by contrast, it is relatively easy to move from one or two examples of the stimulus conditions for, say, cruelty (where these conditions are picked out in physical, value-free terms) to at any rate a class (one of several, we might suppose) of stimulus conditions that are relevant to this kind of (dis)value experience, and accordingly it is relatively easy to control the stimulus conditions for the experience of cruelty. Nonetheless, it remains more difficult, I take it, to provide a phenomenology for the experience of moral and aesthetic properties (of the kind that can be registered directly in experience) than to do the same for sensory qualities. And this is surely, at least in part, because it is more difficult to identify the stimulus conditions for, say, 'beautiful' or 'noble' as distinct from, say, 'red'. So the McDowell-inspired account retains some explanatory power on the question of the relative poverty of our language for describing value rather than sensory qualities.

This suggests that an explanation of the difficulties in describing the phenomenal content of theistic experience can usefully deploy the idea that such experiences are evaluative in character – since this idea will

---

18 So perhaps a revised version of O'Hear's objection could be lodged here; but at any rate, this will have to be a new, more nuanced version of the objection.

direct us to the thought that the phenomenology of value experience in general, including religious experience, is relatively difficult to describe when compared to that of sense experience. However, this approach will not provide a comprehensive explanation. For that purpose, further considerations will need to be adduced, addressing the question of why the mapping of value experiences onto stimulus conditions should prove particularly difficult in the case of theistic value experience. One such consideration is presumably that whereas an experience of cruelty is an experience of some going-on in the physical world, an experience of God, even if it supervenes upon some state of the physical world, is not so straightforwardly tied to a particular state of affairs 'in the world', since God is not a mundane object.[19]

In concluding this discussion of Alston, I want to touch on one final strand of his case where, again, he is seeking to downplay the thought that the phenomenal content of theistic experience is purely affective. Having allowed the in-principle possibility of veridical theistic experience whose phenomenal content is purely affective, Alston goes on to try to show that this possibility need not be allowed as a matter of fact. His interest in sustaining this idea shows, I suggest, his continuing reservation about the role of feeling in religious experience. He writes: 'To further shore up the supposition that mystical perception involves distinctive, *nonaffective* phenomenal qualia, we can advert to the doctrine of "spiritual sensations" that was developed in the Catholic mystical tradition.'[20] According to this tradition, as Alston expounds it, although they are non-sensory, certain spiritual experiences in some way resemble touch, while others resemble taste or smell, and so on.[21] However, the examples Alston gives in support of his thesis appear to retain a strongly affective character. For instance, here is an excerpt from the passage he cites to illustrate the idea of a mystical perception which is reminiscent of the experience of smell (the passage is taken from St Teresa's *Interior Castle*): 'Understand me, the

19 It may be, for example, that in at least some cases the supervenience relation holds with reference to the subject's brain states and not in relation to extra-mental states of the world. McDowell's thesis will still have a role to play on this assumption, by helping to explain why the supervenience of mystical perceptions on brain states does not imply a lawlike correlation between mystical perceptions and states of the extra-mental physical world – again, this absence of correlation is required if the stimulus conditions of mystical perception are not to be open to manipulation. The explanation has to do, once again, with McDowell's account of why we should not expect to be able to map value properties onto properties which are characterised in purely physical terms.
20 *Perceiving God*, p. 51, my italics.
21 Alston allows the possibility in principle that mystical perception may be sensory, but thinks that a non-sensory perception 'has a better claim to be a genuine direct perception of God': *ibid.*, p. 36. Hence his interest in the latter sort of case.

soul does not feel any real heat or scent, but something far more delicious, which I use this metaphor to explain.'[22] The thought that references to 'heat' or 'scent' in this connection are strictly metaphorical, and that such experience is 'far more delicious' than any mundane experience, suggests that the quality in question is registered, at least in significant part, through an experience of delight, which implies that affects remain, to say no more, of fundamental importance to the phenomenology of the experience.[23]

Whether or not this is the right way to read Teresa and others who appeal to analogies between spiritual experience and the various modalities of sensory experience, it remains true, I suggest, that ordinary folk who report religious 'perceptions' (as distinct from elevated mystics such as Teresa) are more likely to describe their experience in affective terms than in terms which suggest a non-affective, non-sensory 'intuition' of the divine.[24] Alston would no doubt reply that even if this is so, it may just reflect the relative poverty of our language for describing non-sensory, non-affective experience (see again his comments above). Nonetheless, if the subjects of 'mystical perceptions' describe their experience in feeling-relative terms, then theists who hold to the epistemic value of religious experience may need to show rather more sympathy than Alston for the thought that the phenomenal content of certain religious experiences is in large part (if not entirely) affective. Moreover, quite apart from this sort of sociological kind of consideration, the notion of a non-sensory, non-affective mode of intuition may anyway be problematic. To think again of Blum's example of Joan and John, it seems at any rate a relatively straightforward matter to imagine how feelings may function to reveal value, whereas the idea of a non-sensory, non-affective kind of experience can seem to require a rather speculative extension of the commonly accepted understanding of the nature of our faculties.

The various arguments I have been rehearsing suggest, I hope, that Alston's view and McDowell's can be fruitfully combined on certain points. The resulting approach will build on the thought that there is no easy correlation between value experiences in general and states of the world characterised in purely physical, non-evaluative terms, even granted

---

22 *Ibid.*, p. 53.
23 For further discussion of 'mystical' experience and its relation to affective experience, see Chapter 7.
24 Compare William James's observation on his Gifford Lectures on religious experience: 'In re-reading my manuscript, I am almost appalled at the amount of emotionality which I find in it': *The Varieties of Religious Experience: A Study in Human Nature* (London: Longmans, Green and Co., 1902), p. 486. He adds that he has been dealing with the 'extravagances of the subject', but also that he chose such examples 'as yielding the profounder informations'.

the supervenience of the first on the second. Alston's account does not articulate precisely this idea, but is broadly consistent with it. And, as we have seen, the idea can help to buttress his position on various issues. First of all, it can help to explain why we do not have a more developed vocabulary for describing the phenomenology of religious experience. Secondly, it can help to rebut the objection that if the phenomenal content of religious experience is purely affective (a possibility which we should take seriously, I have argued), then such experience is best interpreted non-cognitively (since affects, at least typically, lack intentional content in their own right). And finally, appeal to McDowell's discussion can help us to see how we might (if only for ad hominem purposes) allow a non-cognitivist reading of colour experience without thereby being committed to a non-cognitivist reading of religious experience. In these various ways, then, McDowell's proposals can be grafted onto Alston's, to produce an account which is more hospitable to the thought that the affective dimension of religious experience is cognitively significant. Next I want to see if McDowell's approach can also be related fruitfully to another well-known defence of religious experience, that offered in the work of John Henry Newman.

NEWMAN, AFFECTIVE EXPERIENCE, AND THE ACQUISITION OF A 'REAL IMAGE' OF GOD

In his *Grammar of Assent*, John Henry Newman draws a much-cited distinction between having a 'notion' and having a 'real image' of God:

> I have tried to trace the process by which the mind arrives, not only at a notional, but at an imaginative or real assent to the doctrine that there is One God, that is, an assent made with an apprehension, not only of what the words of the proposition mean, but of the object denoted by them . . . The proposition that there is One Personal and Present God may be held in either way, either as a theological truth, or as a religious fact or reality. The notion and the reality assented-to are represented by one and the same proposition, but serve as distinct interpretations of it. When the proposition is apprehended for purposes of proof, analysis, comparison, and the like intellectual exercises, it is used as the expression of a notion; when for the purposes of devotion, it is the image of a reality.[25]

25 John Henry Newman, *An Essay in Aid of a Grammar of Assent* (Notre Dame, IN: University of Notre Dame Press, 1979), p. 108.

So the distinction between having a notion and having a real image of God amounts to the distinction between having a verbal appreciation of the divine nature (for 'purposes of proof' and the like) and having an understanding that is grounded in some direct, experiential encounter with God (having an 'apprehension' of 'the object', as Newman puts it). This suggests that Newman conceives of religious experience in much the same way as Alston: for the experience to which he is alluding is of God (or at any rate, of God's 'voice', as he puts it elsewhere),[26] and not of something else as pointing towards God. He is also (like Alston) talking of a mediated apprehension, for it is by way of the data of conscience, on Newman's view, that we are able to experience God. Hence he can write of 'this instinct of the mind recognizing an external Master in the dictate of conscience, and imaging the thought of Him in the definite impressions which conscience creates';[27] or again he envisages that 'in the dictate of conscience . . . [an infant] is able gradually to perceive the voice, or the echoes of the voice, of a Master living, personal, and sovereign'.[28] So this account is clearly akin to Alston's theory, and can be read as a more precise specification of that theory, in so far as Newman proposes that it is our experience in conscience in particular that provides the medium through which we become aware of God. Newman's account also allows for the affective dimension of religious experience. 'Conscience', he writes, 'considered as a moral sense, an intellectual sentiment, is a sense of admiration and disgust, of approbation and blame: but it is something more than a moral sense; it is always what the sense of the beautiful is in only certain cases; it is always emotional.'[29] So Newman is advancing, I suggest, a cognitivist interpretation of affectively toned religious experience (or 'mystical perception');[30] and his proposal is therefore of the same general type as the Alston–McDowell model I sketched just now. Let us

---

26 *Ibid.*, p. 99.

27 *Ibid.*, p. 102. Newman also allows for a more inferential grasp of God's reality by reference to the data of conscience: *ibid.*, p. 101.

28 *Ibid.*, p. 102. The reference to 'echoes' here suggests that Newman's account also allows for an 'indirect' experience of God.

29 *Ibid.*, p. 100.

30 I think that this is the most natural reading of Newman, but other accounts are consistent with what he says. For instance, perhaps our experience in conscience involves a non-affective awareness of responsibility before God, and perhaps this awareness in turn gives rise to feelings of the kind Newman describes. However, Newman's insistence that emotion is central to our experience in conscience, and his suggestion that it is in the experience of (affectively toned) remorse, for example, that we grasp our accountability before God, and thereby acquire a real image of God, suggests to me that the intentionality of the experience is at least in part affectively constituted.

consider now how Newman's discussion might contribute to the further elaboration of that model.

Alston, as we have seen, is struck by the difficulty of verbalising the phenomenology of religious experience. There is a related idea implied in Newman's distinction between a real image and a notion of God. A notion involves, as we have seen, a verbally expressible understanding. By contrast, the content of a real image of God exceeds our powers of verbalisation, and can only be grasped in full by way of relevant morally and affectively informed experience. Now, Newman may think, with Alston, that it is difficult to describe the phenomenology of religious experience, but what he says is simply that it is difficult to capture verbally, in full, the understanding of God that is vouchsafed in such experiences. How should we understand the relation between these two views?

To appeal to McDowell again, there are reasons for thinking that Alston's perspective on this point implies Newman's. For the upshot of McDowell's discussion is that the phenomenology of value experience is not dispensable for the purpose of identifying its source in the way that the phenomenology of colour experience is dispensable (from the per-spective of some commentators) for the purpose of identifying its source. To rehearse again a point that will be familiar by now, on a projectivist reading of colour experience, the phenomenology of such experience fails to reveal what the world is really like, for the qualities in the world that give rise to the experience are colourless; by contrast, says McDowell, in the case of value experience, we cannot draw the same distinction between what appears (values) and the qualities 'in the world' which give rise to this appearance. So on this view, a difficulty in recording the phenomen-ology of value experience implies also a difficulty in recording the charac-ter of the 'object' which is the source of that experience. Hence, to apply this idea to the case of affectively toned religious experience, a difficulty in describing the phenomenology of such experience (this is Alston's point) implies a difficulty in describing the 'object' (God) which is the source of that experience – and this latter thought is the idea advanced in Newman's proposal that theistic experience involves a real image (as distinct from a notion) of God.

So Newman's cognitivist account of affectively informed religious experience complements the model that we have derived from Alston and McDowell, by advancing a claim that is implied (but not explicitly articulated) in the Alston–McDowell account, namely, the claim that there are difficulties in verbalising (in full) the character of the God who is revealed in affectively toned theistic experience.[31] It is worth noting that Newman's proposal here involves the idea, one I have already attributed to McDowell, that feelings can be intrinsically intentional: that is, they can bear an intellectual content in their own right, and not simply a content that belongs more properly to the discursive (verbalisable) thoughts (or 'notions') with which they are associated – for in the case of a real image of God, he is saying, a certain understanding of God is lodged in feeling, and not otherwise expressible. On this point, his approach offers a striking anticipation of the turn taken in recent philosophical discussion of the emotions.[32]

So the Alston–McDowell model implies Newman's teaching on the distinction between having a notion and having a real image of God. But what justification does Newman himself offer of this teaching? In part, no doubt, Newman thinks of the 'image' of God realised in religious experience as unverbalisable because this is a familiar theme of the mystical literature. But he also has a more philosophical kind of reason for advancing this idea. His thought is, I suggest, that it is difficult to express the content of a real image of God in verbal terms because such an image depends upon an encounter with a particular object. Here Newman is presupposing a distinction between knowledge which involves a kind of 'acquaintance' with its object (resting on a direct experiential encounter) and knowledge by description. Because knowledge by description trades upon the general categories of a language, he seems to think, it will never be able to capture in all its particularity the content of knowledge by acquaintance. On this view, value (including religious) experience is not (in this respect) radically different from sense experience: what I know by acquaintance of the colour of the apple before me also transcends what I can set down in words. That this is Newman's teaching is implied, for example, in the passage I cited above, where he writes that a real assent (one involving a real image) is 'an assent made with an apprehension, not only of what the words of the proposition mean, but of the object denoted by them'. Here we find that the notion/image distinction corresponds to a distinction between the sort of knowledge that turns on knowing the meanings of words (knowledge by description) and the sort that involves knowing an object first hand, by way of direct experiential encounter.

---

31 Alston himself criticises standard accounts of 'ineffability' in *Perceiving God*, pp. 31–2.
32 See, for instance, Peter Goldie, *The Emotions: A Philosophical Exploration* (Oxford: Oxford University Press, 2000), pp. 59–60. For an exposition of these developments, see below, Chapter 4.

We might press Newman on the question of why we should suppose that the content of knowledge by acquaintance is, at least in part, unverbalisable. To revert to the case of seeing an apple, the physicist surely does have the necessary concepts to describe exhaustively what I grasp by acquaintance of a given apple's dimensions, weight, and so on, in so far as what I grasp in these respects can be expressed in quantitative terms. By contrast, we do not have the language to capture in all its particularity the apple's phenomenal appearance as a mix of particular shades of red and green and so on. Why should we have the concepts required to describe the apple in terms of its dimensions and other quantitative properties but not in terms of its phenomenal colours? This is a consequence, I suggest, of the simplifying power of quantitative descriptions: I can grasp conceptually the full number range required to express the mass, dimensions, velocity, etc. of any material object. By contrast, I cannot grasp so simply, in terms of distinguishable concepts, the full colour range required to describe precisely the appearance of an apple. This is not to say that the qualitative appearance of the apple is in principle indescribable (we could, after all, invent a vocabulary for an apple of precisely this colour); but it explains why for practical purposes we lack the necessary richness of language.

So we can elaborate upon Newman's account as follows: the content of a real image of God is not fully expressible in verbal terms because such an image involves knowledge by acquaintance; and, we might now add, knowledge by acquaintance is not fully expressible in verbal terms where it concerns phenomenal colours or, to generalise, where it concerns the non-quantifiable appearance of things. We need to ask now, of course: why is experience of God (of the kind implied in having a real image of God) apt to resist description in quantitative terms? The Alston–McDowell account yields an answer to this question: we should think of the source of religious experience as a set of value-indexed qualities, and not some set of properties which can be adequately characterised in quantitative (or in general, in non-normative) terms.[33] Moreover, whereas it might be

---

33 For another perspective on the difficulty of quantifying value properties, see criticisms of utilitarian attempts to subject value questions to a calculus. Aesthetic experience offers another good example of how value properties may prove to be incommunicable in purely verbal terms, and may require indeed a specially focused kind of first-hand experience, involving repeated exposure to an object. Consider, for example, these remarks of Frank Sibley: 'It is of importance to note first that, broadly speaking, aesthetics deals with a kind of perception. People have to *see* the grace or unity of a work, *hear* the plaintiveness or frenzy in the music, *notice* the gaudiness of the colour scheme, *feel* the power of a novel, its mood, or its uncertainty of tone. They may be struck by these qualities at once, or they may come to perceive them only after repeated viewings,

possible to argue that our knowledge of phenomenal colours is really knowledge of facts which can be specified in purely quantitative terms, if McDowell is right, then the same cannot be said of our knowledge of the phenomena of value experience (including, we might add, the phenomena of religiously informed value experience) – for in this case, we cannot get behind the appearances to a source which can be characterised in non-evaluative, purely quantitative terms. So McDowell's treatment of value experience suggests that a real image of God will involve the sort of knowledge by acquaintance whose content cannot be fully expressed in quantitative terms; and thereby it suggests (with Newman) that the content of a real image of God will not admit of a precise verbal paraphrase. Here is a further example, then, of how McDowell's approach can throw new light on a familiar picture of religious experience.

As we have seen, the Alston–McDowell model also provides an account of why it should be difficult to verbalise the understanding of God that is realised in mystical perception. This account involves, first of all, the thought that it is difficult to identify and control the stimulus conditions of value experience, and therefore difficult to describe the phenomenology of such experience; it then adds that in the case of value experience (including religious experience), a difficulty in describing the phenomenology of the experience implies also a difficulty in describing the source of the experience. By contrast, Newman's account (as developed above) starts from the thought that in general the qualitative appearance of things is difficult to describe (even if those things are physical objects), and it goes on to claim that the source of a mystical perception can only be adequately identified in non-quantitative terms. These accounts are distinct but not in conflict; indeed, they move from their different starting points to their common conclusion (that it is difficult to verbalise the understanding of God that is realised in 'mystical perception') by way of the McDowell-inspired thought that in the case of value experience, there is no route behind the appearances to identify the real source of the experience.

hearings, or readings, and with the help of critics. But unless they do perceive them for themselves, aesthetic enjoyment, appreciation, and judgement are beyond them. Merely to learn from others, on good authority, that the music is serene, the play moving, or the picture unbalanced is of little aesthetic value; the crucial thing is to see, hear, or feel': 'Aesthetic Concepts', reprinted in John Benson, Betty Redfern, and Jeremy Roxbee Cox (eds.), *Approach to Aesthetics: Collected Papers on Philosophical Aesthetics of Frank Sibley* (Oxford: Clarendon Press, 2001), pp. 34–5, Sibley's italics. I am grateful to Peter Goldie for drawing my attention to this passage. As Goldie has noted in correspondence, the verbal incommunicability, or ineffability, of a property need not imply its incommunicability *tout court*: I can, after all, communicate the quality of a piece of music to you by getting you to hear the music for yourself.

We have been exploring the idea that affectively toned theistic experience may be cognitively significant not in spite of but on account of its affective dimension – because feelings may be intrinsically intentional. That is, they may be themselves a mode of perception, and in particular, a way of taking stock of values. This argument hinges, of course, upon the case that McDowell has made for a parallel interpretation of affectively toned ethical experience. In concluding this chapter, I want to examine in a little more detail the cogency of that case. I shall take Simon Blackburn's response to McDowell as a starting point for this question.

BLACKBURN'S CRITIQUE OF MCDOWELL

In his book *Ruling Passions*, Simon Blackburn offers a number of alleged counterexamples to McDowell's cognitivist reading of affectively toned moral experience.[34] Here is one of his examples, which concerns the value term 'cuteness':

Here we imagine a man happily deploying this term, and happily possessed of a perceptual/affective amalgam corresponding to it. He and his cohort see women as cute . . . They have read McDowell, and take themselves to have a new, genuinely cognitive, sensitivity to the cuteness of some women . . . Cuteness, our man says, elicits and justifies various affective reactions. It is hard to specify them except as perceptions of cuteness.[35]

Now, the 'disentangling manoeuvre' is not only possible here, Blackburn maintains, but morally required. He continues:

it is *morally* vital that we proceed by splitting the input from the output in such a case. By refusing to split we fail to open an essential specifically *normative* dimension of criticism. If the last word is that these people perceive cuteness and react to it with the appropriate cuteness reaction, whereas other people do not, we have lost the analytic tools with which to recognize what is wrong with them. What is wrong with them is along these lines: they react to an infantile, unthreatening appearance or self-presentation in women . . . with admiration or desire (the men) or envy and emulation (the women). Cute things are those to which we can show affection without threat, or patronizingly, or even with contempt . . . Applied to women, this, I say, is a bad thing. Once we can separate input from output enough to see that this is what is going on, the talk of . . . a special perception available only to those who have been acculturated, simply sounds hollow.[36]

---

34 Simon Blackburn, *Ruling Passions: A Theory of Practical Reasoning* (Oxford: Clarendon Press, 1998).
35 *Ibid.*, p. 101.   36 *Ibid.*, pp. 101–2, Blackburn's italics.

What should we make of this example? It seems to me that Blackburn is right about the importance of undertaking the 'disentangling man-oeuvre' (and distinguishing 'input' from 'output') in this case. But this example trades on our sense that cuteness is indeed an inappropriate characterisation; this is why we are reluctant to see it as grounded in an affectively toned 'perception', and why it is indeed 'morally vital' to substitute instead a projectivist account of the quality. So even someone who is, overall, in favour of McDowell's account will agree with the appropriateness of a projectivist reading here, providing, of course, that they share Blackburn's moral assessment of cuteness. A more testing example would require a case where the response is deemed morally appropriate. It is precisely this sort of case, and the sense of its distinction from the cuteness kind of case, that generates the cognitivist account in the first place: the cognitivist appeals to the idea of an affectively toned perception of certain values 'in the world' in order to sustain a distinction between those value claims that are grounded in the nature of things and those (such as judgements of cuteness) that are best understood in projectivist terms.

So the cuteness example (along with others that Blackburn cites) is, I suggest, neutral between Blackburn's view and the view of McDowell, since it is (or ought to be) common ground that this example is to be construed in projectivist terms. If Blackburn is to make his case, he needs, rather, to show that he can give a better account than the cognitivist of our sense that some value claims are more worthy of endorsement than others. Naturally, Blackburn also has a view on this further question. In particular, he proposes that we can take ourselves to have knowledge of ethical matters because we can grasp that some of our value assessments are incapable of being improved. Here he quotes Hume's remark: 'Temperance, sobriety, patience, constancy, perseverance, forethought, considerateness, secrecy, order, insinuation, address, presence of mind, quickness of conception, facility of expression; these and a thousand more of the same kind, no man will ever deny to be excellences and perfections.'[37] Blackburn comments:

Hume's list reflects a certain Scottish standpoint, but one sees what he is getting at. Perhaps I can contemplate as a bare possibility that some change should come along and 'improve' me into thinking that these are not after all standards for a

---

37 *Enquiry Concerning the Principles of Morals*, VI.I, in David Hume, *Enquiries Concerning Human Understanding and Concerning the Principles of Morals* ed. L. A. Selby-Bigge, 3rd edn, revised by P. H. Nidditch (Oxford: Clarendon Press, 1975), p. 242.

good character. But I cannot really see how to take off the inverted commas, or in other words imagine how any such change would really be an improvement. The possibility remains idle, unreal. So I can quite properly claim to know that some things count as virtues and others do not.[38]

Blackburn goes on to contrast this sort of judgement with his belief that the government ought to introduce a minimum wage. He notes that it is easy enough to imagine how he might improve his view on this issue, given his sketchy understanding of the relevant economic data and theory.

So Blackburn has an account of what makes some value judgements worthy of the title of knowledge. But from the perspective of a McDowell-style cognitivism, this account still fails, of course, to explain satisfactorily how a value judgement that constitutes knowledge is grounded in the nature of things. All we can say on Blackburn's approach is that value judgements count as knowledge if they properly register the character of relevant non-evaluative facts (facts recorded in economic theory, for example) and if our reactions to these non-evaluative facts are freed from 'insensitivities, fears, blind traditions, failures of knowledge, imagination, sympathy'.[39] If these conditions are satisfied, then we cannot see how our perspective might be open to improvement, and that is sufficient reason for supposing that the perspective counts as knowledge. So on this view, all we have is certain non-evaluative facts and a reaction to them (a reaction we think beyond improvement). A cognitivist account of values will go one step further, and offer an explanation of the appropriateness of the reaction in cases of knowledge: in these cases, the cognitivist will say, the value judgement not only is cognisant of relevant non-evaluative facts, but subjects them to assessment in the light of relevant evaluative facts.

I shall not attempt to adjudicate this dispute here, in general terms (and I shall argue shortly that given our relatively modest aims, there is no need to do so). But it is worth noting that from a theistic perspective, the cognitivist account of our value judgements seems superior, at any rate in the case of value judgements which concern God. On Blackburn's approach, the judgement that God is good can be counted as knowledge if it is the sort of judgement we would reach once acquainted with relevant non-evaluative facts and providing that we have overcome fearfulness, insensitivity, and any failure of imagination, sympathy, etc. But on the theistic view, while it may be true enough that we would form the

---

38 *Ruling Passions*, p. 307.
39 'Reply', p. 175. On this view, such 'insensitivities' presumably count as defects because they imply a failure to grasp non-evaluative facts.

judgement that God is good under the conditions described, there is something further to be said: the reason why someone who is acquainted with relevant non-evaluative facts and who has purged themselves of various failures of affective response will conclude that God is good is that being in such a state enables a right appreciation of the fact of God's being good. To suppose that this further step cannot be taken is to suppose that whether or not God is good is ultimately contingent upon our particular human sensibility (and our tendency to form the judgement that God is good under the conditions specified). But a theist will surely want to say that far from our judgements providing a criterion for the goodness of God, it is the goodness of God that provides a criterion for the adequacy of our judgements. It is only if our judgements issue in the claim that God is good (under the conditions specified) that our sensibility can be said to be trustworthy on this question. So even if we do not resolve the question of whether the further explanatory step taken by the cognitivist about values is in general appropriate, it seems at any rate that some such step is required by traditional theism where judgements about the goodness of God are concerned.[40] (And taking that step in relation to God will surely carry implications for our understanding of the status of evaluative standards more generally, in so far as they are in some way tied to the goodness of God.)

There is a further key point of disagreement between McDowell and Blackburn that emerges in the original symposium exchange. Here we return to the analogy between value and comic experience that I invoked at the outset to make sense of McDowell's proposal. Blackburn writes:

it is notoriously difficult or impossible to circumscribe exactly all those things which a member of our culture finds comic. Any description is likely to have a partial and disjunctive air which would make it a poor guide to someone who does not share our sense of humour, if he is trying to predict those things which we will and will not find funny . . . Let us describe this by saying that the grouping of things which is made by projecting our reactive tendency onto the world is *shapeless* with respect to other features. The puzzle then is why McDowell sees shapelessness as a problem for a projective theory. The necessary premise must be that a reactive tendency cannot be shapeless with respect to those other features which trigger it off, whereas a further cognitive ability can pick up features which are shapeless with respect to others. But why? Do we really support a realist theory of the comic by pointing out the complexity and shapeless nature of the class of things we laugh at? On the contrary, there is no

40 Compare Peter Byrne, *The Philosophical and Theological Foundations of Ethics: An Introduction to Moral Theory and its Relation to Religious Belief* (Basingstoke: Macmillan, 1992), p. viii.

reason to expect our reactions to the world simply to fall into patterns which we or anyone else can describe.[41]

Against this line of thought, McDowell suggests that if the non-cognitivist endorses the shapelessness thesis, then 'there need be no genuine same thing (by the non-cognitivist's lights) to which successive occurrences of the non-cognitive extra [the felt response] are responses'. He continues that in that case, 'non-cognitivism must regard the attitude as something which is simply felt (causally, perhaps, but not rationally explicable); and uses of evaluative language seem appropriately assimilated to certain sorts of exclamation, rather than to paradigm cases of concept-application'.[42]

What should we make of this exchange? Suppose we take for granted that when characterised in non-evaluative terms, the classes of things which elicit our value (including our moral, aesthetic, and religious) responses are shapeless. Both parties to the dispute accept this claim. McDowell continues: since the non-cognitivist does not recognise any evaluative properties 'in the world', they must infer that our value responses involve no consistent sensitivity to a particular class of things (although given the supervenience thesis, or some analogue of it of the kind that Blackburn could accept, there will still be some sort of weakly patterned relationship between stimulus source characterised in non-evaluative terms and value response); and in that case, our value responses do not conform to standard cases of concept application. In reply, Blackburn wants to know why the cognitivist is not in the same boat, since they also subscribe to the shapelessness thesis. Here McDowell would say, I take it, that from the value perspective (but not otherwise), we can see our value responses as tracking shapely properties in the world. I think that both sides have a measure of truth here. Blackburn is right to think that shapelessness does not refute his position: after all, why should the non-cognitivist (of all people) suppose that our value responses do track coherent, 'shapely' properties in the world? But McDowell is also partly right: he shows, I think, how shapelessness is consistent with the thought that our value experience does pick out genuine properties 'in the world', where the qualities in question are normative and only discernible in the light of our value experience. If this is the right way of reading this exchange, then the result is a kind of stand-off. McDowell fails to establish that non-cognitivism is defeated by the shapelessness of

41 'Reply', p. 167.   42 'Non-Cognitivism and Rule-Following', p. 158.

moral and other value properties; and Blackburn fails to establish that cognitivism falls in the face of the same phenomenon.

However, this weaker reading of what McDowell has shown is sufficient, I suggest, for the model of affectively toned theistic experience that we have been exploring. For that model does not seek to provide a simple knock-down disproof of the non-cognitivist approach; rather, it is an attempt to turn aside certain objections to a cognitivist reading of affectively toned theistic experience. And in the ways we have explored, McDowell's account does help to show how various features of religious experience do not after all establish any presumption in favour of a non-cognitivist view. It may be true that the phenomenal content of theistic experience is purely affective; it may be true that we cannot describe the phenomenology of such experience, or its object, at all precisely; it may be true that such experiences are unpredictable – but by reference to McDowell, we can see that none of these considerations constitutes a decisive reason for adopting a non-cognitivist interpretation of affectively toned theistic experience. And if these familiar objections to the veridicality of affectively toned theistic experience can be turned aside, then it will be at any rate more difficult to sustain any presumption that such experiences are in general unreliable.

CONCLUSIONS

In this chapter, after a preliminary exposition of the idea that affective experience can disclose values (by reference to Blum's example of Joan and John), I have sought to bring into fruitful relationship three strands of reflection: on the one side, John McDowell's cognitivist reading of value experience and, on the other side, the view of affectively toned theistic experience that is expounded in the writings of John Henry Newman and William Alston. The resulting account of theistic experience is built around a number of focal claims, notably these. We should not expect to find any lawlike correlation between the values disclosed in 'mystical perceptions' and non-evaluative features of the world, and accordingly, there is no presumption that such experience has as its real object or source some non-evaluative feature of the world rather than a genuine value quality. In turn, this suggests that affectively toned theistic experience may constitute a mode of value perception, and may be veridical even if its phenomenal content is purely affective. This account is consistent with the general drift of what Alston and Newman have to say, and helps to answer certain questions that are raised by their discussions, including questions such as 'Why should the phenomenology of religious experience not be more easily describable?' (an issue for Alston) and 'Why should the understanding of God that is achieved in religious experience not be more easily describable?' (an issue for Newman).

Here is one case, then, where attending to the relationship between emotional experience and religious understanding, in the light of the thought that feelings may constitute modes of perception, promises to yield new perspectives on a basic question in religious epistemology, namely, the question of the cognitive significance of religious experience. I have explored just one dimension of this large issue (examining the implications of one proposal of John McDowell), but I hope that the arguments we have reviewed establish at least the potential fruitfulness of this kind of approach. In the course of this chapter, we have relied upon the idea that value experience is to be treated in broadly the same way in religious and moral contexts. Next I would like to turn more explicitly to the relationship between religious and ethical commitments. This is, of course, to broach another well-worn topic in the history of philosophical theology. Again, our approach to the question will be shaped by particular attention to the contribution of emotional experience to our moral and religious understanding.

CHAPTER 2

Love, repentance, and the moral life

The patients were judged to be incurable and they appeared to have irretrievably lost everything which gives meaning to our lives. They had no grounds for self-respect insofar as we connect that with self-esteem; or, none which could be based on qualities or achievements for which we could admire or congratulate them without condescension . . . A small number of psychiatrists did, however, work devotedly to improve their conditions. They spoke, against all appearances, of the inalienable *dignity* of even those patients. I admired them enormously . . . One day a nun came to the ward. In her middle years, only her vivacity made an impression on me until she talked to the patients. Then everything in her demeanour towards them – the way she spoke to them, her facial expressions, the inflexions of her body – contrasted with and showed up the behaviour of those noble psychiatrists. She showed that they were, despite their best efforts, condescending, as I too had been. She thereby revealed that even such patients were, as the psychiatrists and I had sincerely and generously professed, the equals of those who wanted to help them; but she also revealed that in our hearts we did not believe this.[1]

This passage turns on a distinction between what a person may sincerely profess on some moral matter and what they really ('in their hearts') believe. The psychiatrists are good, well-meaning people: they have an articulate and apparently high-minded understanding of the worth of their patients, and hold to the thought that these patients are genuinely their equals; and yet their behaviour reveals that at some more profound level, they have failed to appropriate this idea: it is not an idea they embody, not something they believe 'in their bones', or can act on with conviction. This account suggests that moral understanding, at its deepest and most effective in action, may be lodged in our felt responses to others

---

1 R. Gaita, *A Common Humanity: Thinking about Love and Truth and Justice* (Melbourne: The Text Publishing Company, 2000), pp. 17–19, Gaita's italics.

(how we think of them 'in our hearts'), rather than in some more discursive account of their significance. There is a parallel here with Newman's understanding of what is required for a religiously deep appreciation of God. The psychiatrists in the passage have as it were a 'notional' appreciation of their patients' value (a verbally formulated account of their worth or dignity); but the nun's appreciation is more profound: she has a 'real image' of the patients, that is, a sense of their importance that is grounded in an affectively resonant responsiveness to them. So the understanding of feeling that is implied in this passage is broadly of the kind that we explored in Chapter 1. There we considered the import of such a view for the topic of religious experience; in this chapter, I want to take the same sort of account of feeling, and consider its implications for the relationship between religious and ethical understanding.

The case of Chapter 1 was developed in dialogue with John McDowell's account of affectively toned value experience. In this chapter, I would like again to take a contemporary commentator's work as the springboard for discussion. This time the author is Raimond Gaita, whose experiences are recounted in the passage above.[2] Gaita defends a view of moral experience and its authority which is distinct from that propounded by contemporary Kantians, utilitarians, and virtue theorists, not least because of the role it accords to our felt responses to other human beings. I shall argue that this account suggests a more fruitful conception of the relationship between ethical and religious commitment than is implied in the prevailing ethical theories. In developing this thesis, my focus will be explicitly upon Christian ethics, and the relationship between Gaita's moral scheme and such an ethics.

Gaita does not consider himself religious, but his work has obvious religious, and specifically Christian, resonances. This suggests two possibilities, both of which I shall examine here. Perhaps Gaita is right to think that his project can be carried through independently of any religious commitment. In that case, his work could be read as a kind of contemporary natural law ethic, in the sense of providing a route to conclusions which Christians will find sympathetic without appeal to explicitly Christian premises. Alternatively, it may be that Gaita's work invites completion in religious terms, in which case it could be read as a prolegomenon to a fuller, more religiously engaged conception of our relationship with

---

2 There are clear parallels between Gaita's work and McDowell's. As we shall see, Gaita thinks that moral qualities are revealed in our felt responses, and cannot be matched up simply with qualities picked out in empirical terms.

other human beings. I shall develop these themes by reference to his books *Good and Evil: An Absolute Conception* (1991) and *A Common Humanity: Thinking About Love and Truth and Justice* (2000).[3] I shall begin by discussing Gaita's objections to a number of standard moral philosophical theories before setting out his alternative conception of the subject and its bearing on our question. His own view, as we shall see, can sound rather counterintuitive on first hearing; it is important therefore to consider the difficulties he finds in other approaches if his own stance, and the role he assigns to feeling, is to seem adequately motivated. We shall see that Gaita's objections to the standard moral philosophical theories already align him with a broadly Christian moral perspective.

OBJECTIONS TO CONTEMPORARY MORAL PHILOSOPHICAL THEORIES

Gaita's writings are characterised by their attention to particular examples of human interaction. I shall quote some of these examples at length since, as we shall see, his general stance suggests that they are not intended to be merely illustrative of ideas that can be adequately conveyed in a more abstract idiom. I shall return shortly to the example cited at the beginning of the chapter; but consider first this further passage which on Gaita's view helps to establish the deficiency of standard philosophical accounts of our moral relations with other people. The character M here is grieving over her recently deceased child.

M was watching a television documentary on the Vietnam War which showed the grief of Vietnamese women whose children were killed in bombing raids. At first she responded as though she and the Vietnamese women shared a common affliction. Within minutes, however, she drew back and said, 'But it is different for them. They can simply have more.' . . . M did not mean that whereas she was sterile they were not. Nor did she mean that as a matter of fact Vietnamese tended to have many children. Hers was not an anthropological observation. She meant that they could replace their dead children more or less as we replace dead pets.[4]

Given this understanding, M is unable to see how the Vietnamese might be wronged as 'we' are wronged. And yet she is able to attribute to the Vietnamese all those qualities that figure in standard philosophical

---

3 See *Good and Evil: An Absolute Conception* (Basingstoke: Macmillan, 1991) and *A Common Humanity*, cited in n. 1 above. Although I shall not refer to it in my discussion, Gaita's autobiographical work *Romulus, My Father* (Melbourne: Text Publishing, 1998) is also an important source for understanding his moral philosophy. See, for instance, the depiction of his father's relationship to the insane Vacek.

4 *A Common Humanity*, pp. 57–8.

accounts of personhood. She can agree that they are self-directing, self-conscious, capable of reflecting upon their first-order desires, and so on.[5] But her recognition of the Vietnamese as 'persons' in this sense fails to provide the conceptual resources for a grasp of their moral significance. Gaita draws the conclusion that standard accounts of the nature of moral requirements are unable to capture their distinctive content:

> If rational negotiators, deploying the Spartan rationality and the kind of raw materials that M can attribute to the Vietnamese, devise rules more or less like our moral rules, covering the same range and kinds of conduct, they would not thereby capture what it means to wrong someone. Whatever reasons we may have to assent to such rules, therefore, they are not the reasons why we accept morality's authority over us.[6]

Here Gaita rejects standard Kantian and contractarian accounts of what is at stake in our moral relations with others. Christian ethicists, I suggest, have their own reasons for finding this conclusion attractive, especially in so far as the contractarian emphasis upon our powers of rational self-direction leaves the moral standing of certain human beings, for instance, the cognitively disabled, open to question.[7]

In this passage, Gaita is also rejecting, at least implicitly, utilitarian theories of the moral significance of others, for M can also attribute to the Vietnamese a capacity for pleasure and pain, or happiness and suffering; but even so, she seems to lack the concepts which are required for a full appreciation of the sense in which, morally speaking, these others set a limit on our will. In fact, much of Gaita's work is concerned with the deficiencies of consequentialist theories of ethics. The fundamental objection to such theories which he poses is that they treat the benefits and harms which are relevant in moral deliberation as adequately characterisable in non-moral terms (and therefore fail to count as theories of moral good and evil).[8] This is to overlook, Gaita maintains, the sense in which evil-doers harm themselves, necessarily, simply by virtue of being evil-doers. This is a theme to which we shall return when we consider Gaita's remarks on the

---

5 Gaita makes this point *ibid.*, pp. 259–60.   6 *Ibid.*, p. 260.

7 Compare, for example, Michael Allen Fox's awkward attempted accommodation of human beings with intellectual disabilities: 'Let us say, then, that although underdeveloped or deficient humans are also, like animals, not full members of the moral community because they lack autonomy, they must nevertheless fall within the most immediate extension of the moral community and as such are subject to its protection': 'The Moral Community', in H. LaFollette (ed.), *Ethics in Practice* (Oxford: Blackwell, 1997), p. 136. I take it that the language of 'immediate extension' must be judged too weak for any properly Christian account of the sense in which people with intellectual disabilities are members of the moral community.

8 He puts the point this way in *Good and Evil*, p. 57.

subject of remorse. But as with his stance on the adequacy of contrac-
tualist theories of ethics, so in this case Gaita's approach is likely to
recommend itself to Christian commentators, because of its insistence
that 'consequences' (characterised as utilitarians typically characterise
them) are not sufficient to fix the moral standing of an action.

Introductory accounts of ethical theory usually enumerate three such
theories, distinguishing virtue ethics from Kantian and utilitarian perspectives. Gaita is also critical of this further account as standardly
construed. From what we have seen already, we know that he will, of
course, reject those versions of virtue ethics which treat the virtues as
causal means to ends which can be adequately characterised in non-moral
terms. But more fundamentally, he takes exception to all versions of
virtue ethics which are focused on the notion of flourishing.[9] The passage
cited at the start of this chapter, where he describes his experience of
working as a ward-assistant in a psychiatric hospital, helps to make this
point. 'Only with bitter irony or unknowing condescension', he notes,
'could one say that the patients in that ward had any chance of flourishing'; and yet, on the moral perspective he wishes to commend, we must
say that these patients are fully the equals of the rest of us, and as worthy
of being the recipients of moral concern. Although this example does not
appear in Gaita's earlier book, the same kinds of issues are addressed
there. There too he wonders about the capacity of an ethic which is
focused on the notion of flourishing to articulate the thought that the
afflicted, or those without any prospect of flourishing, are rightly treated
without condescension. And he notes again that, whatever we might
formally profess on this point, our behaviour typically reveals a sense that
such people are not properly the objects of an 'undiminished moral
response'.[10] So virtue ethics too, where it takes the notion of flourishing
as central to an account of our moral relationships, fails to provide the
necessary conceptual resources for keeping certain individuals fully
'among us', and as we shall see, Gaita therefore looks for another kind
of approach, one which takes the example set by the nun as its starting
point. On these matters too, a Christian commentator is likely to find
Gaita's account sympathetic in so far as his discussion gives a central place
to the weak and marginal – those who show no sign of being able to
flourish – and in so far as he takes the failure of standard ethical theories

9 However, he also argues that this is not the best translation of Aristotle's *eudaimonia*: *ibid.*, pp. 131–3.
10 *Ibid.*, p. 196.

to attend to the full humanity of such people as decisive in establishing the need for another kind of approach.

Gaita's examples of M and the nun show how we can deny the full humanity of other human beings, and relate to them in ways that suggest that their sufferings cannot run deep. Such examples naturally invite the question: how might we reclaim such people (be they mentally ill, the objects of racist contempt, slaves, or afflicted in some other way) as fully members of the human community? As we shall see, Gaita's response to this question turns, eventually, upon appeal to our felt responses in revealing the equality of worth, or the 'humanity', of our fellow human beings. Let us approach this issue by returning to the example of the nun.

Gaita comments that in the light of her love, he came to see the patients as rightly accorded the sort of non-condescending regard that was evident in her behaviour towards them. But, crucially, this realisation did not alert him to any quality in the patients which might be specified independently of the nun's regard:

If I am asked what I mean when I say that even such people as were patients in that ward are fully our equals, I can only say that the quality of her love proved that they are rightly the objects of our non-condescending treatment, that we should do all in our power to respond in that way. But if someone were now to ask me what informs my sense that they are *rightly* the objects of such treatment, I can appeal only to the purity of her love. For me, the purity of the love proved the reality of what it revealed . . . From the point of view of the speculative intelligence, however, I am going round in ever darkening circles, because I allow for no independent justification of her attitude.[11]

On this view it is the nun's love for the patients, as manifest in her non-condescending treatment of them, that establishes their moral standing as fully members of the human community. Elsewhere Gaita enlarges on this point by proposing that we can take others to be fully members of the human community, even if we cannot love them ourselves, only if we can see them as intelligibly the objects of someone's love.[12] Hence a man may ascribe to slaves all those properties that philosophers take to be relevant to being a person, but he can still rape a slave girl without thinking of himself as a rapist (without thinking that she is wronged as

11 *A Common Humanity*, pp. 21–2, Gaita's italics.
12 *Good and Evil*, p. 148.

a white woman would be wronged) because he does not see her as intelligibly the object of someone's love.[13] Similarly, M fails to see the Vietnamese as people who can know real love, or can genuinely reckon with the facts of their mortality or sexuality in the way that 'we' can. This is not, Gaita maintains, simply a matter of a difference of skin colour, nor need it be a matter of attributing to someone a deficiency of an empirically detectable kind (such as a lower IQ). Instead, such attitudes reflect a sense that the others' facial expressions and gestures, and their language and music, lack the kind of expressive depth that is found in 'our' dealings with one another, and fall short of what is required for real love or real depth of feeling.

The examples of M and the nun carry rather different import, I suggest. Gaita's description of M implies that coming to see the full humanity of another person is a matter of seeing that they can appreciate the meaning of the large facts of the human condition: our mortality, vulnerability to affliction, our sexuality, and so on.[14] What M needs to grasp about the Vietnamese, if she is to recognise their humanity, may not be in any straightforward sense empirically detectable, and may be relevant to their being loveable, but in these terms we can specify what she needs to understand independently of reference to anyone's love. By contrast, the example of the nun suggests that coming to see another as fully human may not depend upon coming to see them as having a developed appreciation of the defining features of our humanity, or upon coming to see them in any other light except as the object of someone's non-condescending love. After all, a mentally ill person may be so disturbed that they cannot reckon seriously with their mortality, sexuality, and the rest. But even so, a 'pure' love such as the nun's can reveal their humanity. The second case is more mysterious, and invites a deeper, more radical conception of the contribution that is made by the impartial love of the saints to our sense of the moral reality of other people.

This strand of Gaita's argument is surely, at least initially, offensive to common sense. We are inclined to think: there must be something which the nun sees in these patients, something we can specify apart from her love, which the psychiatrists have failed to see – and it is that reality which conditions her love and justifies it. Christians might say, for instance, that it is the nun's realisation that the patients are made in the image of God that conditions her regard for them, so that her love rests explicitly on

13 *Ibid.*, p. 163. See also *A Common Humanity*, p. 26.
14 *A Common Humanity*, p. 60.

properties which are attributable to the patients only from a theological perspective. Gaita rejects this reading. If metaphysical facts are held to underpin the nun's love, he notes, then it would make sense to suppose that she might be mistaken, for we can after all be mistaken about speculative claims of this kind; but in relation to the nun's love, the concept of a mistake has, he thinks, no clear application.[15]

We can make some progress towards removing the counter-intuitive quality of Gaita's proposal if we recall the commonsensical fact that our sense of the value of others can be sharpened when we see them in the light of their parents' love, a love that need not be conditional upon the child's achievements or other empirically discernible qualities. And as Gaita notes, prisoners are most easily rendered 'morally invisible' to their captors if they are deprived of visits from loved ones.[16] Suppose now that a person is beyond the reach of an ordinary parental love. Following Gaita's line of thought we should say that the 'preciousness' of such a person, and the correlative thought that they are intelligibly the object of someone's love, may be evident only in the light of a saintly love. Specifically, as the example of the nun suggests, such love may reveal the value of afflicted people, and others who are not treated, in the normal course of things, as properly the objects of an 'undiminished moral response'.[17]

We may also be led in the direction of Gaita's view if we recall the difficulties inherent in standard moral philosophical accounts of the value of other human beings. As we have seen, such accounts tend to identify a particular quality, specifiable independently of human response, and to suppose that the moral significance of a person is in some fashion vested in that quality, be it sentience, rational autonomy, or whatever. As commentators other than Gaita have also noted, this sort of approach seems bound to issue in a problematic account of the moral standing of people with cognitive and other disabilities.[18] If such approaches do indeed have this consequence, then (from the standpoint of what is still, I think, moral common sense) we may take that as a *reductio* of their starting point, and infer that some reference to quality of human response

---

15 *Ibid.*, p. 20. 16 *Ibid.*, p. 26. 17 *Good and Evil*, p. 196.
18 Compare this observation of Peter Singer: 'That the imbecile is not rational is just the way things have worked out, and the same is true of the dog – neither is any more responsible for their mental level. If it is unfair to take advantage of an isolated defect, why is it fair to take advantage of a more general limitation?' ('All Animals are Equal', in LaFollette (ed.), *Ethics in Practice*, p. 125). Hence on this view, 'imbeciles' are rightly considered, in themselves, as identical in moral standing with certain non-human animals. For an instructive treatment of these issues, which is similar to Gaita's in general outline, and focused upon this same question, see Peter Byrne, *Philosophical and Ethical Problems in Mental Handicap* (Basingstoke: Macmillan, 2000).

is after all required in our characterisation of the moral worth of human beings.

These reflections suggest that our grasp of the notion of 'humanity' (the key moral notion on Gaita's view, presupposed in any proper assessment of the relative worth of human beings) turns upon the example of figures like the nun. And for our purposes, it is important to add that her example in turn is grounded in what she believes 'in her heart'. After all, Gaita is explicit in the passage I cited at the beginning of the chapter that it is the fact that the nun holds to the equality of the patients with herself in her heart that enables her to act towards them without condescension; and it is the fact that the psychiatrists fail to hold this belief in their hearts that prevents their conduct from having the same revelatory quality as hers. If all of this is so, then it is quality of felt response that lies at the root of our system of moral appraisal (so far as this system acknowledges the equal worth of all human beings): grasping the value of other people (especially marginalised, afflicted people) depends upon this sort of response (and the behaviour which it makes possible), rather than any observation concerning others' happiness, or flourishing, or their capacity for autonomous choice (as in the standard moral theories).

It is natural to wonder whether the idea that the moral standing of another may be visible only in the light of the responses of a figure such as the nun (where those responses inextricably involve feelings) commits us to the thought that the value of other human beings is a kind of projection (has really to do with our sensibilities, and how we respond to others, rather than any truth concerning what they are like in themselves). And by analogy with familiar objections to divine command theories of ethics, where it is the divine decree or regard which establishes the worth of human persons, we might wonder whether Gaita's view implies that our valuing of our fellow human beings is an arbitrary matter, rather than being founded upon any property they possess in themselves. Gaita speaks in this connection of the 'interdependence of object and response'.[19] I take it, then, that he would not endorse the view that the value of others is simply projection; his view appears to be, rather, that we respond to some quality in the other, but a quality that cannot be articulated independently of the response it calls forth. Similarly, in his discussion of the nun's response to the patients, he writes of how he 'felt irresistibly that her

---

19 *Good and Evil*, p. 166. Similarly he writes that 'We love what is precious to us and things are precious to us because we love them. The contrast between inventing or making and discovering cannot be applied in any simple way here': *ibid.*, p. 125.

behaviour was directly shaped by the reality which it revealed'.[20] Here again the response is seen to be conditioned by something in the patients; it is just that what it is conditioned by eludes identification except by reference to the quality of the response. For these reasons, I suggest, Gaita is able to meet the charges of mere projection and arbitrariness.

Some of the mysteriousness can be taken out of Gaita's remarks if we remember that what is revealed is the 'humanity' of the patients, and their humanity is at least in part a matter of their being able to figure in relationships of genuine equality. The nun's behaviour reveals this quality by enacting such a relationship, and this helps to explain why the quality may not be visible apart from such behaviour (without such behaviour, the possibility of full equality would remain merely hypothetical), but also why it is genuinely a property in the patients (the nun could not, after all, sustain such a relationship with a quail).[21] However, I don't think that the humanity of a person is just a matter of their being able to elicit a given pattern of behavioural response; also implied in Gaita's account is the normative thought that in our relations with afflicted human beings, such responses are fitting. It is not only the possibility of the response but its fittingness that is revealed in the nun's behaviour.

These thoughts also throw light on Gaita's claim that the notion of a mistake has no clear application here. We might infer that this is because of the nature of the revelation that is communicated by the nun's behaviour: since we have no independent access to the quality that is revealed in her behaviour, there is no possibility of any countervailing evidence emerging (at any rate, not evidence of an empirical kind) to show that a mistake has been made. Moreover, in so far as she reveals a quality *in the patients*, then we might infer, along with Gaita, that her behaviour does not invite completion by reference to any metaphysical story.

So Gaita's account suggests that it is the quality of felt response (and correlative behaviour) of certain saintly individuals that affords the rest of us a proper sense of the moral significance of other human beings, especially afflicted human beings. It is a consequence of his way of developing this view that the saints do not only provide an epistemic basis for our sense of the worth of others, by revealing their humanity (as distinct from their rationality, their capacity for happiness or flourishing, or their membership of the species *homo sapiens*, for example). The

20 *A Common Humanity*, p. 19.
21 I cite the example of quail since I lived with a pair for some years, and can therefore speak with some authority on this question.

practice of the saints is also required for the very concept of humanity understood in this morally charged sense. This is again because of the mutual conditioning of reality and response in this case: the reality of others' humanity is not available for inspection independently of the revelatory light that is cast by saintly conduct; and accordingly, our sense of what it means to talk of humanity in this context is inextricably connected to that conduct: we cannot expound the quality without pointing to examples of such conduct. Hence the epistemic role of the saints points to a still deeper sense in which our recognition of the moral worth of others is tied to saintly practice: we owe to such practice the very notion of moral worth (in its supra-utilitarian, supra-contractualist sense).

It might be suggested that even if this is so, we do not need actual saints to acquire the concept of humanity. After all, in principle, could not a work of literature record behaviour of the kind that is exemplified by the nun, and thereby reveal what she is said to reveal, without any dependence on some real-life encounter with such a figure? But it is more plausible to suppose, I think, that such a revelation has to be embodied, primordially, in actual examples of saintly living, not least because (as Gaita repeatedly insists) it is so mysterious, so contrary to what a reasoned expectation might suggest. Perhaps it will be objected that it would be enough to construe a person's behaviour as saintly even when it is not (perhaps the nun has no deep-seated regard for the patients, but is only concerned to impress the psychiatrists and others); but here we may adduce again the thought that saintly behaviour appears to be shaped by the reality it reveals, and recall the suggestion that the notion of a mistake has no clear application in this context. Gaita also writes that the wonder inspired by the love of the saints is connected with the tendency of such love to reveal its object while rendering the saint herself as it were invisible (contrast the supposition presented in parentheses just now). Hence he remarks that 'There is a sense in which *she* disappears from consideration.'[22]

GAITA'S ACCOUNT AND CHRISTIAN COMMITMENT

So far we have seen some of the reasons that might lead someone in the direction of Gaita's view (by examining his objections to standard moral philosophical theories), and we have seen how he takes felt responses to reveal the humanity of the afflicted, thereby helping to constitute the very notion of humanity. So Gaita's account provides a further example (to set

22 *Good and Evil,* p. 206, Gaita's italics.

alongside those of McDowell and Newman, for instance) of how emotional experience may be tied to our evaluative understanding. But his discussion is also of interest for our purposes because it offers a way of broaching the question of how moral and religious understanding may be connected. Here we may revert to the two questions I posed at the outset of this chapter.

Assuming first of all that Gaita's account does not tacitly trade on religious assumptions, might this account serve as a kind of 'natural law' route to conclusions which Christians would find congenial? The answer to this question, in relation to the material we have been discussing, must surely be 'yes'. For Gaita's view is that love (rather than happiness, rationality, autonomy, flourishing, or any of the other concepts that are central to the dominant moral philosophical theories) is the central concept in terms of which we should understand the possibility of others' standing in a morally significant relationship to ourselves. Moreover, the sort of love that is most directly relevant here (the sort exemplified by the nun) is unconditional love. Such love is not premised on a particular human achievement (a certain IQ or even a capacity for lucid reflection on the meaning of the big facts of human life), but is instead called forth by the sheer humanity of the other (where 'humanity' is taken once more in a non-biological, morally resonant sense). And love of this kind is surely an instance of (or perhaps simply identical with) what Christians have called neighbour love. And significantly, Gaita's acknowledgement that this sort of response is not simply a projection, but tracks some quality inherent in its object (albeit a quality that cannot be specified without reference to the response) invites the thought that the object of this sort of attachment is not devoid of value in itself, as certain (surely flawed) readings of Christian agape have implied.[23]

So Gaita's account of the role of saintly love, and the felt response to others that is acted out in such love, in constituting our moral scheme suggests that there is a close relationship between religious and ethical understanding to this extent: a philosophical account of the moral significance of others will need to trade in the very concepts (especially the concept of impartial saintly love) that have animated Christian ethical reflection; and it is these concepts, rather than those which have prevailed in the philosophical tradition (autonomy, flourishing, and happiness, for example), that are required for a proper moral understanding. Moreover,

---

23 For a critique of such readings, see Robert Adams, 'Pure Love', in *The Virtue of Faith and Other Essays in Philosophical Theology* (New York: Oxford University Press, 1987), pp. 9–24.

Gaita's view suggests that our moral understanding will be tied to the revelatory example of particular individuals, and as an account of moral epistemology, this view is again strikingly consonant with a Christian sense of the role of the saints and the incarnate God in modelling the nature of our relations with other human beings; by contrast, the philosophical tradition has of course typically committed itself to a more 'reasoned', discursive assessment of what is required of us in action.

So far I have been concerned simply with the broad affinity between Gaita's affect-informed view and the approach of a Christian ethic. The second question I posed was this: does Gaita's account not just sit comfortably with Christian perspectives but invite completion in Christian or other religious terms? Let us turn now to this issue.[24]

I have suggested that Gaita's approach turns on the existence (and not simply the possibility) of 'saints' understood as individuals who are capable of exemplifying the sort of 'pure' love that is manifest in the nun's demeanour. Elsewhere Gaita cites the life of Mother Teresa as an instance of such love[25] and also (drawing on an example of Primo Levi) the actions of a man in a concentration camp who brings relief to a fellow prisoner who has collapsed.[26] So our question could be framed as: does such saintly practice in some fashion invite a religious interpretation? Or might such people be simply secular saints, and might their conduct be fully intelligible in secular terms?

It is clear that Gaita thinks that such love is in significant degree an achievement of culture, rather than, for instance, a natural endowment of certain individuals or the expression of some 'primitive reaction'. Specifically, it depends upon the availability of the language of love.[27] Hence he writes: 'I doubt that the love expressed in the nun's demeanour would have been possible for her were it not for the place which the language of parental love had in her prayers.'[28] We have seen already how parental love need not be closely tied to how a child turns out, and how it

---

24 Gaita is certainly aware of the religious resonances of his thought, and has described his position as lying somewhere between a non-reductive naturalism in ethics and the religious point of view: *Good and Evil*, pp. 228–9. However, I shall try to explore some of the points of affinity in more detail than Gaita has done, and to argue (against Gaita) that his position may at points represent a somewhat unstable middle ground between non-reductive naturalism and a religious point of view.

25 *Ibid.*, pp. 203–7.

26 *A Common Humanity*, p. 151. Indeed, Gaita says: 'As much as the nun's example, perhaps even more than her example, this is goodness to wonder at.'

27 He cites Rush Rhees's remark that there can be no love without the language of love on a number of occasions. See, for instance, *Good and Evil*, p. 121.

28 *Ibid.*, p. 22.

has a special part to play therefore in revealing the value of people who might otherwise seem difficult to love. But of course, Gaita's examples of extreme affliction are meant to suggest that we cannot always grasp the intelligibility of a person's being the object of love by reference to their parents, for there are limits even to parental love. Only reference to the impartial love of the saints will enable us to keep such individuals firmly within the moral community. But in this quotation, Gaita suggests that even when we turn to the love of the saints, the language of parental love, and specifically the language of divine love, may still be in some degree presupposed. Indeed, if Gaita 'doubts' whether the nun's love would have been possible otherwise (since he has no larger knowledge of the nun, I do not see that we should attach special weight to the words 'for her'), that suggests a doubt about whether there is any other language with comparable power to reveal the full humanity of our fellow human beings.

Gaita's view implies, I think, that while there may be no abstract conceptual requirement that saintly love be conditioned by the language of divine love, it may well be that, as a matter of contingent, historical fact, such love needs the language of religion, since that language offers our richest, most sustained exploration of the thought that we are all intelligibly the objects of love, in so far as we are all children of God, and beloved of God. Hence if Gaita is right about the dependence of our moral concern on our ability to see others as intelligibly the objects of love, then a person who shares with Gaita a commonsensical range of moral commitments ought, at least, to be favourably disposed to religious traditions, and to hope that the language of these traditions, where it represents God's love for us as akin to that of a parent, continues to be vital.

In support of this thought, we might note again the recurrent failure of contemporary work in moral philosophy, where it is (as it mostly is) disengaged from religious presuppositions, to articulate fully the worth of people with cognitive disabilities and other 'afflicted' human beings. This tendency in recent moral philosophy lends weight to the thought that a rather specific kind of cultural-linguistic tradition is required if we are to find ways of adequately expounding the value of such people.[29] And Gaita

29 Iris Murdoch's non-theistic appropriation of the language of love, humility, and attention might seem to constitute an exception to this line of argument. But given her use of that language, it is arguable that the sort of move that I am making in relation to Gaita's work can also be made in relation to hers. Her moral objection to theistic interpretations of this language seems to be that such a reading has a tendency to issue in a consoling, self-absorbed fantasy of some sort, but Gaita's example of the nun, along with many other such examples, suggests that failure to attend to the independent reality of other things marks a corruption of genuine theistic understanding. See *The Sovereignty of Good* (London: Ark, 1985), Chapters 2–3.

himself notes that secular equivalents of the idea that human beings are 'sacred', including his own favoured formulation that they are 'infinitely precious', are all 'inadequate'.[30] This is partly, I suggest, because he thinks that moral insights are typically best expressed in a 'natural language', and not in a language devised specifically for the purpose of philosophical discussion.[31]

Of course, there remains a question about whether a person has to subscribe to the language of religion, in the sense of being able to use it in prayer or worship, in order to take it as revelatory on this point. In so far as Gaita's position depends simply on the supposition that others are intelligibly the object of love, it might be thought that there is no need to relate to God in prayer to find the language of theistic religion revelatory of the humanity of afflicted people: isn't it enough to find it intelligible that a God could love such people? But this seems a rather awkward stance, as I shall now argue.

It is worth emphasising that what I am proposing at this point is quite distinct from anything that Gaita envisages; indeed, in as much as it is an argument for the idea that our concept of humanity invites a prayerful, metaphysically engaged appropriation of the language of religion, it is squarely at odds with Gaita's own proposal that the nun's behaviour does not need any kind of metaphysical underpinning. However, the argument will remain in keeping with the spirit of Gaita's approach in so far as it seeks to build on his remarks concerning the role of natural languages, rich in historical resonance, in shaping our moral sensibility and, more specifically, in so far as it seeks to extrapolate from his comments concerning the role of prayer, and the image of God as parent, in shaping the nun's moral sensibility.

If a non-believer thinks (for the Gaita-style reasons that we have been exploring) that the moral worth of other human beings can only be adequately articulated in the language of religion (treating that language 'non-realistically'), this requires the non-believer to take religious tradition as the primary or sole bearer of a most profound truth, concerning the value which attaches to human life. But if the Bible (for example) is revelatory on this point, will there not be some pressure to treat it as trustworthy in other respects? At any rate, the non-believer may well feel obliged at this point to provide some account of why the text is to be

---

30 See, for instance, *Good and Evil*, p. 1. He also speaks of human beings as 'unique' and 'irreplaceable': see, for instance, *ibid.*, p. 51.
31 See, for example, his treatment of Alan Donagan's use of the notion 'rational creature' and its relationship to the expression 'mortal men': *ibid.*, pp. 24–8.

trusted on the question of the worth of human life but not to be trusted on the question of God's reality, when the text itself takes these questions to be related. In other words, the sort of stance that Gaita has sketched seems at least to leave the non-believer with an apologetic task, or at least, the awkwardness of treating a religious text as foundational for their sense of the significance of other human beings (and therefore of life itself) while denying the central, animating conviction of the text.

In reply it might be urged that the story of Jesus, as one who bestows love on the afflicted and is worthy of love in spite of his own affliction, is enough to ground the intelligibility of love for the afflicted, and that there is therefore no need for any reference to God understood metaphysically. But this response still requires us to take the text as revelatory on this point, and so still poses a question about its authority on the other matters of which it speaks, not least because the Gospels themselves evidently consider Jesus' identity as fully comprehensible only by reference to God. So here again, Gaita's account of the role of the language of divine love in making possible a full appreciation of the humanity of other human beings supplies at least a prima facie reason for taking our moral commitments as premised upon a religiously serious appropriation of the language of religion.

It is noteworthy that other commentators on Gaita's work have also wondered whether his approach invites a more religiously engaged stance than he officially allows. Richard Schacht, for example, has suggested that Gaita's emphasis on the revelatory dimension of the nun's behaviour points towards an account of value which is 'metaphysical' and religiously loaded. Speaking of Gaita's discussion of the role of saintly love in establishing our concept of humanity, Schacht writes:

I suspect he is not prepared to embrace the view that the whole configuration of the phenomena to which he here refers is fundamentally *a cultural affair through and through*, answering to and reflecting nothing whatsoever beyond the horizon of human life and history.[32]

So Schacht's difficulty with Gaita's approach is focused upon Gaita's failure to accord a large enough role to language and culture in constituting moral reality. The question I am posing has a rather different character:

32 'Reply: Morality, Humanity, and Historicality: Remorse and Religion Revisited', in D. Z. Phillips (ed.), *Religion and Morality* (Basingstoke: Macmillan, 1996), p. 50, Schacht's italics. This is the text of Schacht's exchange with Gaita at a conference; in his paper, Gaita uses the example of the nun, and makes the same point about the connection between her behaviour and the language of parental love that we noted above. See Gaita, 'Is Religion an Infantile Morality?', in Phillips (ed.), *Religion and Morality*, p. 28.

here it is the acknowledged role of the language of religion in particular in shaping our sense of the humanity of other human beings that is at issue. The question I am asking is: if religion is given such a role, is there not some presumption that the language of religion has authority on other matters too?

However, the question I am pressing is connected to Schacht's in as much as both questions arise from a sense that Gaita wishes to privilege in some way the moral perspective that is implied in the practice of the saints. Compare Schacht's comment, which he takes to be opposed to the drift of Gaita's discussion, that 'there is no more basis for taking this sort of humanity [the sort exemplified in the nun's behaviour] to be *the right one* than for taking English to be the right language for human beings to speak'.[33] So Schacht takes Gaita to be metaphysically committed simply by virtue of according a deeper significance to one value scheme than others, so that the 'revelatory' rather than the 'constitutive' theme 'wears the trousers', as he puts it.[34] My suggestion is more specifically that if it is the language of religion that is tied to the favoured moral scheme, in the ways we have discussed, then Gaita's approach is not merely consonant with religious commitment, but amounts to a prima facie case for making such a commitment. This reading suggests a somewhat novel kind of 'natural theology': a natural theology of this kind takes its rise not from some feature of the world, or even from the character of moral 'reality'; its starting point is, rather, attention to the nature of our moral concepts (here the project retains some affinity with Gaita's own perspective), and the thought that the concept of 'humanity' in particular is not readily explicable independently of the language of religion (where 'humanity' is once more tied to what is revealed in the behaviour of figures like the nun).

To take stock, I am suggesting that Gaita's view (interpreted and developed as I have proposed) suggests a several-tiered account of the workings of our moral language. First of all, there are the saints whose conduct reveals (in the ways Gaita describes in his example of the nun) the full humanity of afflicted human beings and yields our concept of 'humanity'. Some of these saintly figures will use the language of divine love in prayer, and their non-condescending regard of afflicted human beings will be directly an expression of that language; others will be secular saints, but they too (on Gaita's view as I have extended it) will owe their capacity for such conduct to the availability of concepts that ultimately have a religious origin. Then there are individuals like you and

33 Schacht, 'Reply', p. 51, Schacht's italics.   34 *Ibid.*, p. 47.

me. Since we fall short of sainthood, we shall not be able to embody the same quality of undiminished moral response in our dealings with afflicted human beings, but we can still appreciate their full humanity by reference to the revelatory example of the conduct of the saints. Such an appreciation of their humanity will run deeper than that exemplified by the psychiatrists in Gaita's example, providing that we are attentive and sensitive witnesses of the revelatory conduct of the saints, but we may still be unable to love the afflicted person, and while the saints believe 'in their hearts' in the full humanity of their fellow human beings, we shall presumably fall short of that condition, even if our believing has something of the affective charge that is characteristic of saintly loving. All of us, whether saints or not, will have a prima facie reason for taking the language of religion as revelatory in ways that invite a prayerful response, providing that we are committed to the full humanity of the afflicted person.

These reflections suggest that even the psychiatrists in Gaita's example may have a reason for taking the language of religion as revelatory in ways that invite a prayerful response: they may find, for example, that they cannot articulate their commitment to the full equality of their patients in the language supplied by contemporary moral philosophy, or in other ways which do not trade on religious assumptions. However, what puzzles or, rather, amazes Gaita (and what sets his reflections going along the track we are considering) is the nun's ability to reveal the full and not merely the 'notional' humanity of the patients. To this extent, the argument we are considering is also addressed to someone who has a more than notional commitment to the humanity of afflicted people, and therefore shares Gaita's perplexity about how such an understanding is possible.

It is worth noting that this account involves a richer set of distinctions than is implied in Newman's contrast of real and notional assent. For it seems that there are various intermediate cases which lie between those of the nun (unqualified 'real' assent to the full humanity of others) and the psychiatrists (who exemplify, we might suppose, simple notional assent). The converted Gaita models one such case, in so far as he has moved beyond mere notional assent without yet reaching the point of real assent (without believing fully in his heart).

This position invites further clarification, so let us consider some questions that may be addressed to it. It may be asked: if the religious saint depends on the language of divine parental love, then the concept of 'humanity' surely depends fundamentally not on saintly practice but upon something like God's practice; and in that case, what remains of the idea that it is the practice of the saints that underpins our notion of humanity? The view I have expounded does suggest that fundamentally it is God's impartial, parental love of human beings that underpins saintly practice; but saintly practice can still underpin our sense of the humanity of others in the way that is evident in Gaita's example. The young Gaita who witnesses the nun's conduct comes to see the humanity of the patients (in a more than notional sense) because of the revelatory quality of that conduct (and independently of any religious commitment). Hence his sense of their humanity is indebted to saintly practice. But that practice in turn is traced back (directly, in the case of the nun, as Gaita expounds the matter) to God's practice. Moreover, saintly practice is important for a further reason, even if we subscribe anyway to the idea of divine parental love. For that idea can itself be appropriated in 'notional' or 'real' terms. If understood 'really', it will presumably issue in the kind of conduct that the nun displays, whereas if understood merely notionally, it will not. In this respect, the example of the saints is not to be simply subordinated to the idea of divine love: on the contrary, their example shows the 'real' content of that idea, for without that example we would have no deep conception of what it means for us to be the objects of divine parental love and to be equal in the sight of God.

What, then, of the practice of the secular saints? (I take it for granted that there are secular saints – it is surely implausible to think otherwise, though certainly my account would be simplified if we could suppose as much.) The practice of secular saints can also be revelatory: Gaita could have observed a secular figure behaving as the nun behaved towards the patients. But their practice will, naturally, not be dependent directly on the language of parental love as rehearsed in a life of prayer. However, Gaita's view implies, I have suggested, that secular saintly practice still owes its possibility, ultimately, to such a life. Here we have a chain of dependence rather like that posited by versions of the cosmological argument: the ability to exemplify saintly practice can be acquired by exposure to another who exemplifies saintly practice, and so on, but this chain will need to terminate in someone whose saintly practice is grounded in familiarity with the language of divine parental love (this may be someone who reads the Bible non-realistically), and the revelatory force of such language in this respect provides a prima facie reason for its prayerful appropriation. Gaita himself supplies the key premise in this argument when he observes that he doubts whether the nun's regard for the patients would have been possible but for the language of divine love. Implied in this remark, I take it, is the assumption that it is this direct relationship to the language of divine love, rather than the indirect relation that is typical of the secular saint, that accounts for her practice. In this way she can serve as a kind of 'first cause' for the chain of dependence that I have just sketched: her revelatory example is not dependent on the revelatory example of another saint.

So, to return to the second of the two questions identified at the beginning of this chapter, Gaita's appeal to the example of saintly conduct, and the kind of felt response to others that is bodied forth in such conduct, does suggest that ethical commitment invites completion in religious commitment. This is because saintly conduct, and the saintly feeling in which it is implicated, depends for its possibility ultimately upon the prayerful appropriation of the language of divine parental love. Although grounds can be adduced in support of this claim in the way that we have been discussing, it is not a claim which is open to straightforward verification or falsification. Notably, in considering the truth of the claim, it is not enough to make an observation such as: I certainly believe in the full humanity of afflicted people, and I am not religiously committed. This sort of observation fails to engage with the issue for various reasons.

First of all, the claim is that 'real assent', or at least, more than notional assent, to the full humanity of afflicted people (the kind of assent that marks out the saints and those who acknowledge the revelatory force of saintly conduct) is ultimately premised upon prayerful appropriation of the language of religion. (Again, notional assent does not point so readily in this direction: where the psychiatrists are concerned, there is not evidently a revelation whose conditions of possibility call for further reflection.) And it is no easy matter to determine whether I have given more than notional assent to the full humanity of afflicted people. The psychiatrists in Gaita's example evidently thought they had, and discovering that we are mistaken on such a question may call for searching self-examination (and then painful and protracted self-reformation). Moreover, Gaita's account, as I have developed it, involves the idea of a chain of dependence, whereby certain examples of saintly living are enabled by the luminous witness of other examples of saintly living, and so on indefinitely, until we reach a saint whose practice is informed by the language of religion, which in turn provides a prima facie reason for the prayerful appropriation of such language. A counterexample to such a chain would be difficult to produce not only because of difficulties in assessing whether a given individual whom we know personally is a saint (has given a real assent to the full humanity of afflicted people), but also because the further stages of such a chain may lie in the distant past, and beyond the reach of investigation.

To put the point in general terms, Gaita's proposal (as developed here) involves a counterfactual claim whose truth it is difficult to assess: but for the language of divine parental love, western cultures would not have evolved the practice of a more than notional recognition of the 'humanity' of afflicted human beings. (I abstract here from the question of what to say about 'eastern' cultures, which have their own conceptions of divine love, and correlative saintly traditions.) In terms of the history of ideas, there is certainly some connection between the assumptions of the religiously informed cultures of the middle ages and earlier and the practice of saintly love; but the question of whether that practice could have emerged independently of this particular matrix is not a matter which is open to simple empirical investigation. The most we can do, perhaps, is to draw attention to the kinds of facts that we have been discussing – for instance, the tendencies of contemporary religiously disengaged moral philosophical thought.

In summary, using Gaita's account of felt response, saintly conduct, and the language of divine parental love, we have been exploring the thought that moral commitment, of the kind that acknowledges the full 'humanity' of afflicted people, is at least highly consonant with a religiously focused (and more specifically, perhaps, a biblically informed) ethic and perhaps even invites completion in such terms. So here is a view of the relationship between emotional experience and ethical understanding which also carries implications for our assessment of the relationship between ethical and religious understanding. On this view, believing in the full equality of other human beings 'in one's heart' proves to be tied, in various ways, to a certain kind of religious understanding.

REPENTANCE AND THE MORAL LIFE

I want now to explore a further notion (in addition to that of saintly love) which suggests that Gaita's moral scheme is closely aligned with that of a Christian ethics. This time I shall be interested in his notion of remorse. As much the same kinds of move can be made in this connection, I shall treat this strand of his thinking more briefly. Gaita thinks of remorse as 'a form of the recognition of the reality of others'.[35] Again, his account is developed in relation to particular examples. For instance, he considers the case of a man who pushes a beggar to one side, with the unintended consequence that the beggar is propelled into the path of an oncoming car and killed.[36] The man finds himself haunted by his victim, and it is this

---

35 *Good and Evil*, p. 48.   36 *A Common Humanity*, p. 30.

(rather than any sense that he has broken the moral law, or failed to maximise the general happiness, for example) that provides the focus for his sense of the meaning of what he has done. Hence Gaita writes that 'a certain sense of their victim's individuality is internal to a murderer's understanding of the moral significance of what they did and that . . . is part of what it is to be aware of the reality of another human being'.[37]

Here again, as in the case of love, we find that our felt responses to others are crucial in revealing their preciousness; and accordingly our experience of remorse, like our experience of love, is partly constitutive of our sense of moral seriousness. Notice too how it is the felt response which reveals the 'individuality' of the other (the man is not haunted by some representative of humanity, but by this very person), and how this suggests again that feeling may bear an intellectual content in its own right – for the individuality is made known in feeling and is not otherwise fully specifiable. (Notably, this kind of individuality is not reducible to distinctiveness of empirical qualities.)

Once more, this account seems strikingly consonant with the characteristic emphases of a Christian account of the moral life. Specifically, the notion of repentance, as it figures in Christian moral thought, is evidently closely related to that of remorse. So in the case of remorse, as in the case of love, we find Gaita's account of the epistemic and conceptual basis of our moral reflection very much convergent with Christian perspectives. It is worth emphasising that together these two concepts provide the key to his interpretation of our moral commitments. (It is not the case that there are several such concepts, some of which are less religiously resonant than these.) And again, we may think that it is the saints who provide a particularly important source, conceptual and epistemic, for this understanding of the moral life, in as much as the saints are marked not simply by their love, but by the quality of their repentance.

Once more we may wonder whether this sort of attunement of Gaita's categories to those of Christian thought is such that Gaita's thinking invites completion by reference to Christian theology. Here again I think that Gaita's account points in this direction most obviously in virtue of his emphasis upon the role of natural languages in enabling moral reflection. Hence he writes that 'our exploration of what it is to be a murderer, a coward, a traitor, etc, is at its deepest, in a natural language resonant with historical and local association'.[38] Indisputably, the Christian tradition provides one example of a sustained and richly nuanced account of

---

37 *Good and Evil*, p. 51.   38 *Ibid.*, p. 34.

the nature of remorse, and correlative forms of wrong-doing. And again it is arguable that more recent, secular discourses fail to provide a source for our moral thinking of comparable depth. (Think, for instance, of stand-ard consequentialist treatments of killing one person to save several others and the limited acknowledgement of the significance of remorse in such discussions.[39]) So once more we might pose a question of this kind: if Gaita is right to assume that the experience of remorse is presupposed (epistemically and conceptually) in our grasp of the moral significance of other human beings, and if it is the language of religion above all that enables such remorse, then is there not a prima facie reason for thinking that the language of religion is to be treated as authoritative on other matters too?

It might be objected that remorse is less obviously a distinguishing characteristic of saints than impartial love. After all, the man who feels remorse for killing the beggar is not thereby established as a saint. And if that is so, then perhaps there is a route (epistemic and conceptual) into moral discourse that is independent of the route provided by love, and less obviously implicated in a religious scheme of values? I would say that the man's remorse is itself a form of impartial love: it is a recognition of the beggar's 'preciousness' which is not conditional upon attributing to him any particular achievement or distinguishing quality. However, it is true that the example does not require us to suppose that by virtue of his remorse, the man becomes capable of an impartial love of larger scope, one that extends to the afflicted more generally; and it is this sort of impartial love that we take to be characteristic of the saints. This suggests that saintly love has a certain priority vis-à-vis remorse in our moral scheme. For it is of the nature of such love to reach out to human beings in general, whereas remorse typically has a more particular focus, directing us to the humanity of someone we have wronged. This would constitute one kind of response to this objection, one which turns on the thought that remorse fails to provide an alternative route to a generalised sense of the 'preciousness' of our fellow human beings. In responding to the objection, we might also reiterate the thought that remorse is dependent on the language of remorse, that such a language is not easily contrived, and is most fecund when embedded in a long-standing tradition. If that is so, then

---

39 Gaita discusses such examples *ibid.*, Chapter 5. Typically, consequentialists are apt to treat remorse or guilt in such contexts as mere feelings (as akin to unpleasant sensations), which is surely to underdescribe their significance, as Bernard Williams and others have noted. See, for instance, B. Williams and J. J. Smart, *Utilitarianism: For and Against* (London: Cambridge University Press, 1973), pp. 103–4.

while the remorseful person need be no saint, their remorse may be contingent upon concepts which we owe to religious tradition.

So by reference to remorse, as well as by reference to love, we can make a case for the idea that ethical understanding is keyed to our felt responses to other beings, and in turn a case for the idea that this kind of ethical understanding opens out in various ways in the direction of a religious understanding.

EXTENDING GAITA'S PROPOSAL

I have been arguing that Gaita's account of the moral life is grounded in the power of affective response to reveal the value of other human beings, and is also religiously suggestive in so far as it is structured in terms of the notions of love and remorse. But are there points at which Gaita's work is less easily assimilated to a Christian perspective, or requires extension if it is to be compatible with such a perspective? In closing this chapter, I shall take note, fairly briefly, of one such point.[40] This discussion will yield a more nuanced account of the contribution made by feeling in constituting our moral scheme.

Contemporary Christian (and most obviously, Roman Catholic) moral thinking is distinguished by, among other things, its stance on abortion. Characteristically, Gaita does not seek to offer precise prescriptions in this area, but his anti-consequentialism and commitment to the preciousness of life inform his occasional remarks on the question, in ways that suggest once more an affinity with one kind of religiously informed perspective. Here again, Gaita turns to the authoritative example of particular individuals to make his case. For example, he notes how a woman's attitude towards her unborn child might be conditioned by the love she sees another woman show for her (the second woman's) unborn child.[41] And once again he insists that our acquaintance with this value is mediated by our responsiveness to the appearances of the human body. Hence he writes: 'It is important that the child grows in its mother's body, that her body changes with its growth and that these changes can appear to us as beautiful, for this provides a focus for love's tenderness without which

40 There are others in addition to this point. See, for example, Gaita's thought that our concepts of mind are anthropomorphically conditioned, in so far as they reflect human forms of response. (Compare his discussion of the idea that a fly might be in agony: *Good and Evil*, p. 181.) This sort of stance poses a difficulty for metaphysical construals of religious language that I shall not explore here.
41 *Ibid.*, p. 123.

there could be no love.' This sort of point is familiar from our earlier discussion. But he continues:

A foetus growing in a glass jar on her mantelpiece with many of its 'morally relevant empirical properties' in plain view, could not be an object of her love, for her love could find no tender expression (which is not to say that a serious concern for it could find no serious expression).[42]

Given Gaita's stance on the connection between being intelligibly the object of love and being 'precious', the implication of this passage is that in so far as the foetus is unloveable, it cannot be judged 'precious' (under the conditions specified, it is not even, I take it, the possible object of a saintly love). In fact, Gaita does directly add a qualification. He writes: 'Or perhaps more accurately, it could not [be an object of her love] if that were a general practice in a community.' So 'perhaps' the foetus could be loved, and could be deemed precious, if a community were able to fashion a language of love for the 'unborn child' in connection with the normal processes of pregnancy, since this language might then be extended to the foetus in the jar. But this concession still leaves a concern; for the supposition that 'perhaps' the community might then be able to deem the foetus in the jar 'precious' is surely not strong enough. Should we not rather say that if the community recognise the value of a foetus which develops through the normal processes of pregnancy, then they are committed to the thought that one which develops in a jar is of equal value, whether or not they are able to take it as intelligibly the object of someone's love; for the 'morally relevant empirical properties' are indeed the same in these two cases, and whatever moral significance attaches to a foetus surely supervenes upon these properties. Here we are back to the question of whether it is the 'revelatory' or the 'constitutive' theme that 'wears the trousers', as Schacht puts it. Indeed, Gaita's stance here suggests that he is after all closer than I have supposed to Schacht, and to the thought that value in this case is simply constituted by our responses, so that where the responses fail, so must the value.

It may be objected that in making this move (appealing to the need for consistency in our treatment of cases by reference to empirical qualities) I am after all reverting to a more Kantian kind of moral scheme (and the ideal of maxim universalisation), and abandoning Gaita's hard-won insights.[43] But in taking this approach, there is no need to set aside

42 *Ibid.*, p. 122.
43 See Immanuel Kant, *Foundations of the Metaphysics of Morals*, tr. Lewis White Beck, 2nd edn (Indianapolis, IN: Bobbs-Merrill, 1959), Second Section, p. 39.

Gaita's championing of the foundational role of felt response. It is worth recalling that he himself qualifies the connection between felt response and value recognition: after all, he allows that I may regard an individual as 'precious' even if I cannot love them myself, though of course he retains a connection here between felt response and value by requiring that my capacity to take the person as precious should be tied to my capacity to regard them as intelligibly the object of someone's love. (Hence the pregnant woman in the example finds that she cannot love her baby, but still judges that it would be wrong to have an abortion, because she sees her own baby in the light of the other pregnant woman's love.) I am proposing a further qualification of the connection between felt response and value recognition: even if there is no one, not even one of the saints, who is able to take the foetus in the jar as an object of love, we are committed, I am suggesting, to the thought that it is precious, on pain of inconsistency, in so far as it shares its 'morally relevant empirical properties' with an individual whom we know to be precious.

This stance does not imply a breaking of the connection between felt response and value (though it does go further than Gaita, by breaking the connection between supposing that an individual is of value and supposing that it is intelligibly the object of someone's love). For we are still supposing that the value of the individual is revealed by way of felt response; it is just that to recognise the value of an individual I do not need to respond to it feelingly myself (here with Gaita), or even to suppose that it is intelligible that anyone else should do so (here moving beyond Gaita); instead, it is enough to appreciate that this individual shares its base empirical properties with an individual whom I recognise to be precious (whether I respond to that individual feelingly or recognise the intelligibility of someone doing so). So this stance is compatible with Gaita's view that reason cannot pave the way in fixing our moral relations with others, and it remains consistent with his thought that 'Our sense of the preciousness of other people is connected with their power to affect us in ways we cannot fathom.'[44] The position I have been sketching gives reason a muted role, by comparison with the role it is afforded in (for example) traditional natural law ethics, but a larger role than Gaita himself envisages. The foetus example suggests that some such extension is required if Gaita's standpoint is to be

---

44 *A Common Humanity*, p. 26.

consistent with one familiar religiously informed perspective on certain issues in applied ethics; and the move seems justified anyway, quite apart from its implications on this point.

It may be objected that this account makes reference to the saints superfluous after all. For can we not begin by recognising the preciousness of a particular individual, and then infer that human beings in general are similarly valuable, since they share the same base empirical qualities? In that case, we could reach the conclusion that human beings in general are worthy of an 'undiminished moral response' without appeal to the love of the saints. But this sort of argument will be shaky where the afflicted are concerned. It may be thought, for instance, that a cognitively disabled person does *not* possess all the relevant base empirical properties that are exemplified by an adult human being with normal cognitive functions. So here the love of the saints continues to be needed to illuminate the 'humanity' of some of our fellow human beings. The case of the foetus is different, I suggest. As the example is presented, the foetus in the jar differs from the 'unborn child' only by virtue of developing outside the womb. So considered in themselves, there is no empirically discernible difference between the two. Of course, the child in the womb may well be more likely to call forth a loving response from its mother, but doesn't this fact simply reveal the limitations of our powers of sympathetic identification? As we have seen, Gaita himself acknowledges a role for such limits when allowing that the love of a saint may reveal the preciousness of, for instance, an afflicted person to me, even if I cannot myself feel saintly (or any other kind of) love for that person.

CONCLUSION

The question of the relationship between religion and morality has a long and controverted history. I have been arguing that the work of Raimond Gaita suggests a new and more fruitful conception of this relationship than is implied in the currently dominant theories of ethics. If Gaita is right that our moral categories are properly founded upon the quality of our felt responses, and specifically the responses of love and remorse (and not upon notions such as happiness, autonomy, flourishing, rights, and the like), then our relationship to others is to be understood in terms of a broadly similar conceptual framework, whether our perspective is that of morality or that of theistic religion (and perhaps more specifically, that afforded by the Christian faith). More controversially, I have argued that Gaita's scheme invites completion in religious terms, in so far as the impartial love of the saints points ultimately to a religiously serious appropriation of the language of divine parental love. Finally, I have argued that Gaita's scheme needs elaboration in at least one respect if it is to prove fully consistent with the demands of a certain kind of religiously committed ethic.

What thoughts should we carry forward from this chapter? We have seen how a certain kind of understanding may be embedded in 'feeling' (in what a person believes 'in their heart'): on Gaita's view, a morally deep recognition of the humanity of afflicted human beings (the kind of recognition that is displayed by the nun but not the psychiatrists) rests upon some such felt response. As I have suggested, this picture of feeling's role seems closely related to Newman's account of what is involved in a religiously deep understanding of God. And both Gaita and Newman are alert to the way in which feeling, on such a view, serves not only to help us recognise 'humanity' or 'divinity', but also to constitute our sense of the full meaning of those concepts (because felt response offers our only fully adequate route to these qualities). So at least, Gaita can be read as providing a further perspective on the kind of role that is assigned to feeling by Newman (and in some measure, in the ways I have argued, by McDowell and Alston). But there are various reasons why Gaita's account is of further interest in the context of this book. First of all, his view provides a way of elaborating upon Newman's distinction between notional and real assent, providing, as we have seen, for the possibility of various intermediate cases. Moreover, and most importantly, his account offers another way into the thought that felt responses may be religiously important – not in this case because they serve as a vehicle for a 'perception' of God, but because the moral understanding that is realised in feeling proves at least consonant with a religiously engaged ethic (of a Christian and other kinds), and may even invite completion in religious terms, to the extent that it provides a prima facie reason for the prayerful appropriation of the language of divine parental love.

This last thought points to one further respect in which Gaita's discussion offers a development of the material expounded in Chapter 1. In discussing Blum's examples of Joan and John at the beginning of that chapter, I made some reference to the role of character, and in turn of socialisation, in helping to shape a capacity for moral perception. Gaita's observations concerning the role of the language of divine parental love in enabling the nun's moral perspective provide a much fuller account of how a certain kind of moral perception may require the adoption of a range of culturally specific concepts. And it is, of course, his perspective on this point that provides a way of linking felt response, moral understanding, and religious commitment, in the ways that we have discussed. So, in summary, Gaita's account provides an extended and suggestive formulation of the mutual implication of perception, conception, and feeling in moral and religious contexts.

CHAPTER 3

Finding and making value in the world

Odysseus tells Calypso, once again, that he is determined to leave her. Once again, she offers him a bargain that no human being, it seems, could refuse. Stay with me on this island, she says, and you will avoid all the troubles that await you. And best of all, living here, 'in calm possession of this domain', you will be 'beyond the reach of death', both immortal and ageless. The love Calypso offers and has offered is, itself, endless and ageless: no fatigue, no mourning, no cessation of calm pleasure. Odysseus replies, undeflected, choosing death:

> Goddess and queen, do not make this a cause of anger with me. I know the truth of everything that you say. I know that my wise Penelope, when a man looks at her, is far beneath you in form and stature; she is a mortal, you are immortal and unageing. Yet, notwithstanding, my desire and longing day by day is still to reach my own home and to see the day of my return. And if this or that divinity should shatter my craft on the wine-dark ocean, I will bear it and keep a bold heart within me. Often enough before this time have war and wave oppressed and plagued me; let new tribulations join the old.[1]

In this passage, Odysseus makes a choice that may seem strange: he chooses the life of a human being, and its attendant experiences of struggle and loss, in preference to the immortal, ageless, invulnerable existence of the gods. This is a choice which concerns the emotions in two ways, I suggest. First of all, Odysseus is choosing a condition of life in which his emotions will be roused: he is choosing the kind of life in which, for example, his craft can be wrecked, and his wife suffer decline and die; and events of this kind, he is clear, are rightly regarded as 'tribulations', as 'oppressive', and as a 'plague'. So he chooses a life in

---

1 Martha Nussbaum, *Love's Knowledge: Essays on Philosophy and Literature* (New York: Oxford University Press, 1990), p. 365. The quotation from the *Odyssey* is from W. Shewring's translation (Oxford: Oxford University Press, 1980), V.215–24. The earlier quotations are from V.208 and V.209.

which his emotions will figure largely, as ways of registering outward developments, both of success and failure. So this first choice is a matter of allowing the emotions to play the sort of role that we have noted in Chapters 1 and 2: the emotions are stirred by (and in keeping with our earlier discussion, we might add: reveal) good and bad and success and failure, and the life Odysseus is choosing is one in which such goods and bads will arise. By contrast, we might suppose, the lives of the gods are free not only of failure but also in significant degree of success: godly invulnerability means that there is nothing to be achieved, no object of striving, and accordingly in such a life, there is no intelligible place for deeply felt emotion. A life befitting the gods will be, rather, one of 'calm pleasure'.

More speculatively, we may say that Odysseus is not only choosing a life in which the emotions will serve to reveal various values and disvalues, successes and failures; he is also choosing the kind of life in which the emotions can help to constitute certain values. He notes that his 'desire and longing' is to reach his home, and more specifically, it is implied, he aspires to reach home above all because of his desire to be reunited with Penelope. Now, the value which Penelope holds for him is not, it seems, a matter of her outward qualities establishing her superiority over other women: as he says to Calypso, she is 'far beneath you in form and stature'. The importance of Penelope for Odysseus is, we might suppose, in part a matter of their shared history, and the bonds of attachment that have arisen through that history. Given those bonds, Odysseus cannot simply substitute Calypso for Penelope, notwithstanding her superiority of form, or even of intellect or virtue. We might say, then, that the value of Penelope for Odysseus is in part constituted by his felt attachment to her: his feelings mark her out as special in his life, and mean that she cannot easily be replaced. In this respect, the emotions make it possible for one person to sink their good in that of another, and therefore to expose themselves to new possibilities of success and reversal, in keeping with the fortunes of the beloved, and the state of their relationship to the beloved. Again, by contrast, such feelings will presumably have no part in the life of the gods: for their invulnerability extends to their emotional lives, and accordingly their good cannot be put at risk by developments in the lives of others in this (or any other) way.

So the life Odysseus chooses is one in which there are genuine values – those revealed in emotional experience, and also those constituted in emotional experience. In the first case, the emotions help to reveal success and failure, and in the second they make possible certain kinds of success and failure (those correlative to the successes and failures of others whom we love, and our success or failure in sustaining our ties with them). And these values are absent from the lives of the gods, whose existence seems to be free from success and failure alike. This suggests that reflection upon the emotions can help in some degree to make sense of Odysseus' choice of a world such as ours over an Olympian world which is free from the possibility of any kind of affliction. For the emotions both reveal and enable various values which can have no place in the lives of the gods.

An affliction-free world is also, of course, the kind of world that is standardly opposed to our own in discussions of the 'problem of evil'. (The problem is: why did God make a world such as ours, when another world, free from the possibility of affliction, could have been made in its place?) This suggests that reflection upon the emotions may also help to throw into new relief some of the issues posed by the problem of evil. My aim in this chapter is to try to develop this thought, by looking in turn at the emotions as revelatory and constitutive of value.

EMOTIONAL EXPERIENCE AND THE REVELATION OF VALUE

As Blum's example of Joan and John illustrates (see the beginning of Chapter 1), often enough it is through our felt responses that we are alerted to interpersonal values. I want to consider one way, a particularly radical way, of developing this thought. Perhaps it is possible to grasp the value of the world as a whole intuitively, in rather the way that the nun in Gaita's example grasps the worth of the patients intuitively (that is, by means of a kind of perception – contrast again the more discursive kind of appreciation of the patients that is implied in the outlook of the psychiatrists.)[2] And perhaps, more radically still, this sort of insight into the goodness of the world is only available thus, just as Gaita proposes that the true worth or humanity of the patients is revealed only in the light of saintly love, and not otherwise accessible.[3]

---

2 Again, this is not to deny that discursive thought is relevant to her response to the patients (compare in particular the role Gaita assigns to her use of the language of prayer). The thought is just that the insight is realised in an affectively toned perception of value.
3 Compare too the discussion of Chapter 1, where we considered some reasons for thinking that the content of a 'real image' of God may be available only in feeling.

An objector will wonder, of course: why suppose that it is safe to build on these 'radical' assumptions? If you are unpersuaded by Gaita's discussion, or at any rate his treatment of felt responses as uniquely revelatory of certain values, then the enquiry I am proposing to follow will seem pretty unpromising. But if the broad outline of Gaita's programme carries conviction, then the possibility I want to examine will seem, I think, worthy of serious consideration: perhaps it is true that forms of felt response reveal not only the value of this or that item in the world, but the value of the world more generally. Of course, there are further difficulties in this proposal which are not involved in Gaita's thought. Notably, we might wonder whether it is even intelligible that the world as a whole should be the object of a felt response. So I shall begin with a consideration of this question: what would it mean for the world as a whole to be appreciated feelingly?

Philosophers customarily distinguish between emotions and 'moods', where the latter are not about anything in particular. For instance, I may be depressed, but not about anything in particular; in this case, I may suppose that my situation in general, rather than any particular thing or state of affairs, is profoundly unpromising. So the case of moods suggests one way in which an affective state may involve an appraisal of one's circumstances in general, and such an appraisal may in turn lead in the direction of an appraisal of the world as a whole. However, moods do not seem to issue in an assessment of the goodness (or otherwise) of the world in quite the way that we require. It is true that if a person's mood is consistently positive or uplifting, then this may commit them to the thought that their life is good overall; but this thought does not require them to suppose that the life of people in general is good, or that the world as a whole is good. So the route from moods to an assessment of the world as a whole seems to be at best indirect. What we need, rather, is an affective state which is targeted more explicitly at the world. The affective state which involves the discursive thought that the world as a whole is good, where this thought engenders a positive felt response, would satisfy this requirement. But here feelings seem to be assigned a subsidiary role once more, and the goodness of the world is identified in discursive thought rather than in feeling. To preserve the analogy with Gaita's example of the nun, and to retain a distinctive epistemic role for feeling, we need an affective state which is targeted explicitly at the world and involves a kind of affectively toned perception of the goodness of the world. I shall set out two models which seem, broadly speaking, to meet these desiderata.

Quentin Smith has drawn a sharp distinction between what he calls the metaphysics of 'reason' and of 'feeling'.[4] The first is the traditional concern of metaphysical thought in western philosophy, and its goal has been to provide an explanation of the world as a whole (why it exists at all, and why it takes the particular form it does). In place of this enterprise (which he thinks is bound to be fruitless) Smith proposes a 'metaphysics' which is concerned with the value or importance of the world, rather than with its causal or explanatory ground. Summing up this approach, he writes: 'While rational metaphysics is concerned to discover the unconditioned reasons that are reasons for every other reason, the metaphysics of feeling inquires about the ultimate importances. The world has different ways of being important, and the aim is to discover which ways are more fundamental, and ultimately, which is the basic way of being important that underlies every other way.'[5]

Significantly, given our concerns, Smith proposes that global importances are appreciated in feeling. The most basic ways of registering world-encompassing values he calls 'intuitive feelings of global importances', and he expounds their nature as follows:

These feelings are 'intuitive knowings' in the sense that in them the presence of a global importance is felt. A world-importance is manifest in an immediate way, without appearing through the intermediary of verbal significations, mental imagery, or any sort of discursive or inferential thought. These intuitive feelings may vary from a suspenseful and anxious contemplation of an all-pervading ominousness, to a captivated marvelling at the miraculous presence of the whole, to a joyous feeling of global fulfillment. In these intuitions and others, there is a direct sense of a meaningful whole, a whole to which I respond with sensations of feeling.[6]

The position outlined here seems to match the desiderata I set out above. Smith is talking of a non-discursive state that is directed at the significance of the world as a whole; and that significance is registered, he says, feelingly: 'the presence of a global importance is felt'. So here feeling is directed explicitly at the world-whole and thereby reveals its value. In the same vein, writing just before this passage, he comments: 'The appreciative method of metaphysical knowing is not a method that is

---

4 Quentin Smith, *The Felt Meanings of the World: A Metaphysics of Feeling* (West Lafayette, IN: Purdue University Press, 1986).
5 *Ibid.*, p. 20.   6 *Ibid.*, p. 25.

imposed on feeling from the outside, but is found in feelings themselves.'⁷
It is true that in the concluding sentence of the excerpted passage quoted
above, he does differentiate the intuition of the 'whole' and the felt
response to it, and this may suggest again an 'add-on' conception of
feeling, where the real cognitive work is done by a feeling-less intuition
and the feeling is simply tacked on, while lacking any epistemic significance in its own right. However, I take it that Smith's insistence that
this sort of metaphysical knowing 'is not a method that is imposed on
feeling from outside' is enough to cancel that reading: the proposal he is
outlining in the excerpted passage surely involves the idea that the
understanding of global importances is lodged (at least in part) in feeling,
and not otherwise available.

To bring out more fully what Smith has in mind (and to confirm that
feelings are being accorded the role I have just described), it is helpful to
examine a particular example of this sort of feeling. Here is a case which is
central to his overall argument, since it concerns what he takes to be the
most fundamental of global importances:

> I am sitting on a veranda on a summer afternoon, watching the trees as they sway
> gently in the sunlight. My awareness gradually broadens and deepens, and soon a
> joy begins to arise in me, a rejoicing in the *fulfillment* of the very world that is
> composed of myself, these swaying trees, this blue sky, and the indistinctly
> manifest 'everything else' that extends beyond all that I am perceiving. In this
> rejoicing I am experiencing a captivated intuition of the determinately appearing
> importance of global fulfillment . . . The sensuously felt aspect of this appearing
> world-whole can be made explicit first. My perceptible surroundings seem to be
> infused with an upwardly radiated feeling-flow of joy, a joyous feeling-tonality that
> has its source, not in the garden, trees, and sky, but in the fulfilled global interior
> that appears to be 'far behind' and 'far within' these perceptible phenomena. The
> fulfilled global interior joyously radiates everything – including myself –
> upwards, 'on high', to the sensuously felt 'top of the world'. By virtue of my
> being *affected* by the fulfilled whole, everything is felt to be flowingly elevated to
> the highest tonal region of the world.⁸

This description gives some idea of the kind of phenomenology that is
relevant to an evaluative perception of the world as a whole. For our
purposes, it is significant that this insight into the world's value is realised
in feeling. Hence Smith comments that: 'In this rejoicing I am experi-
encing a captivated intuition.' So the intuition is not just the causal source
of the rejoicing, but embedded in the rejoicing. Moreover, this experience
is said to be targeted at the value not just of individual items in his visual

7 *Ibid.*, p. 24.   8 *Ibid.*, p. 151, Smith's italics.

field, but at the significance of the world-whole. In turn this is because the experience is focally directed at the 'global interior', a reality that lies 'far behind and within' the physical objects that are the direct objects of his senses. The seeming mysteriousness of this proposal can be mitigated somewhat by reference to an analogous case that Smith cites. Consider, he says, the way in which someone to whom we feel close may appear to us. In this case, he suggests, the feeling-tonality 'appears to imbue the other's bodily surface' but 'does not seem to arise there, but from further within' (from, as it were, the 'interior' of the person).⁹ He means by this, I think, that we feel ourselves to be related not just to the exterior of the person, which may be infused by a warm glow in our perception, but to their core identity, the real person. In the same way, we might think, the kind of experience recorded in the passage above concerns not just individual features of the world (individual trees and a particular stretch of blue sky), but its core identity.

So here is one kind of example which suggests the possibility in principle of an affectively infused recognition of the value of the world as a whole, where that recognition is communicated in feeling, and not in some discursively articulated assessment of the world's character. If this sort of experience is at least possible, then we have potentially another way of approaching the 'problem of evil', one which does not turn upon the sort of weighing of goods and logically concomitant bads that is typical of standard discussions in theodicy, but involves rather a more direct, intuitive assessment of the world's goodness (or lack of goodness). This is a thought to which I shall return shortly, but first I want to give a further account of the possibility in principle of an affectively toned, intuitive appreciation of the world's value.

In his *Speeches on Religion*, Friedrich Schleiermacher presents a further formulation of the idea that the significance of the 'world-whole' can be grasped intuitively and in ways that implicate 'feeling'.¹⁰ I shall begin by considering the first edition of this work, before offering some comment on the relevance for our topic of the second edition. In the second speech, Schleiermacher proposes that 'intuition of the universe' is 'the highest and most universal formula of religion on the basis of which you should be able to find every place in religion, from which you may determine its essence and its limits'.¹¹ This position seems immediately to meet two of

---

9 *Ibid.*, p. 59.
10 Friedrich Schleiermacher, *On Religion: Speeches to its Cultured Despisers*, tr. Richard Crouter (Cambridge: Cambridge University Press, 1976; first published 1799).
11 *Ibid.*, p. 24.

the desiderata we established above: Schleiermacher is concerned with a state that is targeted at the world as a whole (or 'the universe') and with a state whose content is supplied not by argument or discursive reflection but by 'intuition'. Moreover, he is clear that intuition is closely related to 'feeling'; indeed, he writes (here echoing Kant, of course): 'Intuition without feeling is nothing and can have neither the proper origin nor the proper force; feeling without intuition is also nothing; both are therefore something only when and because they are originally one and unseparated.'[12] Schleiermacher goes on to try to describe more exactly how intuition and feeling may 'originally' be 'one and unseparated'. Although his thoughts on this point are hard to fathom (as Schleiermacher himself freely acknowledges), they are worth citing at some length since the question of how feeling relates to the intuitive grasp of the universe that Schleiermacher is positing is of course important for our concerns. This is what he says:

That first mysterious moment that occurs in every sensory perception, before intuition and feeling have separated, where sense and its objects have, as it were, flowed into one another and become one, before both turn back to their original position – I know how indescribable it is and how quickly it passes away . . . Would that I could and might express it, at least indicate it, without having to desecrate it! It is as fleeting and transparent as the first scent with which the dew gently caresses the waking flowers, as modest and delicate as a maiden's kiss, as holy and fruitful as a nuptial embrace; indeed, not *like* these, but *is itself* all of these. A manifestation, an event develops quickly and magically into an image of the universe. Even as the beloved and ever-sought-for form fashions itself, my soul flees toward it; I embrace it, not as a shadow, but as the holy essence itself. I lie on the bosom of the infinite world. At this moment, I am its soul, for I feel all its powers and its infinite life as my own; at this moment it is my body . . . With the slightest trembling the holy embrace is dispersed, and now for the first time the intuition stands before me as a separate form; I survey it, and it mirrors itself in my open soul like the image of the vanishing beloved in the awakened eye of a youth; now for the first time the feeling works its way up from inside and diffuses itself in the blush of shame and desire on his cheek. This moment is the highest flowering of religion; if I could create it in you, I would be a god . . . This is the natal hour of everything living in religion.[13]

Whatever the difficulties of interpretation here, it is clear at least that Schleiermacher is alluding to a unitary kind of 'awareness' in which subject and object of experience are not yet fully differentiated. And he seems to be suggesting, plausibly, that a mode of awareness of this kind is

12 *Ibid.*, p. 31.   13 *Ibid.*, pp. 31–2. Schleiermacher's italics.

bound to be non-linguistic, and its content difficult to record therefore in verbal terms. So on this view, 'feeling' is in some fashion involved in the most fundamental way of cognising the significance of the world-whole, but at this point it has still to be differentiated from intuition, and its sense is not readily verbalisable.

Richard Brandt has suggested that in the first edition of the *Speeches*, the term 'feeling' is being used in a 'nonintentional sense': 'here [Schleiermacher] does not assert that the feeling is a *feeling of* anything, but only that there is a feeling of a certain sort "appropriate" to certain intuitions'.[14] If this is right, then we should resolve any uncertainties in the interpretation of the above passage in favour of the view that feeling's role is after all derivative: it is not in itself of cognitive significance. But in the second edition (of 1806), Brandt suggests that 'Intuition is given over to science', and accordingly it is now feeling (rather than intuition, as in the first edition) that is the essence of religion.[15] This poses a question about how we should understand the relationship between feeling and scientific understanding in the second edition, and whether feeling is now derivative from science (rather than intuition). Brandt's preferred interpretation of the second edition is this: 'at this time Schleiermacher himself, although he recognized the possibility of religious experience apart from knowledge in some circumstances, believed that religious experience ultimately cannot occur without interpretations of the world which are bound up with scientific and philosophical thought'.[16] However, he also acknowledges that 'it is impossible to exclude absolutely the possibility of Schleiermacher's having thought that the religious feeling is immediate in the sense of being altogether unmediated by thought, directly brought about by the contact with the universe, and hence independent of scientific or philosophic knowledge'.[17] Here Brandt contrasts two interpretations of the role of feeling in the second edition: on one reading (his favoured reading), feeling depends upon the mediating influence of discursive (scientific or philosophical) thought; on the other, feeling results directly from some encounter with 'the universe'. Quite apart from textual considerations, Brandt evidently considers the second reading philosophically problematic, and his reasoning here is of some relevance for the general stance that we are examining in this book. In the following

14 Richard B. Brandt, *The Philosophy of Schleiermacher: The Development of his Theory of Scientific and Religious Knowledge* (Westport, CT: Greenwood Press, 1941), p. 107, Brandt's italics. I am grateful to Peter Byrne for drawing this reference to my attention.
15 *Ibid.*, p. 176.   16 *Ibid.*, p. 193.   17 *Ibid.*, p. 191.

passage, he is discussing the idea of an 'intuition' of the universe which is unmediated by scientific or other discursive understanding:

> If Schleiermacher did mean that religious feelings include such intuition which is an independent act of the religious consciousness, then he could consistently believe that religion is independent of science in that it is experience independent of thought which may nevertheless be expressed in judgments which may be true or false. Unfortunately for this view, it is difficult to see of what importance certain judgments would be even if they did somehow express religious intuitions of this sort. For the religious man would have little reason to believe these judgments to be true. At best they could be only a crude kind of opinion, which could not enjoy the high degree of probability of confirmation of judgments integrated with the whole system of thought and knowledge. And if conflicts arose between these judgments and scientific thought, the latter would have all the advantage due to the logical weight of the whole integrated system of which it is a part. It is difficult to believe that Schleiermacher meant this, although some passages do suggest the interpretation.[18]

Here Brandt allows the possibility (both in itself and as a reading of Schleiermacher) that feeling may register the nature of things independently of discursive thought; but he thinks this possibility of little epistemic significance because such an understanding must always defer to what is made known in 'scientific thought'. The understanding of feeling that we have been exploring may offer Schleiermacher a way out of the difficulty that is posed here. The example of Newman and Gaita suggests that feeling may build upon discursive thought and offer a deeper reading of it (see, for example, Newman on the relationship between a 'notional' and a 'real' understanding of God). On this perspective, the potential clash between discursive thought and what is revealed in feeling, which Brandt takes to establish the epistemic worthlessness of feeling, will not arise – and yet feeling's content is not being treated as simply reducible to that of discursive thought. A good example of this possibility, whereby feeling takes up the concepts that have been framed in discursive understanding and takes them further, is provided by Fritjof Capra in *The Tao of Physics*:

> I was sitting by the ocean one late summer afternoon, watching the waves rolling in and feeling the rhythm of my breathing, when I suddenly became aware of my whole environment as being engaged in a gigantic cosmic dance. Being a physicist, I knew that the sand, rocks, water and air around me were made of vibrating molecules and atoms, and that these consisted of particles which interacted with one another by creating and destroying other particles. I knew also that the Earth's atmosphere was continually bombarded by showers of

---

18 *Ibid.*, pp. 192–3.

'cosmic rays', particles of high energy undergoing multiple collisions as they penetrated the air. All this was familiar to me from my research in high-energy physics, but until that moment I had only experienced it through graphs, diagrams and mathematical theories. As I sat on that beach my former experiences came to life; I 'saw' cascades of energy coming down from outer space, in which particles were created and destroyed in rhythmic pulses; I 'saw' the atoms of the elements and those of my body participating in the cosmic dance of energy; I felt its rhythm and I 'heard' its sound, and at that moment I *knew* that this was the Dance of Shiva.[19]

The perception that is described here is, I suggest, affectively informed – considering the setting of the experience, the general tone of the description, its existentially significant content, and the author's suggestion that he 'felt' the rhythm of the cosmos. So the passage provides an example of an affectively toned, conceptually structured value perception of the nature of the cosmos as a whole. On this view, what is apprehended in feeling is certainly informed by what has been understood scientifically, and to this extent is in harmony with such an understanding, but at the same time it is not simply reducible to what can be set out in discursive terms. It may be, then, that Brandt's interpretation of Schleiermacher involves a needless shrinking of the possibilities, and that feeling can contribute to an appreciation of the value of the world as a whole, without thereby being independent of discursive understanding or reducible to such an understanding.

We have been considering Schleiermacher's *Speeches* as a further way (to set alongside the model we derived from Quentin Smith) of developing the thought that it is possible to grasp the value of the world in an affectively toned intuition of the whole. I suggest that when read in the light of Newman and Gaita, along with Capra, his position can at any rate be developed in broadly this direction.[20] This account seems somewhat different from Smith's: notably, unlike Smith's approach, the Schleiermacher–Capra model (as I have presented it) is explicit that the

19 Fritjof Capra, *The Tao of Physics: An Exploration of the Parallels between Modern Physics and Eastern Mysticism*, 3rd edn (London: Flamingo, 1992), p. 11, Capra's italics. I am grateful to Kate Masel for this reference.
20 The question of what exactly Schleiermacher himself thought is no doubt a complex matter, and one that I am happy to hand over to his commentators. The suggestion that he may have failed to resolve certain ambiguities in his notion of 'feeling' is confirmed by some remarks of Robert Roberts on Schleiermacher's appeal to the 'feeling of absolute dependence' in *The Christian Faith*. Roberts comments: 'Schleiermacher's account of this religious emotion cries out for critical comment. He vacillates between the highly "cognitive" interpretation of the feeling that I have just expounded and a concertedly non-cognitive one': Robert Roberts, *Emotions: An Essay in Aid of Moral Psychology* (Cambridge: Cambridge University Press, 2003), p. 271.

value perception is structured by concepts that have been fashioned in discursive thought.[21]

This concludes my survey of two ways in which we might expound the possibility of an affectively toned, non-discursive apprehension of the value of the world as a whole. I conclude that this sort of experience, unusual though it sounds and is, is not unintelligible. On the contrary, there are various ways (in particular those provided by Smith and a certain reading and development of Schleiermacher) in which we might try to understand its possibility, and provide the beginnings of an associated phenomenology.[22]

In philosophical discussion, the 'problem of evil' is standardly addressed by considering the relations between various goods and bads, the theodicist claiming that these goods and bads constitute 'integral wholes' (since the goods logically cannot be achieved without the bads) which are overall good, and the sceptic denying this claim. Of course, there are other stances too in this debate – for instance, the proposal that this sort of exercise is objectionable on religious grounds, perhaps because it purports to assume a divine perspective on the order of things. The thoughts that we have been exploring in this chapter suggest that alongside these familiar strategies of argument we may set another kind of view, namely, the view that an assessment of the goodness or otherwise of the world may depend, at least in part, upon an insight into its character which is available, and only available, in feeling. Again, the analogy with Gaita's discussion of the nun is instructive. The psychiatrists in his example have developed an analytically sophisticated account of the worth of the patients (by appeal to notions such as 'dignity' and 'equality'); and similarly, moral philosophers (using the language of rationality,

21 As I have indicated, Smith comments simply: 'A world-importance is manifest in an immediate way, without appearing through the intermediary of verbal significations, mental imagery, or any sort of discursive or inferential thought': *The Felt Meanings*, p. 25. This account seems compatible with the idea (which Brandt delineates) that the character of the world is registered in an 'intuition' that is wholly unmediated by scientific or other discursive thought.

22 It is worth noting that Schleiermacher's text offers another and in some ways more easily comprehensible intimation of how we might understand the possibility of a non-discursive, affectively toned assessment of the goodness of the world. He is clearly impressed by the thought that if 'the universe' constitutes an organic whole, then any part of it can in principle function to reveal the whole; and in this vein, he can write that 'to accept everything individual as a part of the whole and everything limited as a representation of the infinite is religion' (*On Religion*, p. 25). Accordingly, if it is possible to grasp the character of some part of the world in feeling (compare Gaita), then that insight might also serve as a revelation of the character of the whole. I do not want to explore this possibility further here, but a similar kind of idea will be under discussion in Chapter 6.

autonomy, flourishing, and so on) have considered the worth of various classes of human being, including 'afflicted' human beings. But if Gaita is right, no amount of such discursive reflection is enough to reveal what is revealed in feeling. A person may have just the right discursive account of these matters (rather as the psychiatrists do, on his view), and may sincerely hold to this account, and yet fail to grasp the relevant values in depth. If we can have an affectively toned impression of the goodness of the world as a whole, then at least in principle, a similar assessment of the role of discursive reflection in matters of theodicy is possible. This is a bold claim that calls for closer examination, but first of all, I would like to consider two more general objections to the idea that feeling can be relied upon to reveal values.

Gaita's own sense of the value of the patients on the psychiatric ward seems to turn upon a moment of intense 'visionary' experience. (I take it that this experience has a degree of felt intensity: certainly it made a deep and lasting impression upon him and made for a fundamental reorientation of value perspective, and this suggests that the experience was in some degree affectively toned.) Similarly, Quentin Smith seems to have in mind moments where we feel forcefully the significance of the world as a whole. This sort of epistemology of value recognition poses an obvious difficulty: such moments of vividly experienced feeling are typically transient (we cannot, realistically, live enduringly in such a state of heightened sensitivity). Even allowing that we continue to acknowledge the authority of the original experience once the feeling has subsided, there is a question therefore about how we are to appropriate its meaning at later times, and appropriate that meaning 'really' and not just 'notionally'. Smith's discussion offers one response to this issue, by setting out ways in which the meaning of an initial 'intuitive feeling of global importance' may be recovered at later times. He deals first of all with what he calls 'afterglowing reappreciations' of such intuitive feelings:

These intuitive feelings and their sensuous accompaniments eventually begin to decline and dissipate, and the global importance begins to lose its immediate presence. But there lingers an 'afterglow' of the feeling and of the appearance of the importance . . . I could reappreciate the importance by allowing its vividly retained presence to evoke in me thoughts and linguistic formations that capture and articulate its nature. In the reappreciative afterglow of a marvelling affect, for instance, the global importance of miraculousness could evoke in me the verbal significations that are appropriate for expressing and conveying its felt importance. I could be moved to exclaim inwardly, 'It is amazing that the world exists! It is a miracle!' These significations are felt to capture the very tension and vibrancy of the intuited importance; in them the world's importance reverberates and rekindles my sensuous feelings, although in a subtle and diminished way.[23]

On this account, the original intuitive feelings of importance give rise, I take it, to dimmer ('afterglowing') copies of themselves at later times, and these dimmer copies in turn may give rise to verbal formulations, which can be used to evoke or 'rekindle' (rather than simply describe the content of) something like the original experience. But this way of recalling the original feeling will also give out with time, Smith thinks. And this suggests the need for a further way of appropriating the meaning of such feelings, and here he appeals to feelings 'of concentrative interest'.[24] The movement from an afterglowing feeling to a feeling of concentrative interest involves a shift from one sort of vocabulary to another. In the case of afterglowing feelings, we are still trying to recall the content of the original feeling at the level of intuitive insight, albeit with the assistance of language (a language that is, Smith says, 'intimative, suggestive and evocative',[25] rather than more formal or descriptive). (Compare Schleiermacher's use of poetic and erotic language to convey the character of a non-dualistic awareness of the universe.) The feelings of concentrative interest, by contrast, involve an attempt to cast some of the content of the original insight in the language of discursive prose. What this means in practice is evident from Smith's further reflections on the experience of 'global fulfillment' that I cited earlier. Let us take a representative comment: 'this global interior', he remarks, 'is intuitively felt to be a plenum, a fullness, a positivity'.[26] Clearly, at this juncture, the content of the original feeling is no longer being conveyed at the level of intuition, or evoked using metaphorical or allusive language; instead, Smith is offering a prosaic account of what has been understood.

Some might suppose that the content of the original feeling can be captured in full in prosaic terms. Alternatively, in the spirit of Gaita's discussion, we might suppose that the truth of a claim such as 'the global interior is a plenum' (compare: 'the patients are fully my equals') cannot be apprehended in depth apart from the original feeling (because the sense

23 *The Felt Meanings*, p. 25.   24 *Ibid.*, p. 26.
25 *Ibid.*, p. 25.   26 *Ibid.*, p. 152.

of the relevant concepts cannot be fully explicated independently of what is revealed in feeling). However, even on a Gaita-style view, such discursive claims will still have a part to play. First of all, discursive thought will make possible a partial, relatively superficial understanding of what is revealed in feeling. Moreover, discursive thought can specify its own limits, and acknowledge that there is a deeper-than-can-be-articulated insight whose content can be understood in full only in the light of feeling. This offers a discursively formulated way of remaining open to what (by assumption) can be grasped only in feeling. For instance, given such an account, a person may resolve to treat afflicted human beings as genuinely the equals of other people, while granting that from the perspective of discursive thought (the only perspective to which the person has direct access in the present), there is something in this stance that remains, at least, mysterious.

These responses to the problem of how to assign an enduring role to what is revealed in feeling assume that the content of the feeling cannot be fully specified at later times. Another response (a preferable response, I think) would appeal once more to the idea that feelings of the kind that Gaita identifies can be embedded in character and situated in narrative terms (such as the narrative of divine parental love). This response allows feeling to play a still larger role in our evaluative lives: here its deeper content need not be simply gestured at retrospectively in the language of discursive prose; instead, feeling itself remains available as a source of continuing understanding. This sort of case is embodied in the witness of the nun. Her believing in the full humanity of the patients 'in her heart' involves an enduring disposition to certain kinds of affective-cum-behavioural response to afflicted people. It is worth adding that these various replies to the objection from the transitoriness of feeling need not be mutually exclusive: it may be plausible to take one response in relation to some feelings, and another in relation to others.

Before returning explicitly to questions of theodicy, there is one further objection to the Gaita-style model that I would like to note. Here the objection is not that feeling cannot be recreated, or its content apprehended in some other way at a later time, but that even if it can, such moments of visionary experience are not a secure starting point for evaluative reflection, because they are not properly integrated with our knowledge more generally.[27] Martha Nussbaum rehearses an objection of

---

27 Compare Brandt's objection to his less-favoured reading of Schleiermacher for a different formulation of this difficulty.

this kind in her critique of knowledge claims which are grounded in the forcefulness of passing emotional experience. She considers this example of such alleged knowing:

Françoise brings him the news: 'Mademoiselle Albertine has gone.' Only a moment before, he believed with confidence that he did not love her any longer. Now the news of her departure brings a reaction so powerful, an anguish so overwhelming, that this view of his condition simply vanishes, Marcel knows, and knows with certainty, without the least room for doubt, that he loves Albertine.[28]

Nussbaum comments: 'Proust tells us that the sort of knowledge of the heart we need in this case cannot be given to us by the science of psychology, or, indeed, by any sort of scientific use of intellect. Knowledge of the heart must come from the heart – from and in its pains and longings, its emotional responses.'[29] This view is clearly akin to the thought that we have been exploring, that feeling vouchsafes a kind of intuitive understanding whose content is not otherwise available. Given this parallel, it is very much to the point to enquire why Nussbaum finds this account of human understanding defective.

Nussbaum's critique has various strands, and I shall note just two. First of all, she asks: 'Can any feeling, taken in isolation from its context, its history, its relationship to other feelings and actions, really be cataleptic? Can't we be wrong about it and what it signifies?'[30] Suppose we read these remarks as an objection to Gaita's proposal that it makes no sense to doubt what is revealed in the conduct of the nun. Nussbaum is surely right to suppose that an experience carrying a strong emotional charge is not thereby rendered immune from error. So she is right to think that such experiences, and what they appear to disclose, may properly be doubted, and subjected to testing. But this view is compatible, I suggest, with Gaita's claim that he was 'certain about the revelatory quality of [the nun's] behaviour' and that the concept of a mistake has no application here.[31]

In general, there are two kinds of reason for doubting the veracity of an experience. First, one might find some difficulty with the experience itself or its context (the conditions under which it occurs, and 'its context, its history, its relationship to other feelings and actions'). Secondly, one

---

28 'Love's Knowledge', in Nussbaum, *Love's Knowledge*, p. 261. The passage to which she is referring is, of course, from Proust's *Remembrance of Things Past*.
29 *Love's Knowledge*, pp. 261–2.
30 *Ibid.*, pp. 269–70. Here Nussbaum is alluding to the Stoic understanding of science as a system of *katalēpseis*, that is, certainties which are grounded in self-verifying experiences (see *ibid.*, p. 265).
31 *A Common Humanity*, p. 20.

might find that while the experience seems trustworthy enough in itself and in its context, what it appears to disclose conflicts with what appears to be disclosed by other sources which have as much claim to reliability. Nussbaum is concerned with doubt which pertains to the first kind of challenge. As it happens, the nun's experience (and perhaps Gaita's too) seems to satisfy this sort of challenge. Her experience is not merely isolated, but integrated with her epistemic commitments in other respects: since this kind of sensitivity is grounded in her character, the experience fits with experiences she has had at other times, and it is consistent with her use of the language of divine parental love in her prayers. Allowing that an experience meets this sort of challenge, we can then consider its susceptibility to the second kind of challenge. And by contrast with, say, my belief that I saw the Speke bus this morning, Gaita's belief in the revelatory quality of the nun's behaviour seems invulnerable in principle to this second sort of challenge, because by assumption we have, apart from her revelatory example (and the revelatory example of others like her), no means of access to the quality of 'humanity'. So there is in principle no way in which what is disclosed in the experience could be open to challenge by reference to some other epistemic source. On this point, Gaita's claim that the concept of a mistake has no application here seems to hold good.

In these ways, I take it that the sort of perspective we have been exploring can after all accommodate Nussbaum's first kind of objection. She frames a second objection as follows:

> Proustian catalepsis is a solitary event. This is emphasized in the narrative, where true knowledge of love only arrives in Albertine's absence, indeed at a time when, although he doesn't know it, Marcel will never see her again. The experience does not require Albertine's participation or even awareness; it has no element of mutuality or exchange. And it certainly does not presuppose any knowledge of or trust in the feelings of the other . . . We said that the cataleptic impression can coexist with skepticism about the feelings of the other. In fact, it implies this skepticism. For on the cataleptic view an emotion can be known if and only if it can be vividly experienced. What you can't have you can't know. But the other's will, thoughts, and feelings are, for Marcel, paradigmatic of that which cannot be had.[32]

Nussbaum's objection this time is that the model of feeling as revelatory (developed as Proust develops it) issues in a kind of solipsism: I commune with my own inward states, but do not have any real encounter

---

32 *Love's Knowledge*, p. 271.

with other people, since their inward states are inaccessible to me. Again, this is a criticism that brings some features of the approach that we have been exploring into new focus. The nun believes in the equality of the patients with herself 'in her heart', but this belief is not therefore impenetrable to others. On the contrary, what she believes is communicated in bodily terms. It is her demeanour towards the patients and the inflexions of her body that, from the vantage point of the young Gaita, light up their humanity. Indeed, her behaviour is not just evidence of what she feels, but helps to specify what it is to hold such a belief 'in one's heart'. So here too the model of feeling that we have been considering can accommodate Nussbaum's concerns.

Nussbaum goes on to offer her own preferred account of the nature of love's knowledge. After relating Ann Beattie's story 'Learning to Fall', she comments:

> This knowledge [achieved in love] is 'kind of slow'; it unfolds, evolves, in human time. It is no one thing at all, but a complex way of being with another person, a deliberate yielding to uncontrollable external influences . . . We can barely imagine how we (or Zeno) might describe and defend the cataleptic view of love in an article without reference to any whole literary work – using, perhaps, schematic examples. We can imagine this because the experience in question is fundamentally self-contained and isolated. And it announces a set of necessary and sufficient conditions: it tells us what love *is*. With Beattie's view, a treatment even by schematic examples is bound to seem empty, lacking in the richness of texture that displays knowledge of love here. We seem to require no unit shorter than this actual story, with all its open-endedness. The view says that we cannot love if we try to have a science of life; its embodiment must be a text that departs, itself, from the scientific.[33]

Again, these reflections throw into new relief the view that we have been developing in relation to Gaita's work. Here Nussbaum maintains that the kind of knowledge that belongs to love cannot be conveyed abstractly or by means of schematic examples, but has instead to be communicated narratively.[34] Once more, the example of the nun fits this

---

33 *Ibid.*, p. 281, Nussbaum's italics.
34 It is worth noting that in according this sort of importance to story, Nussbaum is not thereby denying the place of first-hand feeling. As she says in relation to Beattie's story: 'The cataleptic view has its role to play inside these experiences . . . There are powerful feelings here – sexual feelings, feelings, I think, of profound joy and nakedness and giddiness and freedom: the feelings of falling. But he's too intrinsic to it all for us to say that those feelings just *are* the falling, the loving' (p. 279, italics in the original). Again, the view of feeling that we have been exploring can accommodate this sort of concern: the requirement that feeling open out to the other is implied in Gaita's view, where feeling is taken to have an 'aboutness' in its own right.

requirement, in so far as her conduct and feeling towards the patients have to be understood (in the ways explored in the last chapter) in the light of the language of divine parental love, where the nature of this love in turn is communicated not in schematic examples or the language of theoretical psychology, but in the biblical narrative, and the richly articulated story of God's dealings with humankind that is recorded there. And we could see the nun's own love as having a narrative dimension: it is, after all, not just a state of consciousness, but is acted out in relationship to the patients. So Nussbaum's criticisms of the 'cataleptic view' of emotional knowing are helpful in drawing out various features of the Gaita-style account that have not received due attention so far, notably: the particular kind of certainty that attaches to the nun's revelatory example; the integration of feeling and bodily conduct on this view, so that lodging belief in feeling need not imply a kind of epistemic solipsism; and the role of narrative in communicating the nature of the nun's love, and also the divine love which makes hers possible.

THE PROBLEM OF EVIL

We have been reviewing various objections to the idea that an intuitive grasp of values (and specifically, the goodness of the 'world-whole') can be realised in states of feeling. Allowing that these objections can be turned aside, or accommodated, in the ways we have supposed, we can return to the issue of theodicy, and the relevance of such feelings in this regard. If it is possible to have an intuitive, affectively toned appreciation of the goodness of the world as a whole, where what is communicated in this appreciation is not otherwise fully accessible, what difference should this make to our assessment of questions of theodicy? If nothing more, this possibility should at least mean that we conduct theodicy in the conventional style (where goods and bads are weighed against each other, by means of discursive argument) with a degree of humility; for perhaps this kind of discussion is of its nature incapable of the kind of understanding of the world's goodness that can be achieved in felt intuition. (Compare again the attempt to understand in purely discursive terms the worth of individual human beings, including afflicted human beings; on the Gaita-style view, such an account is bound to neglect what is revealed in feeling and inaccessible to a more theoretical kind of enquiry.) If there is in fact another, deeper understanding of the world's goodness, available only in feeling, then this suggests that the findings of a more conventional theodicy will always be provisional. Analogously, the failure to find a satisfactory way of articulating the worth of afflicted human beings in the language of (for example) moral philosophy ought not of itself to establish that such people lack equal worth with the rest of us; for perhaps that kind of insight lies by its nature beyond the reach of that kind of enquiry.

But what of a person who is not in receipt of an affectively toned appreciation of the goodness of the world? Can these deliberations have any relevance for them? Naturally, someone in this position will want a reason for supposing that this sort of affectively toned perception is indeed available; in the absence of such a reason, they might conclude either that the very idea of an affectively toned appreciation of this kind is confused, or that this is a possibility which has at any rate to be set aside for all practical purposes, so casting us once more on the resources of discursive thought. Thinking again of the role the nun plays for the young Gaita (in exemplifying the possibility of an affectively toned appreciation of the patients), we might wonder whether there is any counterpart for her behaviour in the case where it is the goodness or worth of the world as a whole that is in question. Perhaps we can find such a counterpart in the lives of people who despite great adversity and even affliction continue to testify, though their dealings with other people and the world more generally, that the life of a human being is a worthwhile undertaking. This sort of witness may be conveyed in a refusal to give way to despair, or in a continuing capacity to find meaning in daily life in the face of affliction. Again, historically, it is the example of the saints which speaks most powerfully of this possibility: such individuals show a kind of indomitable trust in the goodness of the world which is not vanquished even in the face of great tribulation. Simon Tugwell offers an account of how St Francis of Assisi's open-handedness towards not just his fellow human beings but nature itself might be interpreted in broadly these terms:

Whatever happens is God's gift to us. This is the source of Francis' famous love of nature. But we shall misunderstand it entirely if we only look at the obviously attractive features of it. It is easy enough to enjoy the story of Francis taming the wolf of Gubbio or making friends with a cicada, and there is something pleasantly sentimental about his getting a passer-by to purchase for him a solitary lamb that was left in a field full of goats. But Francis' acceptance of all creatures was intended to mean a radical unprotectedness precisely in the face of *all* creatures. So Francis bids his followers not merely to be obedient to all human creatures, but even to be subject (*subditi*) to wild animals. And subjection does not even stop there. On one occasion Francis' habit caught fire, and he tried to stop his companion putting the fire out, saying to him, 'Dearest brother, do not harm brother fire.' Francis only permitted the fire to be extinguished because the superior insisted on it . . . It is this quality of total resignation to the will even of inanimate things which gives Francis' poverty its special nuance.[35]

Perhaps this sort of example can play a role in relation to the problem of evil analogous to that played by the nun in relation to the question of the worth of afflicted human beings: just as the nun's behaviour reveals the full humanity of the patients, so Francis's conduct reveals the unconditional goodness of the world, that is, a goodness which does not depend upon things going well for me. It is worth emphasising, however, with Tugwell, that the kind of happiness or meaning that Francis thinks is attainable in this life, whatever may befall a person, is not what is conventionally meant by happiness; and his sense of the character of the world's goodness needs to be understood accordingly. As Tugwell comments:

[Francis] is indeed most insistent on happiness, so much so that when he is tormented himself for some reason or another, he tries to keep himself out of the way for fear of scandalising the brethren. But the happiness he preaches is a long way from the simple happiness of a child of nature. It is the rigorously supernatural happiness of those who find all their joy in being identified with the Lord in his passion. The exposure to nature which is a genuine part of Franciscan tradition is not primarily a matter of fresh air and fun, it is most typically a sharing in Christ's exposure to maltreatment and rejection.[36]

In this way, rather as with the example of the nun, we can understand how the life of the saint depends for its possibility upon the biblical story, where this story makes possible a reappraisal of conventional value categories, whether those categories concern the worth of afflicted human beings or the possibility of 'happiness' in and not merely in spite of affliction.[37] Again, feeling is relevant here, on the model we have been expounding, in so far as the quality of life exemplified by figures such as Francis rests upon what a person believes 'in her heart', and cannot be achieved on the basis of theoretical or discursive or even narrative understanding alone.

---

35 Simon Tugwell, *Ways of Imperfection: An Exploration of Christian Spirituality* (London: Darton, Longman and Todd, 1984), p. 130, Tugwell's italics.
36 *Ibid.*, p. 132.
37 These two kinds of saintliness, exemplified by the nun and by St Francis, seem closely related, in so far as each draws its inspiration from Christ's affliction: St Francis can find meaning in affliction because of Christ's 'maltreatment and rejection'; and Christ's affliction may also enable the nun's conviction that disability does not diminish a person's moral worth, but rather constitutes a form of identification with the incarnate God.

However, it is worth noting that the feelings which arise here are not evidently of the kind described by Schleiermacher or Smith: St Francis's conduct reveals the goodness of the world, and not just his immediate circumstances, not evidently because he has a felt intuition of the goodness of the whole, but because his conduct is grounded in his character, and therefore involves at least implicitly a commitment to behave in similar ways in any circumstances in which he finds himself. In this respect, his example resembles that of the nun, in so far as her conduct towards these particular afflicted human beings is grounded in her character, and therefore implies a similar commitment to the worth of afflicted people in general. The possibility suggested by Smith and Schleiermacher provides another kind of parallel with the nun: just as her commitment to the worth of these particular individuals (present here and now) is grounded in her affectively toned perception of them, so (if we follow Smith and Schleiermacher) someone's commitment to the worth of the world may be grounded in their affectively toned perception of the world. While St Francis may not have embodied this possibility, others may do so.

We have been considering the possibility of an affectively toned apprehension of the value of the world, and I have been arguing that even if someone is not in receipt of such an apprehension themselves, they may still be moved (and properly moved) to judge the world good on account of the authoritative example of others whose conduct bears witness to the possibility of such a perception. In drawing these reflections to a close, I would like to return to the position of Quentin Smith that was outlined earlier. Smith is writing from an avowedly atheistic point of view, and would no doubt think of the problem of evil as a legacy of the 'metaphysics of reason'. However, it is perhaps significant that he considers the most fundamental world-importance to be that recorded in global 'rejoicing', where this rejoicing is directed at the world's very existence, rather than its character in some particular respect. Smith evidently thinks that for this reason this global intuition should trump all others, since they are concerned with the importance of the world from one or another partial perspective, whereas here we are concerned with its significance simply as existent. For instance, he offers this assessment of 'despair', which is directed at the fact that the world appears to happen for no purpose: 'the truth of despair is itself an indication and even a "proof" that the world-whole is deserving of joy, for the truth of despair includes the truth that the world-whole happens rather than does not happen'.[38] So using the framework that Smith provides, we could undertake an exercise somewhat analogous to discussion of the problem of evil by examining various global importances, and trying to determine which of them is the most fundamental. The conclusion that Smith reaches, when supposing that global rejoicing picks out the most fundamental global importance, seems to sit at least somewhat comfortably with the theistic thought that, overall, our assessment of the world should be that it is good.

But suppose that someone is sceptical of the larger framework that Smith provides, and sceptical of the idea of felt intuitions which are targeted at the goodness of the world as a whole. This standpoint does not render the kind of experience that Smith describes simply irrelevant to the problem of evil. For that kind of experience can be read, independently of Smith's larger theoretical commitments, as a simple matter of taking joy in the very existence of the world (and that is surely a familiar enough kind of experience). And such an experience will presumably make a difference to a person's assessment of the goodness of the individual states of affairs that make up the world (and rightly so, given the kind of perspective on feelings as modes of value perception that we have been exploring). And a transformed sense of the goodness of such individual states of affairs will in turn contribute to a person's assessment of the goodness of the world as a whole if the goodness of those states is compounded in the way proposed in traditional theodicies. So for this further kind of reason, we might suppose that there is something that eludes such theodicies, namely, the full value of individual states of affairs, where this omission can only be made good by reference to the kind of understanding that is made available in feeling and not otherwise. This way of appealing to what is revealed in feeling does not involve as radical a departure from standard discussions of theodicy (because it leaves intact the idea that assessment of the world's goodness is a matter of compounding the goodness of individual states of affairs), but again it invites us to put a question mark against such theodicies or anti-theodicies. And to generalise the point, however sophisticated a person's manipulation of the kinds of argumentative strategy employed in the theodicy debate (on both sides), that person may remain mostly blind to what is really at issue, because of deficiencies in their emotional life, which mean that they do not have a keen grasp of the values and disvalues that are at stake in everyday experience. (Compare Blum on the role of

38 *The Felt Meanings*, p. 185.

feelings in disclosing values.) Again, this is to suggest that we should engage in theodicy (and its critique), if we do, with deep-seated humility. It may be that only a saint (only someone whose emotions run true) is really fitted for the task.

EMOTIONAL EXPERIENCE AND THE CONSTITUTION OF VALUE

In keeping with the central theme of this book, we have been mostly concerned so far with the question of how affective states may reveal values. But as I commented at the beginning of the chapter, emotions are relevant in a further way to the question of the world's goodness, in as much as they not only reveal but also constitute certain values. I want now, more briefly, to develop this thought.

In the passage below, Graham Nerlich offers one perspective on how our emotional attachments may help to constitute the value of other human beings. He is commenting on the nature of grief in particular:

A priori, it might seem that a person could just accept the fact of death and irrecoverable loss, and turn to a new life and new values. But the problem is not like that of accepting new sentential information. Grieving is valued because of facts on which the abstract picture of personhood sheds no light. Conversely, understanding the concept of a person gives no hint why we may be chilled at the absence of grief in one who appeared so attached to another who has just died. Grief can do no obvious service to the dead. It pays its due to the deep and complex array of threads that tie one to a beloved. It is a *human* debt, paid because we are, quite contingently to personhood, creatures who need a time for recovery from the tearing-away of those manifold connections. But it is also personal, in the sense that many of these inarticulately forged connections and judgements constitute the value placed on the person for whom one grieves and were a part, perhaps quite dimly perceived, of the process of coming to value her.[39]

These remarks help to amplify various themes that we have examined already. Registering the significance of the death of a loved one is not fundamentally, Nerlich notes, a matter of 'accepting new sentential information'. Here he offers another perspective on the idea that the value of others is not accessible simply, or most basically, through discursive thought. On Nerlich's view, this is because given the facts of human nature (as distinct from the nature of other kinds of possible person), love for another typically implies being bound to them by ties of affection; and if

39 Graham Nerlich, *Values and Valuing: Speculations on the Ethical Lives of Persons* (Oxford: Clarendon Press, 1989), p. 164, Nerlich's italics.

these ties are deep-seated, then when they are severed with the death of the beloved, that will (in the normal case) be registered in feeling. This can sound like Proust's cataleptic view again, but Nerlich notes that the bonds in question have a history (typically, there will be a process of coming to value the beloved, he notes), and this suggests that their character cannot simply be grasped by way of a self-verifying experience in the present. And the ties are anyway 'manifold and complex', which implies again that their nature cannot be straightforwardly registered in a single moment of feeling. Of course, this picture needs to be complicated further: it is, after all, possible for a person to be deeply attached to another and yet feel no grief on the other's death. Yet this sort of case is presumably non-standard: our sense of what it means, in the human case, to have formed deep-seated ties to another is connected to what we know about how such ties typically find expression in grief or sorrow in appropriate circumstances.

So in this sort of way, the grief I feel at the death of another may help to reveal the value that they held for me; and on occasion, this response may reveal more than I could have understood by discursive reflection alone. At the end of the passage, Nerlich notes that 'many of these inarticulately forged connections and judgements constitute the value placed on the person'. The thought that judgements may be 'inarticulate' could be understood in the terms we have been exploring – by supposing that the content of affectively constituted judgements cannot be rendered, in full, in 'notional' terms. But this remark is also significant because here Nerlich recognises that emotions may be important in constituting the value of the other person – and not just in so far as they help to reveal that value. This relationship of constitution is in part a consequence of the fact that, as Nerlich notes, we human beings need a time to recover from the tearing away of emotional bonds. It follows that the death of someone I love will disable me, at least for a time: following their death (or our enduring separation for some other reason), I will feel grief, and by its nature, grief involves an incapacity to take on new kinds of meaning-sustaining activity. This is one way in which the beloved proves to have irreplaceable value: even if there are others who are qualitatively very like them, they remain irreplaceable in as much as the tearing away of the bonds that bind me to them leaves me unable to take on other relationships that might substitute for my relationship with them.

On this view, grief has a dual significance. It can function to reveal the value of a person to me. And it is bound up with the role of the emotions in constituting the value of other people: it is in part because of my emotional ties to a person that I find them irreplaceable; and grief is the enactment of this irreplaceability, a state which prevents me from simply 'moving on'.

Now that we have taken note of one way in which values may be contingent upon emotions, let us consider the relevance of this theme for the problem of evil. To return to Nerlich's example, it is striking that the emotions can help to constitute the value of other human beings because of their status as forms of vulnerability. My affective attachments to others leave me vulnerable to the kind of disruption of meaning that is implied in grief; and it is this vulnerability which, in part, constitutes the value the other person has for me, by ensuring that they are of irreplaceable worth. The idea that there is some such connection between emotion, vulnerability, and value may help to make Odysseus' choice, as described at the beginning of the chapter, more intelligible. Reflecting upon this choice, and the significance of grief in particular, Martha Nussbaum writes:

Our preference for Odysseus's life with Penelope over his life with Calypso actually stems, I think, from this more general uneasiness about the shapelessness of the life Calypso offers: pleasure and kindliness on and on, with no risks, no possibility of sacrifice, no grief, no children.[40]

Here Nussbaum proposes that a life that is lacking in the possibility of grief, or more generally a life that is devoid of vulnerability (with 'no possibility of sacrifice'), is thereby rendered 'shapeless'. In speaking of the shapelessness of such a life, she is suggesting that in such circumstances, nothing matters very much: it does not matter whether I do X or Y because in any event I cannot be damaged or suffer any setback (not even the setback of not achieving as much as I might have done). In this sense such a life lacks evaluative structure, since events cannot be marked out as having a positive or negative significance for my well being. Similarly, Nussbaum comments that the Olympians' 'social life is free-floating, amorphous, uninspired by need', so that 'there is a kind of playfulness and lack of depth about the loves of the gods'.[41] Here again, invulnerability means that nothing matters very much: even the loves of the gods are 'playful' and superficial, because their loves do not involve openness to hurt or reversal. This suggests that vulnerability and the emotions to the extent that they are forms of vulnerability are connected to a most profound value, a value which seems to be foundational for all others: namely, the value of things mattering at all. So generalising from Nerlich's example of grief, we

40 *Love's Knowledge*, p. 366.   41 *Ibid.*, p. 376.

may suppose that the emotions constitute values because of their status as forms of vulnerability: notably, they enable us to sink our well being in that of others, and thereby they make possible new kinds of success and failure, correlative to the fortunes of the beloved, or our success and failure in sustaining our relationship to the beloved.

The role of vulnerability, including emotional vulnerability, in constituting values is of course directly relevant to the problem of evil, because that problem is typically rooted in precisely a consciousness of our being vulnerable. I do not think that noticing the deep-seated connection between vulnerability and the foundational value of things mattering at all resolves the problem of evil in favour of the theodicist. But if Odysseus can intelligibly choose a world such as ours (in which craft can be wrecked and loved ones suffer and die) in preference to a life of ageless invulnerability, then at least some formulations of the problem of evil seem misguided: granted the intelligibility of such a choice, then whatever the problem of evil is, it is not a matter of our being subject to some degree of vulnerability rather than none at all. It is worth noting that this kind of perspective is not reducible to the 'soul-making' approach that is typical of many theodicies. It is no doubt true that vulnerability makes possible the acquisition of courage and certain kinds of fidelity, along with other virtues (think again of the life story of Odysseus). But in Nussbaum's remarks, the kind of value that is enabled by vulnerability is not fundamentally that of our ability to acquire certain character traits; it is the value which consists in other people, and things more generally, mattering to us, and this seems a more basic kind of value than any concerned with the acquisition of virtues: it is, after all, only because it matters how things turn out (because we human beings are vulnerable) that there is any point in acquiring the virtues.

There is, of course, an ancient and enduring philosophical tradition which has insisted upon invulnerability as a condition to which we should aspire. And this tradition has, unsurprisingly, viewed the emotions with suspicion, as ways of acknowledging vulnerability (think again of grief), and as forms of vulnerability (think of the attachments which make us liable to the disabling consequences of grief). In the *Phaedo*, for example, Socrates famously maintains that philosophy is a preparation for death, since it requires its practitioners to give up any emotional attachment to worldly things as a condition of achieving a proper perspective on the relative worth of the material world and the realm of the Forms.[42] On this

---

42 *Phaedo*, tr. David Gallop (Oxford: Oxford University Press, 1993), Section 64, p. 9.

view, events in the outer world ought not to disturb our mental equilibrium, since the good of the soul, or the real self, is located in another, non-material world. Similarly, the Stoics represented freedom from emotional disturbance as an ideal, and here a similar value judgement is implied, namely, that what really matters is virtue as distinct from things in the outer world, which are subject to the movements of fortune. The view I have been expounding stands this tradition on its head: our well being is indeed at stake in developments in the outer world, and the emotions have a proper place in human life both as a way of acknowledging these vulnerabilities and as themselves forms of vulnerability. On this account, vulnerability is bound up with the good of a human life.[43]

Of course, the value scheme that is involved in the Stoic–Platonic perspective is naturally correlated with a theology, according to which God (or the realm of perfection otherwise conceived) is taken to be invulnerable and accordingly as passion-less, changeless, immaterial, and impassible. We might wonder whether the kind of value scheme that we have been exploring is committed to a different conception of God. This is a large question, and I shall touch on just one dimension of it. Nussbaum notes in passing that 'the Christian idea that god is also fully human and has actually sacrificed his life is, if it can be made coherent, a most important element in the thought that god actually loves the world'.[44] This is, of course, the other side of her thought that the loves of the Olympian gods involve 'a kind of playfulness and lack of depth'. Her suggestion is, I take it, that only someone who is vulnerable can love deeply, and more exactly, only someone whose love is itself a form of vulnerability to the beloved can love deeply: a love will run deep only if it implies sinking one's own good in that of the beloved, so that one's own well being is tied to that of the other, and thereby put at risk. There is nothing amiss, surely, in regarding the case in which someone forms a steady resolution to uphold the good of another person without putting

---

43 Compare John Cottingham's remark that: 'Joy would not be *human* joy without the possible yield of pain of which Keats spoke so elegantly – the pain of potential loss which dwells in the very "temple of delight". Without that special human dimension, all that can remain as positive "joy" for the Stoics is simply a calm "expansion of the soul" signalling the presence of what reason perceives as worthy of pursuit, namely a purely moral value. It is, if not exactly a chilling picture, at least a strangely colourless one which takes us to the very edges of recognizable human emotion': John Cottingham, *Philosophy and the Good Life: Reason and the Passions in Greek, Cartesian and Psychoanalytic Ethics* (Cambridge: Cambridge University Press, 1998), p. 57, Cottingham's italics.

44 *Love's Knowledge*, p. 376.

their own good at risk in any way as genuinely a case of love. But such a love has not proved itself to the same extent as a love which implies making oneself vulnerable. And perhaps such a love is of its nature more superficial: it is not just that the lover has not gone to the same lengths to show their love; in this case, there is less of a tie between lover and beloved, less that unites them, because the well being of the lover has not been identified, in some significant degree, with that of the beloved.

These reflections do not straightforwardly establish that the Christian God must be vulnerable (and therefore, arguably, material, passible, and the rest). There is surely no failure of orthodoxy in supposing that, in relation to human beings, and bracketing for the moment the question of incarnation, the Christian God exemplifies simply the love of benefi-cence.[45] Nonetheless, the considerations we have been rehearsing do suggest that a love which makes itself vulnerable is thereby a 'deeper' kind of love, and the notion of depth here does seem to be evaluatively laden: such a love is thereby more perfect, we might say, because it gives more to the beloved (it gives the self of the lover, in so far as the well being of the lover is genuinely at stake in the relationship). And if we wish to think of God as perfect, and of love as a defining divine attribute, then that provides some reason for supposing that the divine love of human beings implies, so far as this is possible, a real making vulnerable. Of course, in turn, this raises a question about the extent to which this is really possible: is it even intelligible that a God who is the creator of all should make his/her well being conditional upon that of creatures? The idea of incarnation supplies one very direct answer to this question: if it is intelligible that God should become fully human, then it is surely no less intelligible that God's love should be a vulnerable love. This may suggest that there is more at stake in the doctrine of incarnation than is sometimes supposed: the paradox of God becoming human is perhaps one and the same as the paradox (not always recognised as a paradox) of God being capable of a love that is perfect.[46]

---

45 Compare Anselm's treatment of the idea of divine compassion in *Proslogion*, Chapter VIII, in *The Prayers and Meditations of St Anselm with the Proslogion*, tr. B. Ward (Harmondsworth: Penguin, 1973), Chapter 8, p. 249.
46 There are other strands of the argument we have been developing which invite extension in an incarnational direction. Notably, we have been considering the possibility that certain kinds of understanding are lodged in feeling and not otherwise available. This perspective may suggest that there are epistemic reasons for thinking of God as capable of emotion, as well as reasons having to do with the perfection of God's love. (And these epistemic reasons may in turn relate to the perfection of God's love, in so far as they have to do with achieving a more than notional grasp of the 'humanity' of human beings.) For a related argument, which sees limitations of

CONCLUSIONS

The first two chapters of this book were concerned with the possibility of an affectively toned perception of God and of other human beings. In this chapter, we have been examining the possibility of an affectively toned perception, or at least assessment, of the world. I have argued that there is some reason to suppose that this sort of assessment is possible (appealing to the models of Smith and Schleiermacher, and also Tugwell's discussion of St Francis), and that if it is possible, then our discursive enquiries into questions of theodicy should be conducted with humility. In the course of this discussion, we have also clarified the sense in which the insights made available in feeling admit of certitude, are enduringly available, and are capable of embodiment and communication to others. Finally, we have considered how emotional attachments may also help to constitute certain values, and how this possibility may contribute to a reassessment of the problem of evil, by pointing to a larger connection between vulnerability and the fundamental value of things mattering at all.

So this chapter has extended the discussion of earlier chapters by applying the idea of feeling as revelatory of value to another subject matter (the world as a whole), and by introducing the thought that feelings may also help to constitute certain values. Now that it has been shown how emotional experience may be relevant to religious understanding in the various ways we have discussed in the first three chapters, it is time to consolidate a little, by turning our attention more explicitly to some theories of emotional feeling. This is the task of the next chapter.

power as a precondition of some kinds of knowledge, see David Blumenfeld, 'On the Compossibility of the Divine Attributes', in T. V. Morris (ed.), *The Concept of God* (Oxford: Oxford University Press, 1987), pp. 201–16. Blumenfeld suggests that a response to this sort of argument which appeals to the idea of incarnation amounts to heresy, because it implies that God had to become human (p. 214, n. 10). The argument I have given implies only this conditional: if God makes human beings, then the perfection of God's love of them may depend on incarnation. This does not imply that the perfection of God's love depends on incarnation *tout court*.

CHAPTER 4

Emotional feeling: philosophical, psychological, and neurological perspectives

hearing the dominant seventh evokes a desire, and sometimes something akin to a longing, for its resolution. That is a state of consciousness directed to an intentional object; it is also an affective state of consciousness. It is *not* the entertaining of an evaluation which (magically) leads to certain bodily disturbances. One may, if one is so disposed, regard the desire for the tonic resolution as ground for the evaluation that such a resolution would be 'a good thing', but it would be a total distortion to suppose that the desire, or the longing, *is* an evaluation, one which inexplicably leads to certain physical effects. It is a mode of 'feeling towards' its intentional object.[1]

In this passage, Geoffrey Maddell is seeking to rebut one widely influential account of the character of the emotions. On this model, we should see the emotions as compounded of thoughts and feelings: the thought component of the emotion may take the form of a belief or judgement or some non-assertional thought (such as an imagining), and this component is taken to give rise to the emotion's affective component. Take, for example, the emotional state described in this passage:

The thought that no call from him would ever again evoke the answer of her voice made him drop heavily into the chair with a loud groan, wrung out by the pain as of a keen blade piercing his breast.[2]

Here it appears that a discursive thought gives rise to a feeling of pain, and the associated behaviour of dropping into the chair and crying out. And extrapolating from this sort of case, we might say that grief is in general composed of a thought component (say, the belief that one has suffered some significant loss) and a felt response to that thought (broadly, one of pain rather than pleasure). And generalising further still,

---

1 Geoffrey Maddell, 'What Music Teaches about Emotion', *Philosophy* 71 (1996), p. 76, Maddell's italics.
2 The passage is taken from Joseph Conrad's *Nostromo* as cited in David Pugmire, *Rediscovering Emotion* (Edinburgh: Edinburgh University Press, 1998), p. 104.

we might seek to differentiate emotional states from one another by reference to distinctions in either their thought component or (less commonly) the affective state engendered by the thought. Hence, very roughly, we might see embarrassment as comprising the thought that I have done something that would lower my standing in the eyes of others, where this thought gives rise to a feeling of pain rather than pleasure; and pity and *schadenfreude* we might take to comprise one and the same thought (that someone has suffered some misfortune) and differing affective responses to that thought (of pain and pleasure respectively).[3]

In the passage above, Maddell takes exception to this model of the emotions, on the grounds that it fails to reckon seriously with the capacity of affective states to be themselves kinds of thought or understanding. On the view he is expounding, the felt response to the music is itself a way of taking stock of the music's character, and the experience to which he is alluding is therefore not to be understood in terms of some affect-independent judgement, or 'evaluation', of the music's character giving rise to a bodily change which in turn is registered in feeling. In other words, Maddell is arguing for what we might call the intrinsic intentionality of feeling: feelings may be about something, may have some content, intrinsically, that is, in their own right, and not simply because of their association with some thought or evaluation, which represents the world as having a certain character and thereby gives rise to a bodily-cum-affective response, where the affective response is considered as rather like a sensation, that is, as a feeling of some bodily condition, rather than being directed at the world.

Of course, Maddell's position on this issue is of the same general type as the view that we have been exploring in the first three chapters of this book. Against the 'add-on' theory of feeling (where feelings are considered as addenda to thoughts, lacking in any intrinsic intentional significance) we have been considering the possibility that God's presence may be registered directly in our felt responses (rather than being apprehended in some other fashion, which in turn engenders a felt response), and the possibility that the moral considerability or 'humanity' of our fellow human beings may be recognised directly in feeling (rather than being understood discursively or by way of an affectively neutral perception of their significance, which in turn gives rise to a felt response); and lastly,

---

3 For a clear exposition of this kind of programme, together with questions it needs to address, see Malcolm Budd, *Music and the Emotions: The Philosophical Theories* (London: Routledge & Kegan Paul, 1985), Chapter 1.

we have been considering the possibility that the goodness of the world (and its parts) may be registered in an affectively toned appreciation of its character (and not in some affect-independent way). So in these respects, we have been examining the idea that feelings may themselves be the bearers of understanding, or ways of acknowledging the character of things. And more radically, we have considered the thought (especially in relation to Newman and Gaita) that the content of such an understanding may not be available otherwise. This sort of approach does not require a blanket rejection of the add-on model, but it does suggest that this model is at any rate incomplete.

So the position we have been exploring implies taking a stand in contemporary discussion of the emotions, and indeed, a stand which runs contrary to a widely received view, which has represented feelings as devoid of intrinsic intentional significance. However, there is a growing body of opinion which is in sympathy with the kind of perspective that I have been expounding, and in this chapter, I would like to set out several such accounts, drawn from philosophy, neurophysiology, and psychology. So the object of this discussion is to provide a broader theoretical context for the construal of emotional feelings that I have been expounding, and applying to various issues in philosophical theology, in Chapters 1–3. I shall then be in a position, in Chapter 5, to offer a general account of the relationship between feeling and religious understanding in particular.

The primary reason for speaking in this connection of 'emotional' feeling is to mark a distinction between feelings which are purely bodily in character (feelings of gnawings, throbbings, or dizziness, for example) and feelings which have more obviously some kind of intellectual content (such as feelings of anguish, inspiration, and triumph). Again, what is distinctive about emotional feelings is that we can take them to have a subject matter, and can therefore ask questions such as: what are you feeling triumphant about? By contrast, while we can evidently enquire into the cause of a throbbing feeling, such a feeling is not naturally construed as being about anything. There are other uses of 'feeling' too, of course. I can feel the air temperature, or feel in the cupboard for the packet of Weetabix, or feel in anticipation the ring being placed on my finger on my wedding day, or feel an itch (to revert to the case of feelings of bodily condition), or feel sluggish, or feel that there is something amiss in what has been said, or feel like going for a walk.[4] None of these

---

4 Here I am illustrating the seven senses of 'feeling' distinguished by Gilbert Ryle. They are, respectively: 'perceptual', 'exploratory', 'mock', of bodily condition, of 'general condition', of

examples seems equivalent to the case of emotional feelings. It is true that the feeling that there is something amiss in what has been said has an intellectual content: this feeling is about something. But the term 'feeling' in this case could be used (and is perhaps most naturally used) to refer to an intuitive but non-affective registering of error.

Again, the case that interests us is that in which the intentional content of a 'feeling' is embedded in an affective response. An example would be my feeling downhearted, or a buzz of excitement, or a glow of gratitude, where these states are taken to have a content which resides, at least in part, in feeling. For instance, I may hear some news, and I may register its import to some extent at least through my downheartedness (or my excitement or gratitude, where these states are taken to be affectively toned). This is the sort of case that concerns Newman, Gaita, and Smith. For instance, Newman supposes that through the affectively toned recognition of my wrong-doing (through remorse), I may come to some new and more profound understanding of the divine nature; and Gaita and Smith speak similarly of how a new understanding of the 'humanity' of others or of the 'meaning' or goodness of the world may be realised in an affectively toned response to other people or the world. This reading of feeling and its significance is to be distinguished from two others. First: the view which sees affects as engendered by some intellectual content but as devoid of any intentional significance in themselves; for instance, I may recognise in a purely discursive (affectively neutral) way that someone has done me a favour, and thereupon I may experience a warm glow (where the warm glow is taken to be simply a thought-induced sensation). And secondly: the view which treats feelings as sensations which give rise to interpretive thoughts; for instance, I may experience a churning sensation in my stomach, and infer that I am anxious about the approaching exam. In these cases, the feeling is represented as simply an accompaniment to cognition (because in each case, feeling is being understood in terms of sensation, whether a sensation that follows on from some thought or one that engenders a thought). What we are interested in is the possibility that feeling may itself be the vehicle of thought.

I add one final point of terminological clarification. Although for the most part we shall be concerned with emotional feelings, I do not wish to conflate emotional feelings and emotions in general: it is true that what we call emotions in ordinary language are often emotional feelings (think again of a buzz of excitement or glow of gratitude), but some emotions are

tentative judgement, and of inclination. See Gilbert Ryle, 'Feelings', in *Collected Papers*, Vol. II (London: Hutchinson, 1971), pp. 272–86. Ryle does not intend the list to be exhaustive.

best thought of as dispositions rather than experiential episodes, and even when episodic, certain emotions need not be felt.[5]

Let us turn first of all to some recent philosophical accounts of feeling. In this way I hope to articulate four models of the relationship between emotional feelings and understanding; we shall then be in a position to consider, in Chapter 5, how these accounts might be applied to the question of feeling's contribution to religious understanding in particular. I shall begin with John Deigh's proposal that in certain 'primitive' contexts, we can take stock of the character of the world through feeling, and independently of the mediating influence of any discursive thought.[6] In developing this proposal, Deigh notes a distinction between 'being sensible of something' and 'having a concept of it':

Many people are sensible of flats and sharps, for instance, though they have no concept of half steps in a diatonic scale. Wild geese are no doubt sensible of changes in the weather, though they have no concept of seasons. To be sensible of a property is to be able to detect its presence and to discriminate between those things that have it and those that do not. To have a concept of a property, by contrast, is to be able to predicate it of some object and, hence, to locate it in a system of propositional thought.[7]

For example, a mouse might be transfixed by the gaze of a cat, where this is not a matter of the mouse thinking of the harm that might befall it were the cat to get much closer, but a non-conceptually mediated apprehension of some quality of the cat. In this case, we could say that the mouse is 'sensible' of the cat's scariness without bringing the cat's appearance under the 'concept' of danger. This sort of example suggests that we can be sensible of a given quality (as distinct from having a concept of it) not only by virtue of affectively neutral sensory experience (as when I distinguish between sharps and flats on the basis of their sensory qualities alone), but also by way of our affective responses. That is, my recognition of something's scariness, for example, may be realised in the affective response, where this response does not involve any conceptually articulated thought. Deigh picks up this sort of case when he remarks that:

---

5 For example, when speaking of someone as an angry person I may be alluding simply to their disposition to undergo episodes of anger; and even when a person is episodically angry, they may not feel anything at the time, and may only later (if ever) appreciate that they were angry.

6 Compare the view (described in Chapter 3) that Brandt considers, and rejects, as an interpretation of Schleiermacher.

7 John Deigh, 'Cognitivism in the Theory of Emotions', *Ethics* 104 (1994), p. 840.

Roughly speaking, one feels fear at what is scary, horror at what is gruesome, and disgust at what is foul. These properties characterise the way things look, sound, taste, smell. A scary mask, for instance, will have certain exaggerated features that are designed to alarm or frighten the innocent or unsuspecting viewer, and a scary voice will have a certain unusual cadence and pitch that unsettles the listener . . . the important point is that the scary differs from the dangerous in being at least sometimes a true or direct property of the way something looks and sounds. Something that looks dangerous is something that one can infer is dangerous from the way it looks, whereas one need make no inference to see that something looks scary.[8]

Here we have the beginnings of an account of how affects may constitute a mode of perception which operates independently of any conceptual articulation of the world's character. An objector might say: perhaps we recognise an object as scary independently of affect (via an affect-independent perception or thought), and this recognition then gives rise to the sensation of being scared? Or perhaps we recognise an object as having some quality other than scariness, and this recognition causes the sensation of feeling scared? Or perhaps an object causes me to feel some sensation and I then infer that I am scared? But these possibilities (all of which separate recognition or understanding from feeling) are surely false to the phenomenology of our experience in at least some cases: sometimes (I would say, typically) the recognition of a thing's scariness is realised in an affectively toned perception of its character (in the feeling of being scared by it). No doubt, it is sometimes possible to recognise a quality as scary independently of one's own felt responses, but it would make no sense to suppose that the quality of scariness could in general be detached from the feeling of being scared: if a quality is properly denominated as scary, then it must in at least some significant number of cases cause people to feel scared. What I am proposing, in addition, is that in at least some cases, the quality of scariness is recognised in the felt response, and not (for instance) in an affectively neutral perception of scariness which in turn gives rise to the sensation of being scared.

The kind of case that Deigh is describing is particularly radical because it involves the idea of an entirely non-conceptual grasp of the world's character. But we might suppose that these primal, non-conceptual apprehensions of the world can interact with conceptual understanding, and thereby contribute to larger complexes of feeling which are informed by conceptualisation. Deigh notes that as a child develops,

---

8 *Ibid.*, p. 842.

It learns, for instance, to distinguish what is harmful from what is merely scary, what is rotten from what is merely foul. Acquiring the concepts of these objective conditions and the understanding of the world that having these concepts entails weakens the impact of the sensory phenomena, the scary and the foul. Accordingly, the child's susceptibilities to fear and disgust change. While it may continue to feel uneasy in the presence of large dogs, say, it is no longer afraid of them and may at some point cease even to regard them as scary; while it may continue to dislike liver, it is no longer disgusted by it, and the dish may at some point cease even to taste foul. These emotions, in being educated, as it were, for governance by the conceptual understanding of the world one acquires, thus become responsive to reason.[9]

So in some cases, the sensory presentations associated with foulness, scariness, and so on may with time lose their power to excite an affective response, as the child comes to insert these phenomena within some larger, discursive picture of the world. In this sort of case, the feeling of being scared will no longer function as a mode of perception. In other cases, a 'primitive' feeling such as that of being scared by heights may prove entirely unresponsive to reason. But there is also an intermediate kind of case, surely, where an object retains some of its power to excite a 'primitive' (non-conceptually-articulated) response but where this response is infused in some degree by a conceptually informed understanding of the world. Deigh gives an example of this sort of case in a passage that he cites from Proust:

If only night is falling and the carriage is moving fast, whether in town or country, there is not a female torso, mutilated like an antique marble by the speed that tears us away and the dusk that drowns it, but aims at our heart, from every turning in the road, from the lighted interior of every shop, the arrows of Beauty, that Beauty of which we are sometimes tempted to ask ourselves whether it is, in this world, anything more than the complementary part that is added to a fragmentary and fugitive stranger by our imagination over stimulated by regret.[10]

The response which Proust describes here is, clearly, affectively toned (the female figure 'aims at our heart'). And in part at least, this response is presumably grounded in a kind of primal appreciation of the female form (that is, an appreciation that involves being struck by the form independently of any conceptual articulation of its qualities). But what the passage emphasises, of course, is the contribution that is made to this sort of experience by the imagination, which expands upon the rather

---

9 *Ibid.*, p. 851.
10 Marcel Proust, *Remembrance of Things Past*, tr. C. K. Scott Moncreiff (2 vols., New York: Random House, 1934), Vol. I, p. 540; cited in 'Cognitivism', p. 853.

fragmentary sensory presentation; and it is plausible to suppose that when engaged in this sort of way, the imagination is heavily informed by cultural constructions of various kinds (notably, a particular, culturally specific ideal of female beauty, together with a culturally particular sense of what such beauty signifies). So what Proust is describing is an affectively toned perception which is infused by a primal responsiveness to the female form, but also bears the mark of a conceptually articulated (and culturally specific) appreciation of that form.

In terms of its phenomenology, such a perception is surely not to be disaggregated into a number of separate components: a certain sensory presentation, grasped in a primal feeling, and then laid upon this (and remaining distinct from it) a conceptually informed assessment of what has been seen, together with associated images and feelings. Against this picture, we should say that the primal affect does not remain in itself as it would have been but for the operation of these concepts, as though the concepts (together with any images and feelings that are associated with them) simply exist alongside of it. Rather, concepts and primal responsiveness are fused so as to produce a unified, affectively toned perception of the form. What is significant for our purposes is that while primal affects in this case no longer offer a direct (concept-independent) awareness of the character of the world, nonetheless the resulting state of mind depends for its content (depends for its sense of what the world is like) on the contribution of a primal, affectively toned sensitivity to the female form. Analogously, while the kind of responsiveness that we associate with romantic love is not reducible to any primal affective sensitivity, neither is it fully intelligible without such sensitivity.

Since the possibility of concepts infusing a primal affective awareness in this sort of way will have some importance for our later discussion, it is worth noting a further example. Here is Holmes Rolston writing in an autobiographical vein of something like a 'primitive' experience of natural value:

One steps into the tunnels enroute [*sic*] here, lower in the gorge, with an initial shudder. He enters the stone bowels of the Earth as though they were haunted with the jinn of Hades. The darkness is lonesome and alien. Intuitions of the savage persist, modern as I am. But the shudder passes, and, as in the case with one's initial encounter with the sea, there follows a fascination born of the intuition of connection, or reconnection.[11]

---

11 Holmes Rolston III, *Philosophy Gone Wild* (Buffalo, NY: Prometheus Books, 1989), p. 233.

Here Rolston speaks of a kind of visceral, non-'conceptual' (in Deigh's sense) response to the natural world, whereby the character of his environment is registered in feeling. (Compare again Deigh's discussion of the felt recognition of an object's scariness.) In the rather beautiful passage which follows, Rolston describes how his feelings undergo further evolution, under the pressure of a scientifically informed conception of his surroundings:

Earth's carbonate and apatite have graced me with carbon, calcium, and phosphate that support my frame. The iron of hornblende and augite is the iron of the blood that courses through my life. Those stains of limonite and hematite now coloring this weathered cut will tomorrow be the haemoglobin that flushes my face with red. So now would I, this rock parasite, return to praise my natural parents. Ephemeral, anomalous, if so I am, erudite, conscious, proud, I can no longer suppress, but yield to, rejoice in, and humbly confess yet another primitive intuition, only enriched by my intellectual sophistication. Here is my cradle. My soul is hidden in this cleft of rock.[12]

Here the 'intuition' of connectedness to which Rolston refers in the first passage is deepened, by appeal to a conceptually articulated, scientifically informed account of how his own life and that of the rock are interwoven. The result is, I take it, a unitary state of mind which is affectively toned (see the references to 'rejoicing' and 'humbly confessing') and at the same time conceptually structured. Moreover, the initial, 'primitive', affectively toned sense of connectedness is not simply set aside here, but infuses the awareness of the rock as 'my cradle'. In this way, we can see how an initial, pre-reflective sense of the world's meaning can be penetrated by a growing conceptual awareness, without thereby surrendering its own distinctive contribution to the resulting affective complex.

Deigh's remarks suggest the following account of how feeling may be related to understanding in religious contexts. Perhaps there are certain primal, affectively toned responses to the world which can be taken up into larger affective complexes which are structured by concepts and by the work of the imagination; and perhaps it is in this way that affects can contribute to an affectively toned perception of God, or of other human beings, or the world (in the ways described in Chapters 1–3, for example). The possibility of integrating primal responses within larger complexes in this way is, of course, significant if we wish to see how this sort of responsiveness may contribute to religious understanding; for religious understanding typically has a fairly complex conceptual structure (think,

12 *Ibid.*, pp. 233–4.

for example, of what is involved in believing that there is a God). Accordingly, if primal affective responses are to inform this sort of understanding, it is most likely to be by way of their contribution to some larger affective complex, one which owes its character in part to such responsiveness and in part to conceptualisation.

Let us take this sort of model, which derives from Deigh, as a first prospective account of the relation between feeling and religious understanding (to be developed in the next chapter). I want now to examine some other ways of representing this relationship. Consider first of all the following passage from Peter Goldie's book on the emotions. Here he is describing how a person who has fallen on ice may come to think of the dangerousness of ice in a new, 'emotionally relevant' way:

> Coming to think of it in this new way is not to be understood as consisting of thinking of it in the old way, plus some added-on phenomenal ingredient – feeling perhaps; rather, the whole way of experiencing, or being conscious of, the world is new . . . The difference between thinking of *X* as *Y* without feeling and thinking of *X* as *Y* with feeling will not just comprise a different attitude towards the *same* content – a thinking which earlier was without feeling and now is with feeling. The difference also lies *in* the content, although it might be that this difference cannot be captured in words.[13]

Here Goldie is resisting (like Deigh) the add-on conception of feeling – the idea that emotions in general consist of a conceptually articulated thought, or an affectively neutral perception, and an affective state which is engendered by the thought or perception, where the intentional significance of the emotion resides in the thought or perception and not in the feeling. Hence he insists that feelingly thinking of ice as dangerous involves a different understanding of ice (not just a different attitude to ice, understood in a certain way).

How does this account relate to Deigh's? Deigh's model involves an initial, concept-independent affective responsiveness being penetrated by conceptual kinds of thought, and the imagination, to produce a new, richer kind of affectively toned sensitivity to the world. Goldie's model seems to work in the other direction. Here we begin with a conceptually articulated understanding of the world: the person in his example already has some sense of the dangers presented by ice (perhaps they have been told of what can happen, or they have seen what can happen from observing others). Here affect builds upon an already achieved conceptual

---

13 Peter Goldie, *The Emotions: A Philosophical Exploration* (Oxford: Oxford University Press, 2000), pp. 59–60, Goldie's italics.

understanding, and runs beyond it – the feeling makes possible a new and deeper appreciation of the dangers presented by ice. Goldie notes that this deeper understanding may not be susceptible of linguistic formulation: perhaps it is the sort of understanding that can only be realised in feeling. This proposal is, of course, reminiscent of the accounts of Newman and Gaita. Newman suggests that a felt experience may take us beyond a 'notional' understanding of God, by providing a 'real image' of God, whose content cannot be captured in words. And Gaita notes how as a young man he had a certain verbal understanding of the worth of the patients on the psychiatric ward (in terms of their equality with himself, for example), but adds that this understanding proved to be relatively superficial when set beside the affectively toned understanding exemplified by the nun.

Goldie gives a further example to bring out the meaning of his proposal. Imagine that you are at a zoo watching a gorilla move about in its cage, while thinking of how dangerous such creatures can be. Suppose that you then notice that the cage door is open, and suppose that, for a moment, you fail to put together the belief that the gorilla is dangerous and the belief that the cage door is open. Now suppose that all of a sudden you do put these two beliefs together. Goldie comments: 'now your thinking of the gorilla as dangerous is new; now it is dangerous in an emotionally relevant way for you.'[14] As Goldie notes, the new state of understanding is naturally reported in just the same terms as the old (the gorilla is dangerous and the cage door is open), but there is some new content involved in the new understanding, and following Goldie, we might suppose that that additional content is grasped in the feeling of fear (rather than, say, being grasped in some non-affective way, which in turn gives rise to the feeling of fear). This example might be interpreted in somewhat different terms from the first: whereas the example of ice involves someone who, post-fall, will have a new understanding of the dangers presented by ice *in general*, the gorilla example is concerned with the understanding of a particular gorilla and the dangers it presents in these particular circumstances here and now. But these two kinds of understanding (the general case and the here and now) are plausibly seen as related (the first arises out of the second), and the two examples are naturally read as making the same sort of point about the intrinsic intentionality of feeling.

14 *Ibid.*, p. 61.

The example of the gorilla helps to bring out the fact that the additional content achieved in feeling is action-guiding content. What you grasp now and did not grasp fully before is the import of the situation, and what it requires of you by way of action: to be fearful in this situation is to be predisposed to move away from the cage, or in some other way to take self-protective action. Similarly, if a person has fallen on ice, and thereby acquired an affectively informed understanding of the dangers of ice, then, in the normal case, they will be predisposed to take additional care on ice. We might see a further parallel here with Gaita's example of the nun, for her understanding is also evidently action-guiding. Indeed, it is the nun's enacted relationship to the patients that reveals to Gaita what she believes 'in her heart'.

So Goldie's remarks suggest that alongside the relationship between feeling and discursive thought that Deigh has described, we can set a further account which is in some respects its inverse. Deigh notes how a primal affective responsiveness may be infused by conceptual understanding, so as to give rise to a new, unitary, affectively toned sensitivity to the world. Goldie is describing how an initial conceptually articulated, affectively neutral kind of understanding may be carried further by feeling. In this latter case, feeling builds on what has been achieved conceptually, rather than (as with the 'primitive' experiences of feeling that Deigh describes) operating independently of it. For example, the felt appraisal of the dangers presented by ice, post-fall, surely presupposes and builds on a discursive understanding of those dangers. Again, this is because we do not have here two distinct understandings which simply sit alongside one another: the affectively toned appreciation of the dangers, and the non-affective, purely verbal understanding. There is, rather, a unitary, affectively toned, conceptually structured appreciation of the dangers. It is because the new understanding includes all that was involved in the old understanding, and more, that Goldie is able (plausibly) to represent the new understanding as a deepening of the earlier. By contrast, if we were to treat the new, feeling-relative understanding as a concept-independent kind of understanding, it would be, to say no more, difficult to place this understanding and the earlier understanding on a common scale to compare which runs deeper. Similarly, in the example of the gorilla, the new, affectively toned understanding of the dangers presented by the gorilla will be shot through with a conceptual grasp of the nature of gorillas, cages, and the like. So this case is not like that of the mouse (to revert to our earlier example) which is transfixed by the stare of a cat. If this is the right way to read these examples, then Goldie's account has to do with how conceptual understanding may come to be penetrated by feeling, whereas Deigh's has to do with how feeling may come to be penetrated by conceptual understanding.[15]

Accordingly, we can in principle see religious understanding as related to feeling in two kinds of way: sometimes, conceptually inarticulate feelings may lead the way and then be deepened by concepts and the working of the imagination; and sometimes, discursive thoughts may lead the way, and then be extended by feeling. We might wonder if these two models can interact, so that some kinds of religious understanding arise from the reciprocal influence of these two movements: for example, perhaps a primitive feeling is penetrated by concepts, resulting in some new and richer affective sensitivity; and perhaps this sensitivity in turn enables new ways of talking about God or the world, and perhaps these ways of talking can in turn be deepened by new kinds of feeling. Again, the usefulness of this sort of model is a matter to be examined in the next chapter, where we shall consider how these accounts of the relationship of feeling and understanding may be applied to the case of religious understanding in particular.

It is worth noting one further point of distinction between Goldie's proposal and Deigh's. There appears to be no direct counterpart in Deigh's discussion for Goldie's thought that feeling may achieve a kind of understanding that cannot be verbalised. Deigh maintains that the understanding that can be achieved in feeling does not require concepts for its spelling out, since primitive emotional responses operate independently of conceptualisation. But this thought leaves open the possibility that what is understood in feeling could be otherwise understood. Goldie is suggesting that in some cases at least, feeling may offer not only an additional understanding that does not require discursive formulation, but one that cannot be articulated in such terms. Here feeling is not only sufficient for achieving the relevant understanding, but necessary. On this point Goldie's model suggests a way of extending Deigh's (or making it more explicit): if the affectively toned complexes which Goldie is discussing (such as the affectively toned appreciation of the dangers presented by ice) have a content which cannot be identified fully in feeling-neutral terms, then we might think that the affective complexes which figure in Deigh's account (such as the complex described by Proust) are to be

---

15 This difference between Goldie and Deigh is partly a function of their different concerns: Deigh is interested in the question of how conceptual thought develops from the kind of understanding that is typical of an animal or young child, and Goldie in the question of how to distinguish, in the case of adult human beings, the content of feeling-relative and feeling-independent thought.

understood similarly, that is, as resisting any exhaustive, affectively neutral specification of their content.

We have been considering how feeling may function as a mode of perception, sometimes infused by concepts and sometimes not: Deigh notes how 'primitive' qualities may be identified in feeling, and how other qualities may be identified in affective complexes which depend for their character in part upon conceptualisation and in part upon a primitive, affective responsiveness; and Goldie notes how felt response may involve a deepened, action-guiding perception of what is at stake in a situation. This understanding of affects as modes of perception is, of course, the account that occupied us for much of the first three chapters, where we considered in turn the possibility of an affectively toned perception of God, our fellow human beings, and the world. Next I want to consider a rather different way in which understanding may be tied to feeling.

It is a familiar enough fact of everyday life that our emotions can predispose us to focus on certain issues rather than others, and in turn to reach certain conclusions rather than others. For instance, if I am angry with someone, I may find myself thinking about their behaviour towards me, and I may be predisposed to find that behaviour offensive. My predisposition to find the behaviour offensive is no doubt, in part, to do with the fact that I view it from a certain perspective, by putting to myself the question: in what respects is this behaviour offensive? I am also no doubt predisposed, in normal circumstances, to favour answers to this question which prove that my angry response was warranted. As Robert Stocker puts the point, states such as anger and self-pity can be mood-like, and accordingly 'they seek out and collect, even create, sustaining or concordant facts (or "facts"), which they then use to justify and sustain that emotion, which then leads to further seeking, collecting, creating and coloring'.[16] Of course, this way of putting the matter suggests that an already-established emotional state is simply being rationalised. However, there is another, more benign understanding of how initial emotional commitments may help to direct our enquiries. For instance, Ronald de Sousa has suggested that emotions can play a role akin to that of scientific paradigms: 'paying attention to certain things [as we do when our emotions are engaged] is a source of reasons', he writes, 'but comes before them. Similarly, scientific paradigms, in Kuhn's sense, are better at stimulating research than at finding compelling and fair reasons for their

16 Robert Stocker with Elizabeth Hegeman, *Valuing Emotion* (Cambridge: Cambridge University Press, 1996), p. 94.

own adoption. They are too "deep" for that, too unlike specific, easily formulated beliefs."[17] De Sousa is suggesting that our emotions may have a proper part to play in setting the agenda for our thinking, where this is not a matter of just ratifying prejudice. Analogously, in science, paradigms help to give structure to the data (to constitute the data as informative), and thereby they identify certain lines of enquiry, and certain kinds of question, as potentially more fruitful than others.

We could put de Sousa's point otherwise by saying that before reason sets to work, we need a subject matter, something to think about. And the emotions are well suited to supplying such a subject matter, because of their role (one we noted in Chapter 1) in constituting patterns of salience. To register some feature of a situation emotionally is to accord that feature weight, or to judge it to have some sort of importance. So the objects of the emotions are already lit up for us as deserving of attention, and in that case, we seem to have good prima facie reason for allowing our emotions, especially perhaps strongly felt emotions, to set the agenda for our thinking. Again, this perspective seems to issue naturally from our earlier discussion: if the emotions have an important part to play in alerting us to values (as I have argued), that is a reason for thinking that they are prima facie trustworthy on the question of what deserves attention. These considerations apply most obviously to emotions which I am currently feeling. But similarly, we might argue that we also have good reason to attend to the object of our long-range emotional attachments (here thinking of emotions more in dispositional terms); for these attachments are in part constitutive of the value of their objects (consider again the example of Odysseus and Penelope in the last chapter), and therefore the existence of the attachment is a good prima facie reason for thinking that its object is indeed worthy of attention. Indeed, even if I have some reason to doubt the fittingness of a particular long-range attachment, that will still give me reason to think about its object, as a way of determining more exactly what my attitude should be, and of weakening the hold of the attachment if that should prove appropriate.

A similar perspective on the rational significance of the emotions emerges in evolutionary treatments of their rationale. For instance, Keith Oatley and Jennifer Jenkins have asked: why should emotions be important for human beings, but not for ticks and gods?[18] What is it about

---

17 Ronald de Sousa, 'The Rationality of Emotions', in Amélie Rorty (ed.), *Explaining Emotions* (Berkeley, CA: University of California Press, 1980), p. 139.
18 See Keith Oatley and Jennifer Jenkins, *Understanding Emotions* (Oxford: Blackwell, 1996), p. 257.

human living and thinking that makes the emotions practically and rationally indispensable for us, but not for other kinds of creature? They answer that ticks have no epistemic need of the emotions, because they can only take in a limited range of environmental stimuli, and they process those stimuli in a purely mechanical manner (on registering the appropriate scent, the tick drops from the tree onto the host animal, and so on). On the other hand, the gods have a wide range of stimuli to interpret, but they also have a comprehensive understanding, and therefore they too have no epistemic need of the emotions. We human beings find ourselves in an intermediate position: we are presented with a wide range of stimuli (here like the gods), but have only limited understanding (here like the ticks). And this poses a problem: given all the information we receive from the world, and all the correlative prospective topics of thought, how should we decide where to direct our attention? The emotions help to rescue us from this predicament, for they constitute patterns of salience, lighting up some matters as deserving of attention and leaving others at the periphery of our awareness. And, we might suppose, this is why at least some characteristic human emotions emerged in the first place. For example, perhaps we are predisposed to respond with fear to snake-shaped objects, for the reason that paying close attention to such objects is apt to promote survival in the conditions under which human beings evolved. So we could see de Sousa's proposal as building upon the sort of role the emotions (or some of them, at any rate) are equipped to play for evolutionary reasons; or again, we could see his thought as consonant with our earlier discussion of the role of the emotions in revealing values, and thereby picking out objects which are worthy of attention.

So by lighting up features of our environment, emotional feelings can help to train our attention on certain matters rather than others, and (I have been arguing) rightly so. But once our attention has been engaged in this way, we are predisposed not only to think about a certain subject matter, but also to reach certain conclusions about it, because the subject matter is picked out not neutrally, but from a certain point of view, as arousing certain kinds of concerns. (Think again of the example of anger, and how viewing another person's conduct with a certain question in mind – what is offensive in this behaviour? – may help to shape the conclusions we reach about the behaviour.) Now, sometimes the emotions may improperly lead us to a certain conclusion. For instance, if I am angry, and I arrive at the conclusion that another person's behaviour is offensive solely for reasons of self-justification, then my procedure will be epistemically at fault (because it is not targeted at the truth of the matter). But suppose instead that my anger simply makes it more likely that I shall come across whatever evidence there is in support of the idea that the person's behaviour was offensive (because I review their behaviour with that question in mind); and suppose that it does not thereby lead me to downplay any countervailing evidence, or to close off avenues of enquiry that might bring such counter-evidence to light. In this case, while my anger may well lead me to reach certain conclusions (suppose that there are good reasons for taking the behaviour as offensive, and that my anger helps me to identify those reasons), it is not on that account epistemically suspect. Here anger shapes the conclusions I reach not by prejudging the issue, but by leading me to attend to certain kinds of question (and associated evidence or counter-evidence). And once more, we may suppose that this sort of bias is justified, given that the emotions reveal not only what sort of subject matter is worth attending to (for example, this person's behaviour), but also in what respects that subject matter is worth attending to (by posing the question of whether the behaviour is offensive).

These considerations point to a further kind of relationship between emotional feelings and understanding. Here again we start with the idea of feelings as vehicles for the revelation of value; but now the thought is that this sort of revelation can serve as the springboard for a new and richer discursive understanding of a given subject matter, both by lighting up that subject matter as deserving of attention and by encouraging us to put certain questions to it rather than others. (Analogously, as de Sousa suggests, scientific paradigms offer a certain way of 'reading' the world – they pick out topics for reflection and suggest the appropriateness of putting certain questions, rather than others, to the world so construed.) As with the models we have derived from Deigh and Goldie, there is in principle at least no reason why this model should not be extended to the question of the relationship between emotional feeling and religious understanding in particular: by setting an agenda for our thinking, and by guiding that thinking in certain directions, the emotions may, in principle, pave the way for the formation of a certain kind of religious understanding. Again, we may wonder about the relationship between this model and the others we have examined. And once more, it seems easy enough to see them as contributing, potentially, to an overarching account. For instance, perhaps an affectively toned complex of the kind posited by Deigh (where this complex draws in part upon some primitive affective responsiveness) will help (quite properly) to shape the character of our subsequent discursive reflection in ways that are of some religious significance.

This is one way in which an affectively toned perception of value (of the kind identified by Deigh and Goldie) may provide the springboard for the development of further understanding. The quotation at the beginning of this chapter suggests a further respect in which such perceptions of value may direct the understanding in new ways. Geoffrey Maddell writes of how 'hearing the dominant seventh evokes a desire, and sometimes something akin to a longing, for its resolution'.[19] Here Maddell is alluding to the familiar fact that passages of music may be experienced in terms of 'tension' and 'resolution'. And he supposes that such qualities in the music may be registered (as their names suggest) in feeling: I grasp the tension not in purely musicological terms (though no doubt in a given case this is also possible), but in my felt responses to it. As we have seen, this account represents a further criticism of the add-on theory of feeling: on Maddell's view, feelings are intentional in their own right, and in particular, in the case under discussion, they pick out features of a musical composition in their own right.

Maddell's proposal presents an obvious parallel with Deigh's discussion of primitive feelings in so far as both authors are concerned with affective states which are non-conceptual in content (assuming again that my appreciation of music is not musicologically informed). However, what is of particular interest for our purposes in Maddell's remarks (and this sets him apart from Deigh) is how this sort of affectively toned understanding (of tension) provides for a further kind of intentionality: on account of its felt recognition of the tension, the mind is cast forward, in desire, to an anticipated moment of 'resolution'. In Maddell's example, the character of this resolution is grasped not musicologically, or in purely auditory terms (after all, it is not available to be heard as yet), but by way of the felt yearning or longing which points more or less precisely towards what is required if a resolution of this particular musical tension is to be achieved. So here Maddell identifies a further way in which affects may relate us to some object. As with de Sousa's model, an affectively toned perception provides the springboard for some further understanding: here it is the affectively toned perception of tension that grounds the thought of the resolution. But in this case the further understanding (concerning the character of the resolution) is itself non-discursive; but at the same time it is not just another affectively toned

19 'What Music Teaches about Emotion', p. 78.

perception of the kind we have been discussing, because the object of the affect is only anticipated, and not directly perceived. Again, I shall reserve further consideration of the possible religious significance of this model for the discussion in Chapter 5.

It is noteworthy that Maddell takes this account of feeling's role in the appreciation of music as a clue to its role in emotional experience more generally. In particular, he supposes that there is in all emotional experience an element of 'feeling towards' (this expression is designed, of course, to bring out the intentionality of feeling in its own right: it is feeling itself that is directed towards some object or state of affairs). For instance, he sees a person's fear that the stock market will crash as comprising a discursive thought (that the market will crash) and a fearful feeling towards the event picked out in this thought. However, this more general claim is not essential for our purposes: for us it is enough that Maddell's model has application in some cases; there is no need to suppose that the model is comprehensive.

To take stock, drawing on the contemporary philosophical literature, we have identified four kinds of relationship between emotional feelings and understanding. Sometimes emotional feelings may function as non-conceptual perceptions of 'primitive' qualities such as scariness, and this sort of responsiveness may contribute towards the formation of larger affective complexes which owe their character in part to a conceptual appreciation of the world (this is Deigh's model, of course). Or our affective responses may help us to deepen a purely discursive understanding of some situation, in ways that cannot be exhaustively specified in verbal terms (Goldie). Or an affective complex may serve to direct our attention to a given subject matter, and encourage the putting of certain questions to that subject matter, thereby helping to shape the development of our discursive understanding (de Sousa). Or an affectively toned perception of 'tension' may cast the mind forward to some as yet unexperienced but anticipated resolution or culmination, where the character of this resolution is grasped not discursively but in feeling (Maddell). As I have intimated, these proposals need not be in competition, and can be interwoven in various ways to form part of an overarching account.

Next I want to take note, fairly briefly, of some themes in the recent literature in psychology, neurophysiology, and philosophy which seem to corroborate the kind of picture that we have been developing. The object of this discussion is not to propose a further model to set alongside these four, but just to locate these models within some larger context, and thereby to suggest ways in which they may be further elaborated. I do not claim that there is a clear consensus on the issues which I am going to discuss, or even that the sources I cite represent the majority opinion; however, the views I mention do at least command respect in their respective fields, and to that extent they will provide broad corroboration for the kind of perspective that we have been considering.

PLACING THE FOUR MODELS IN CONTEXT

The models of Deigh, Goldie, and Maddell suggest that feeling can sometimes take the form of a non-verbal mode of understanding. This is an idea that can also be found in the recent psychological and neuro-physiological literature on the emotions. For example, John Teasdale and Philip Barnard have proposed what they call an 'interacting cognitive subsystems' (ICS) framework for understanding the working of the mind.[20] The key idea in this proposal is that there are

qualitatively different kinds of information, or mental codes, each corresponding to a different aspect of experience . . . Each different kind of information is transformed and stored by processes that are specialised for dealing with that particular kind of mental code and no other. These specialised processes are arranged in distinct subsystems, each subsystem storing and transforming only one kind of information.[21]

Teasdale and Barnard propose that there are nine of these codes in all. The most basic are those relating to sensory perception and proprioception (the latter having to do with the registering of body state), and these codes provide the input for various others. The authors state that the two most important codes for cognition are the 'propositional' and 'implicational' codes, which derive 'meaning' from the input provided by more basic codes. For our purposes, it is important to note that implicational meaning is made conscious in the form of feeling, where feeling is understood to be distinct from sensation. Thus implicational meaning can be grasped by way of a felt awareness of a non-propositionally encoded content. This sounds rather like what Deigh is proposing in his discussion of primitive affective responses and, depending upon how propositional and implicational codes are related, may also converge with the kind of picture offered by Goldie, where feeling builds upon a

---

20 John D. Teasdale and Philip J. Barnard, *Affect, Cognition and Change: Re-Modelling Depressive Thought* (Hove: Lawrence Erlbaum Associates, 1993). I am grateful to Maria Hearl for this reference.
21 *Ibid.*, p. 50.

discursively articulated understanding. Given these analogies, it is worth spelling out the Teasdale–Barnard model a little further.

The model proposes, naturally, that information in one mental code can be transformed into information in another. (Otherwise the information deriving from sense perception, say, would never be able to inform propositional thought.) But the 'higher' codes do not merely replicate the content of more basic codes; rather, they tend to synthesise it, and thereby extract new meaning from it. Here is a simple example of how this process is supposed to work. I have left in Teasdale and Barnard's acronyms, to mark the various cognitive subsystems that are meant to be in play:

an upsetting personal encounter could be encoded and stored in parallel (1) in separate sensory codes describing the scene in terms of, respectively, the qualities of sound (AC), light (VIS), and proprioceptive (BS) patterns involved; (2) in more perceptual codes that encode the scene in terms of the visual objects (OBJ) and speech components (MPL) present; (3) in a semantic code (PROP), which captures the meaning of the situation in the form of sequences of propositional elements; and (4) in an integrative schematic code (IMPLIC), which captures prototypical features of the situation corresponding to generic aspects of experience extracted from previous episodes. IMPLIC code might represent, for example, the schematic model related to the prototypical 'argument with person I care for but who does not understand me' theme.[22]

It is striking that on this model the IMPLIC code emerges as both the most integrative kind of understanding (at the top of this hierarchy of codes) and as the kind of understanding that is most directly attuned to the interpersonal or existential meaning of a situation, since the implicational 'schematic model' gives the personal significance of the situation. Analogously, Goldie's example of the gorilla suggests that affectively toned understanding may integrate the various propositionally expressed elements of a situation ('the door is open', 'the gorilla is dangerous', and so on) so as to identify their existential and action-guiding import. Moreover, Teasdale and Barnard also state, as we have seen, that implicational meanings can be grasped affectively. This happens by way of what they call the COPY process, whereby newly acquired information is stored in a particular code. In general, it is the COPY process that generates subjective experience, including affective experience:

---

22 *Ibid.*, p. 56. Compare Nerlich's comment, quoted in Chapter 3, that registering the death of a loved one is not like grasping new sentential information.

Subjective emotional experience is distributed over the COPY processes of several subsystems, primarily those handling Implicational and Body-state information codes. Emotional experience often includes feelings which have an implicit information content. For example, it is implicit in a sense of apprehension that something awful is about to happen, a feeling of hopelessness implies that my efforts to get what I want will be doomed to failure, and it is implicit in feeling confident that I will be able to cope and things are likely to turn out well. Such subjective feelings with implicit information content mark the processing of related Implicational code patterns by the COPY process of the implication subsystem. Holistic 'senses' or feelings of this type are the phenomenal experience corresponding to activity in the Implicational subsystem, just as phenomenal experiences of pitch or timbre mark activity in the Acoustic subsystem. Subjective emotional experience also includes sensations that have a much more 'physical' quality, devoid of an implicit information content. For example, we may feel tense when anxious, we may experience pangs of grief, or we may feel we are shaking with fury.[23]

Here information-bearing 'feelings' are clearly differentiated from 'sensations'; and such feelings are said to be capable of expressing implicational meaning, which of its nature is not reducible to propositional meaning, since it represents a more integrative or holistic kind of understanding. Here again, there are parallels with Goldie's model, and his thought that the integration of discursive thoughts that is achieved in feeling may not admit of any precise verbal paraphrase. The thought that implicational meaning is the most integrative kind of meaning is also reminiscent of de Sousa's analogy between emotions and paradigms. In general, 'paradigms' confer intelligibility upon experience by providing an overarching account of its sense, within which our particular enquiries may be set. Similarly, implicational meaning, since it is the most integrative kind of meaning, assigns a sense to all the other elements of our experience, and thereby provides an overarching context in terms of which further reflection upon individual items of experience can proceed. This feature of implicational meaning is important for Teasdale and Barnard's attempt to understand continuing depressive thought. For the paradigmatic quality of implicational meaning suggests how the mind may get locked into a particular (for instance, depressive) way of reading the world; this is because paradigms can be in some degree self-sustaining, since they provide the interpretive framework that governs the assessment of any new evidence.[24] Similarly, de Sousa comments that paradigms are too 'deep' to be subject to the normal processes of rational enquiry.

23 *Ibid.*, p. 84.
24 Teasdale and Barnard discuss 'self-regenerating depressive interlock' *ibid.*, pp. 168–71.

Of course, assigning such a central role to implicational meaning in the explanation of depression poses a problem for therapy: since implicational meaning is non-propositional, it cannot be straightforwardly articulated and thereby examined or contested. (Contrast the approach favoured by some forms of 'cognitive behaviour therapy'.) Teasdale and Barnard suggest that this difficulty can be overcome in part by the use of evocative verbal tags:

Our solution to the problem of communicating implicational meaning is to refer to Implicational schematic models by verbal tags such as ['self as failure'] or ['argument with someone I care about but who does not understand me']. These convey, very partially, the *topic* of the Implicational schematic model, but obviously not its constituent breakdown.[25]

The difficulty Teasdale and Barnard seek to address here is very like the difficulty Quentin Smith poses when asking how we are to communicate in verbal terms the content of intuitive feelings of global importance. Smith suggests that we can recall such feelings at the level of intuition by the use of verbal formulas which 'are vague in their sense but rich in connotations'. (He gives as an example: 'The world-whole is fulfilled! Everything joyously radiates with its fullness!')[26] In the same place, Smith notes that metaphor may also have a part to play in communicating the content of these intuitive, nonpropositional, integrative, meaning-apprehending feelings. And here again there is a parallel with the Teasdale–Barnard account. They note in particular how poetry (along with other creative arts) may communicate an implicational meaning: a poem's meaning is not reducible to what might be conveyed in a literal, line-by-line paraphrase, and in part, this is because it is an integrative kind of meaning, one that is grasped in an 'immediate sense' or unitive appreciation of what the poem as a whole means.[27] And again, this sort of content may be grasped in feeling. In Teasdale and Barnard's terms: 'Subjectively, the synthesis of the generic meaning conveyed by a poem is marked by a particular holistic "sense" or "feeling".'[28] The role of feeling in art appreciation is a matter to which we shall return in Chapter 6, where we shall think further about the possible connections between the arts and the pervasive, 'paradigmatic' making sense of the world that is characteristic of religious understanding.

25 *Ibid.*, p. 66, square brackets in the original.
26 *The Felt Meanings of the World: A Metaphysics of Feeling* (West Lafayette, IN: Purdue University Press, 1986), p. 25.
27 *Affect, Cognition and Change*, pp. 73–4.   28 *Ibid.*, p. 73.

To take stock, I have been suggesting that the Teasdale–Barnard account of cognitive function presents a number of parallels with some of the models we have been examining in this chapter. Notably, Teasdale and Barnard's suggestion that information can be encoded in non-propositional, implicational, and feeling-accessible terms formulates in other terms what Deigh and Goldie both affirm (that feeling may have an action-guiding, non-verbalisable content). The Teasdale–Barnard model also allows, as we have seen, that propositional meaning may infuse implicational meaning (when the latter kind of meaning involves an integration of propositional meanings), and this suggests a parallel with Goldie's model of how affect may build upon propositional or discursive understanding. But Teasdale and Barnard also allow that implicational meaning can build directly on sensory inputs without these inputs having been mediated by any propositional understanding, and, on this point, their view is of the same type as Deigh's account of 'primitive' feelings.[29] They also suppose that implicational code may be transformed into (without its content being reduced to) propositional code, here echoing Deigh's suggestion that non-propositional content may be taken up into some larger affective complex which owes its character in part to concep-tualisation.[30] Lastly, we have considered how implicational meanings in the Teasdale–Barnard model function rather like the paradigms in de Sousa's account of the emotions, and this provides another way of developing the idea that an affectively apprehended meaning may con-tribute to the shaping of our discursive understanding of the world. This strand of their model is of obvious religious significance, potentially, given that religious understanding often has a paradigmatic quality, and provides an overarching interpretive framework for making sense of various regions of experience.

Before proceeding I would like to offer an autobiographical footnote to this discussion. I have often found that a current experience can trigger a memory where the memory does not replicate in any way the content of the current experience (in terms of people, objects, or places, for example), and where the event recalled is not causally related to my current experience, or related in terms of physical or temporal proximity. (Compare Hume's three principles for the association of ideas: resem-blance, contiguity in time or place, and cause and effect.[31]) Rather, the

---

29 See their discussion of 'prewired procedures' *ibid.*, pp. 87–9.

30 Compare this remark: 'all four "central" codes (OBJ, MPL, PROP, and IMPLIC) have transformation processes for reciprocal conversions of mental code': *ibid.*, p. 57.

31 David Hume, *A Treatise of Human Nature*, ed. L. A. Selby-Bigge, 2nd edn revised by P. H. Nidditch (Oxford: Clarendon Press, 1978), Book I, Part I, Section IV. The same distinction is

only connection that I can discern is one of emotional structure, and this parallel of structure can be quite detailed, and is typically difficult to identify in propositional terms. This phenomenon could be readily understood in terms of the Teasdale–Barnard model: cast in the terms of that model, the content of my current experience is being encoded in implicational terms, and therefore sorted in the mind according to a resemblance that is most readily specified in terms of emotional resonance (rather than in sensory or propositional terms). It is worth noting too that this process whereby later events are mapped onto earlier in terms of their implicational structure is not, in my experience, readily brought to conscious awareness. Even when I consciously recall an episode from my past, I have often found that it takes some effort to 'catch' it, since the recollection tends to be fleeting, and is typically not the subject of thematic awareness. This fits with Teasdale and Barnard's suggestion that the implicational structuring of experience involves the use of 'implicit' schematic models. (Here they contrast the ICS model with others which understand depression more in terms of 'consciously accessible negative thoughts'.[32]) So while feelings may give us access to implicational meanings, those meanings can serve to structure our experience quite independently of any awareness we may have of them, and indeed in the normal case we shall not be aware of their operation. If the mind understands the significance of current experience by mapping its content onto implicational meanings that have been laid down in memory, and if non-propositional feelings are the way in which this kind of making sense of things is most readily accessed, even if with difficulty, then all of this is of some importance for any philosophical and theological anthropology.

To turn now to another developing body of literature on the emotions, a number of neurological studies have also endorsed the idea that affects can convey information independently of propositionally apprehended meanings. For example, Joseph LeDoux has argued that there are two distinct brain pathways which lie behind emotional experience, and only one of these passes through the cortex (the seat of discursive thought). The other pathway is not thereby devoid of informational content; but its content is cruder, and can therefore be registered more quickly. Summarising this approach, LeDoux writes:

made in the first *Enquiry: Enquiries Concerning Human Understanding and Concerning the Principles of Morals*, ed. L. A. Selby-Bigge, 3rd edn revised by P. H. Nidditch (Oxford: Clarendon Press, 1975), Section III.

32 See *Affect, Cognition and Change*, p. 218.

Information about external stimuli reaches the amygdala by way of direct pathways from the thalamus (the low road) as well as by way of pathways from the thalamus to the cortex to the amygdala. The direct thalamo-amygdala path is a shorter and thus a faster transmission route than the pathway from the thalamus through the cortex to the amygdala. However, because the direct pathway bypasses the cortex, it is unable to benefit from cortical processing. As a result, it can only provide the amygdala with a crude representation of the stimulus. It is thus a *quick and dirty* processing pathway. The direct pathway allows us to respond to potentially dangerous stimuli before we fully know what the stimulus is. This can be very useful in dangerous situations. However, its utility requires that the cortical pathway be able to override the direct pathway.[33]

This sort of account sits very comfortably with Deigh's model of 'primitive' affective experience: if there is a brain system which can process information independently of the cortex, then we have a neurological foundation for the idea that we can take stock of our environment independently of any conceptual appraisal of its character. Moreover, on LeDoux's account, this taking stock, when registered in consciousness, can take the form of affective awareness. Hence he comments that: 'feelings come about when the activity of specialised emotion systems gets represented in the system that gives rise to consciousness'.[34]

Moreover, like Teasdale and Barnard, LeDoux postulates a separate, implicit 'emotional memory' system, to be distinguished from the explicit 'declarative memory' system (compare Teasdale and Barnard on the implicational and propositional encoding of current experience). And again, as with Teasdale and Barnard's implicational and propositional meanings, these two systems can be engaged jointly so as to produce a single unified experience. LeDoux gives the example of a person who had a traumatic car accident in which the car's horn somehow became stuck so that it continued to sound after the accident. Suppose that the person now hears the sound of a horn at a later time:

The sound of the horn (or a neural representation of it), having become a conditioned fear stimulus, goes straight from the auditory system to the amygdala and implicitly elicits bodily responses that typically occur in situations of danger . . . The sound also travels through the cortex to the temporal lobe memory system, where explicit declarative memories are activated. You are reminded of the accident. You consciously remember where you were going and who you were with . . . There is a place, though, where explicit memories of emotional experiences and implicit emotional experiences meet – in working

33 Joseph LeDoux, *The Emotional Brain: The Mysterious Underpinnings of Emotional Life* (London: Phoenix, 1998), p. 164, LeDoux's italics.
34 *Ibid.*, p. 282.

memory and its creation of immediate conscious experience . . . The fact that you are aroused becomes part of your current experience. This fact comes to rest side by side in consciousness with your explicit memory of the accident. Without the emotional arousal elicited through the implicit system, the conscious memory would be emotionally flat . . . Actually, these two events (the past memory and the present arousal) are seamlessly fused as a unified conscious experience of the moment.[35]

Here we find a number of familiar ideas: emotional memories (laid down in a non-propositional, implicational code) provide a kind of template in the light of which we can assess the significance of current experience. This kind of assessment can be undertaken independently of any conceptual appreciation of our circumstances, and can be registered very quickly in the form of feeling (on all of this, compare Deigh's model of 'primitive' feeling). But such an assessment can also be interwoven with a more discursive understanding, so giving rise to a unitary state of mind, which is both affectively toned and conceptually structured (compare Deigh's discussion of how primitive affects may be penetrated by concepts).

Antonio Damasio has also argued, on neurological grounds, that felt responses can provide a quick and non-discursive, but also rational, way of assessing our circumstances, especially for the purpose of determining what sort of behavioural response would be appropriate. He cites in illustration a patient of his who is suffering from ventromedial pre-frontal damage and associated flatness of affective response; in this passage, he and Damasio are trying to decide when they should next meet:

I suggested two alternative dates, both in the coming month and just a few days apart from each other. The patient pulled out his appointment book and began consulting the calendar. The behavior that ensued, which was witnessed by several investigators, was quite remarkable. For the better part of a half-hour, the patient enumerated reasons for and against each of the two dates: previous engagements, proximity to other engagements, possible meteorological conditions, virtually anything that one could reasonably think about concerning a simple date . . . It took enormous discipline to listen to all of this without pounding on the table and telling him to stop, but we finally did tell him, quietly, that he should come on the second of the alternative dates. His response was equally calm and prompt. He simply said: 'That's fine.' Back the appointment book went into his pocket, and then he was off.[36]

35 *Ibid.*, pp. 201, 203.
36 Antonio Damasio, *Descartes' Error: Emotion, Reason and the Human Brain* (Basingstoke: Picador, 1995), pp. 193–4.

This example reveals that, despite his brain condition, the patient's capacity for relatively abstract, discursive thought is unimpaired; and accordingly, he is able to rehearse with ease a whole range of considerations that might have some relevance to the scheduling of the appointment. But while he is able to perform this relatively sophisticated cost-benefit kind of analysis, there remains something irrational about his behaviour. He fails to register the social inappropriateness of taking so long to reach a decision, or that given his circumstances, it matters little what decision he takes. Damasio remarks: 'This behavior is a good example of the limits of pure reason. It is also a good example of the calamitous consequence of not having automated mechanisms of decision-making.'[37] What the patient lacks, Damasio goes on to say, is a 'somatic-marker device' that would signal the 'useless and indulgent nature of the exercise'. A somatic marker is a visceral or non-visceral feeling that marks out an option as bad (or, less importantly, as good) independently of any discursively articulated assessment of the option.[38] More colloquially we could talk of registering the character of an option in a 'gut feeling'. It is because of our gut feelings that we do not get lost in the kind of indefinitely extended examination of possibilities that is occupying the patient in Damasio's example: there are times when it is rational to desist from further reasoning; and gut feelings can help to set limits to our reflection, by excluding some options (those that are marked by a negative feeling) from further consideration. A person of normal affective responsiveness would not proceed as the patient does in this example, because they would have a negative gut feeling (perhaps a feeling of self-consciousness or awkwardness) that would alert them to the need to reach a decision (any decision) quickly. Such a person would give less time to a reasoned examination of the issues, but their behaviour would, even so, be rationally more appropriate than that of the patient.

This picture of the contribution of the emotions to rational decision-making echoes LeDoux's thought that feelings may offer a 'quick and dirty' (non-conceptually-articulated) route to choices of action. It also recalls Goldie's suggestion that the action-guiding understanding that is embedded in feeling may not be reducible to anything we have articulated (or could articulate) in verbal terms. For somatic markers are not themselves propositionally articulated thoughts, but they move us to action anyway, in ways that involve some genuine taking stock of what is at stake in a situation. Damasio's model is also reminiscent of de Sousa's

37 *Ibid.*, p. 194.   38 *Ibid.*, p. 173.

suggestion that the emotions may function as paradigms; for somatic markers help to frame our problems of practical decision-making, by highlighting some possible choices as worthy of further consideration and excluding others, and thereby they may help to determine the course of our discursive reflections.

In concluding this section, I want to swing back briefly to the philosophical literature and to note several further themes which will help to corroborate some of the proposals we have been examining in this chapter. We shall then be in a position to examine, in Chapter 5, the relationship between emotional feeling and religious understanding in particular.

In recent philosophical discussion there has been a division between 'cognitive' and 'non-cognitive' accounts of the emotions, where the first school differs from the second in maintaining that the emotions must involve cognitions or judgements. However, the two sides of this dispute have tended to unite on the thought that feelings belong to the non-cognitive side of our mental life. In keeping with the general approach we have been following in this book, a number of recent theories of emotion have sought to challenge this way of understanding the distinction between cognitive and non-cognitive theories, by expanding the notion of cognition, so that it encompasses not only conceptually articulated assessments but also feelings. Jesse Prinz puts the issue in these terms:

> we have a serious puzzle. The fact that emotions are meaningful, reason sensitive, and intentional suggests that they must be cognitive. The fact that some emotions arise without the intervention of the neocortex suggests that emotions cannot *all* be cognitive. The emotions that arise in this way seem to be meaningful. This suggests that being meaningful does not require being cognitive. Noncognitive states are explanatorily anaemic and cognitive states are explanatorily superfluous. Noncognitive theories give us too little, and cognitive theories give us too much. Call this the Emotion Problem.[39]

The Emotion Problem is, I take it, one of how emotions can be 'meaningful' (content-bearing) even if not 'cognitive' (having a content which can be propositionally articulated). Non-cognitive theories provide too little, because they do not explain meaningfulness; cognitive theories provide too much, because the sort of meaningfulness they acknowledge is conceptually articulated. Prinz's own solution to the Problem is to suppose that there are 'embodied appraisals', that is, appraisals which are

---

39 Jesse Prinz, 'Emotion, Psychosemantics, and Embodied Appraisals', in Anthony Hatzimoysis (ed.), *Philosophy and the Emotions* (Cambridge: Cambridge University Press, 2003), p. 78, Prinz's italics.

not conceptually articulated, but which nonetheless serve to represent and evaluate the world in some fashion. Expounding this view, he writes:

> The beep emitted by a smoke detector might be said to represent 'smoke from fire here now', but it does not decompose into meaningful sub-beeps. It is semantically primitive. Complex contents do not need complex representations. Defenders of cognitive theories assume that emotions can only designate core relational themes if emotions are judgments, thoughts, or some other kind of concept-laden, structured states. This simply isn't true. To represent appraisal core relational themes, emotions need only occur, reliably, when those themes occur.[40]

Here Prinz is beginning to explore (from a philosophical rather than a neurological perspective) the possibility of a non-conceptual mental content. Applying the smoke detector kind of example to the case of emotional content, he considers the possibility that a state of bodily arousal may be reliably correlated with images (to be distinguished from judgements) of snakes, bugs, looming objects, and the like. In this case, he thinks, we should suppose that this particular body state is a 'danger detector': although the concept of danger is not deployed, the body state is reliably triggered in circumstances that potentially pose a hazard, and in this sense it can be said to represent danger. This model evidently offers another way of expanding upon Deigh's claim that 'primitive' affective responses can be concept-independent and yet content-bearing. If this sort of programme can be carried through, Prinz thinks, then we should conclude that 'Cognitive theories have been right about content, and noncognitive theories have been right about form.'[41] In other words, emotions are indeed constituted of cognitions, but these cognitions may be realised in feelings of bodily states, rather than conceptually articulated judgements.

A similar kind of perspective has been defended by Patricia Greenspan. She also postulates a 'primitive', non-conceptually-articulated kind of intentionality on which discursive thought may build:

> emotional affect has an evaluation as its content. The assumption of intentionality at this level of basic feeling can sound mysterious, but in principle it is no more so than in more familiar cases involving units of language and thought. In fact, I suspect that the historical or evolutionary account of thought

---

40 *Ibid.*, p. 80. An example of a core relational theme in this context would be 'there has been a demeaning offence against me and mine' (the theme corresponding to anger). Prinz has borrowed the concept and this terminology from R. S. Lazarus, *Emotion and Adaptation* (New York: Oxford University Press, 1991).

41 'Emotion', p. 82.

would start with feelings, assigned 'meanings' by their significance for the organism in a sense that includes their role in behavioural response – meanings in a sense that becomes mental only with later cognitive development. Thought content in this sense, even at the later states of development, need not be a separable mental element; it is the content of a feeling.[42]

The penetration of primitive affect by discursive thought that is postulated in Deigh's model is represented here in evolutionary terms: perhaps thought itself is first of all feeling, and this sort of intentionality then provides the basis for the richer kind of intentionality achieved in conceptual thought.[43]

This passage suggests too that the kind of intentionality realised in feeling is inseparably action-guiding intentionality: the meanings borne by feelings are defined in part by the role of those feelings in guiding behaviour. For instance, a feeling may be a 'danger detector', to use Prinz's terminology, if it reliably gives rise to flight or fight behavioural responses. This thought is significant for our purposes because it suggests the possibility of a kind of intentionality that is inherently evaluative and action-guiding; for this is, surely, the kind of intentionality that belongs to at least some kinds of religious (as well as ethical) understanding.

Greenspan's account also invites the thought that feeling achieves its intentionality by virtue of its connection to a state of the whole body (including body posture and the condition of the heart, lungs, muscles, and nervous system) – because on this view the meanings of emotional feelings are fixed (at least in part) by their role in behavioural response. More exactly, we might suppose that emotional feeling achieves its intentionality as a mode of awareness of the state of the whole body, with particular reference to the body's readiness to express itself in action. This thought seems to be an improvement on the idea that emotional feeling is basically a registering of the state of a particular body part, an account which seems more suited to sensations. However, if we understand emotional feeling as registering the state of the body as a whole, there remains a question about why the intentionality of feeling is not directed simply at the body, rather than at the world.[44] Hanna Pickard's account of the emotions offers a suggestive response to this difficulty:

42 Patricia Greenspan, 'Emotions, Rationality, and Mind/Body', in Hatzimoysis (ed.), *Philosophy and the Emotions*, p. 123.
43 Greenspan wants to speak of emotions as having a 'propositional content', but 'not necessarily propositional thoughts held in mind in some independent sense' ('Emotions', p. 122). In other words, the content can reside in the feeling itself.
44 The problem is noted in Anthony Hatzimoysis, 'Emotional Feelings and Intentionalism', in A. Hatzimoysis (ed.), *Philosophy and the Emotions*, pp. 108–9.

when the object of the emotion is actually present, then and there in the subject's vicinity, it is possible that the body itself possesses all the intentionality which is required. In such cases, the body is likely to be spatially oriented in relation to the object. Most basically, it may be withdrawing or approaching: literally directed towards or away from the object. But within these basic modes, there are many kinds of bodily engagement. For this reason, a subject's awareness of her body from the inside can be an awareness of it as directed towards or away from objects in the world: the bodily feeling has an intrinsic intentionality.[45]

Following Pickard's examples, we might say that in emotional feeling I am aware of some state of the world by virtue of being aware of my body's readiness to act in the world. It is tempting to think that this case is no different, structurally, from the case of sense perception: in seeing a computer, say, what I am directly aware of is the computer, but I am aware of it by virtue of my state of consciousness. However, in the case of seeing the computer, I am not (in the normal case) consciously attending to my body (and I need not be feeling anything), whereas in the case of emotional feelings, I seem to be aware (however peripherally) both of the state of my body and of the world. Robert Solomon's account of anger provides a further illustration of how this dual yet integrated directedness is possible:

Anger involves taking up a defensive posture. Some of the distinctive sensations of getting angry are the often subtle and usually not noticed tensing of the various muscles of the body, particularly those involved in physical aggression. All of these are obviously akin to kinaesthetic feelings, the feelings through which we navigate and 'keep in touch with' our bodies. But these are not just feelings, not just sensations or perceptions of goings-on in the body. They are also *activities*, the activities of preparation and expression.[46]

On this view, perceiving the world by way of emotional feelings involves an awareness (however peripheral) of body state, and for this reason we can speak of 'feeling' here; but this feeling is at the same time directed towards the world, because it is an awareness of the body as a whole as ready for action in the world.

---

45 Hanna Pickard, 'Emotions and the Problem of Other Minds', in Hatzimoysis (ed.), *Philosophy and the Emotions*, p. 97.
46 Robert Solomon, 'Emotions, Thoughts and Feelings: What is a "Cognitive Theory" of the Emotions, and Does it Neglect Affectivity?', in Hatzimoysis (ed.), *Philosophy and the Emotions*, p. 14, Solomon's italics.

It is time to take stock. Emotional feelings are embodied appraisals, which are correlated with danger, offensive behaviour, and other situations of existential import (here with Prinz); they are, more exactly, appraisals which involve the body's readiness for action (with Greenspan); and therefore, more exactly still, emotional feelings have a dual directedness, being targeted both at a bodily gestalt (understood as readiness for a certain kind of action) and thereby at the world (whose character is registered in the readiness for this particular kind of action) (here with Pickard and Solomon). I am not proposing that this model will work in all cases (naturally, it is most easily applicable when our emotions concern an object which is present here and now, and which invites a behavioural response). But it marks one suggestive way of developing the intrinsic intentionality of feeling thesis. Solomon gives this pithy summary of the model: 'There are feelings, "affects" if you like, critical to emotion. But they are not distinct from cognition or judgment and they are not merely "read-outs" of processes going on in the body. They are judgments of the body . . . ' And he goes on to say (here giving his solution to what Prinz calls the Emotion Problem): 'this is the "missing" element in the cognitive theory of emotions'.[47]

CONCLUSION

In this chapter, we have elaborated four models of the relationship between emotional feeling and understanding, and we have considered how those models may be placed in a larger context, and to some degree further specified and corroborated, by reference to recent work in psychology, neurophysiology, and philosophy. In brief, these models are those of Deigh (primitive affects may be intrinsically intentional and may be infused by a growing conceptual appreciation of the world); Goldie (feeling may take further the understanding achieved by discursive reflection, in ways that perhaps escape verbal articulation); de Sousa (feeling may present a kind of paradigm that can help to govern the unfolding of our reflective enquiries); and Maddell (feeling may be targeted at some as yet unrealised but anticipated consummation). The first two of these models offer an elaboration of the understanding of feeling that we have been using in Chapters 1–3; the last two present a rather different account,

---

47 *Ibid.*, p. 16. Solomon is one of the best-known advocates of the 'cognitive' theory, so it is significant that in this essay he is defending cognitivism by appeal to an expanded conception of cognition, which allows for the cognitive significance of emotional feelings.

although one that is still founded on the idea of feeling as revelatory of value. I hope that I have done enough in this chapter to show that all of these models make a real claim on our attention, and are securely enough established to provide a worthwhile basis for further reflection. I want now to consider how the four models might be applied to the question of the relationship between emotional feeling and religious understanding in particular.

CHAPTER 5

Emotional feeling and religious understanding

When I call theological formulas secondary products, I mean that in a world in which no religious feeling had existed, I doubt whether any philosophic theology could ever have been framed. I doubt if dispassionate intellectual contemplation of the universe, apart from inner unhappiness and need of deliverance on the one hand and mystical Emotion on the other, would ever have resulted in religious philosophies such as we now possess. Men would have begun with animistic explanations of natural fact, and criticised these away into scientific ones, as they actually have done . . . But high-flying speculations like those of either dogmatic or idealistic theology, these they would have had no motive to venture on, feeling no need of commerce with such deities. These speculations must, it seems to me, be classed as over-beliefs, buildings-out performed by the intellect into directions of which feeling originally supplied the hint.[1]

Here William James accords feeling a kind of priority over the findings of the discursive intellect. In this chapter, I would like to see how the four models of emotional feeling elaborated in Chapter 4 can be used to give further definition to James's proposal – by helping us to specify various respects in which feeling may indeed appear to come before religious understanding, as well as certain senses in which it appears to follow on behind. I shall proceed by examining the stance of several authors who have written explicitly on the relationship between emotional experience and religious or metaphysical understanding, giving particular attention to the work of John Henry Newman, Jonathan Edwards, Rudolf Otto, William James, and Pierre Hadot.

---

1 William James, *The Varieties of Religious Experience: A Study in Human Nature* (London: Longmans, Green & Co., 1902), p. 431.

APPLYING THE MODELS OF DEIGH AND GOLDIE

As we saw in the first chapter, Newman thinks that it is possible to have an affectively toned awareness of God, an awareness which yields what he calls a 'real image' (as distinct from a notion) of God, whose content cannot be specified in full in discursive terms.[2] It is striking that Newman thinks that such an image can be possessed by young children, which suggests that it need not be dependent on any developed conceptual understanding of God or the world. Speaking of the impression of God that a young child may have, he writes:

It is an image of the good God, good in Himself, good relatively to the child, with whatever incompleteness; an image, before it has been reflected on, and before it is recognized by him as a notion. Though he cannot explain or define the word 'God', when told to use it, his acts show that to him it is far more than a word.[3]

Here the child is said to have some understanding of God even though he lacks any discursively articulated concept of God. In saying that the child can have an image which has yet to be 'recognised' as a notion, Newman means, I take it, that the content of an image can in part be spelt out in discursive terms, but that the child has yet to do this. (Indeed, it seems that he must think that the image has some notional content; after all, the image is of God, and God can be understood at least in part in notional terms – as the creator, for example.) So the child's image contains within it implicitly a notion of God – although, once more, on Newman's view, the content of such an image cannot be specified in full in notional terms. More exactly, Newman's view is that through an affectively toned recognition that they have acted wrongly, a child may have a sense of themselves as accountable before God, and therefore an 'image' of God. Contained in this image is the thought that God is 'an invisible Being, who exercises a particular providence among us, who is present everywhere, who is heart-reading, heart-changing, ever-accessible, open to impetration',[4] since all of these thoughts are implied in the sense of oneself as accountable before God. These thoughts are partly composed, I take it, of implicit notions, but without being reducible to what

---

2 I have noted that his text does not force precisely this reading upon us, but this does seem the most reasonable interpretation: see Chapter 1, n. 30. Certainly, Newman is clear that we encounter God through the data of conscience, and that those data are affectively toned.

3 John Henry Newman, *An Essay in Aid of a Grammar of Assent* (Notre Dame, IN: University of Notre Dame Press, 1979), p. 105.

4 *Ibid.*, pp. 103–4.

can be expressed in purely notional terms. On this last point, Newman's position is like that of Goldie, when he supposes that the content of an affectively toned thought may elude any precise affect-neutral paraphrase. On this view, the idea of divine 'accessibility', for example, can only be grasped in religious depth with the aid of feeling, and not by purely discursive (or 'notional') means.

This sort of picture is reminiscent of the first of our models of the relationship between emotional feeling and understanding. On Newman's view, we are capable of something like a 'primitive' (non-conceptually-articulate), affectively toned responsiveness to God, one that is grounded in our awareness of ourselves as morally responsible. A rather similar proposal has been advanced, famously, by Rudolf Otto in *The Idea of the Holy*. Otto also postulates an affectively toned, non-discursive awareness of the divine, although the kind of awareness to which he is referring is not moral in content:

Taken, indeed, in its purely natural sense, *mysterium* would first mean merely a secret or a mystery in the sense of that which is alien to us, uncomprehended and unexplained; and so far *mysterium* is itself merely an ideogram, an analogical notion taken from the natural sphere, illustrating, but incapable of exhaustively rendering, our real meaning. Taken in the religious sense, that which is 'mysterious' is – to give it perhaps the most striking expression – the 'wholly other' . . . that which is quite beyond the sphere of the usual, the intelligible, and the familiar, which therefore falls quite outside the limits of the 'canny', and is contrasted with it, filling the mind with blank wonder and astonishment.[5]

Otto's teaching here echoes Newman's distinction between having a 'notion' and having a 'real image' of God. It is possible to understand the meaning of 'mysterium' in purely notional terms; and in that case we shall assign it a sense by reference to our experience of worldly mysteries (what is unexplained within the world, for example). But this does not give the real, religious content of the idea. For that content, we have to defer to the kind of mysteriousness that is revealed in affectively toned, specifically religious experience, for instance, the experience Otto labels 'stupor', which involves 'blank wonder, an astonishment that strikes us dumb, amazement absolute'.[6] Otto's talk of 'blank wonder' and 'an astonishment that strikes us dumb' perhaps suggests that, like Newman, he is thinking of a kind of 'primitive' (non-conceptually-articulated),

---

5 Rudolf Otto, *The Idea of the Holy: An Inquiry into the Non-Rational Factor in the Idea of the Divine and its Relation to the Rational*, tr. John W. Harvey (Harmondsworth: Penguin Books, 1959), p. 40, Otto's italics.
6 *Ibid.*, p. 40.

affectively toned recognition of value. At any rate, this sort of experience does not appear to be a matter of building upon a conceptually ordered understanding and deepening it by reference to what is revealed in feeling.

So Otto and Newman both seem to subscribe to the idea of a 'primitive' awareness of value. On this point, their accounts recall the first strand of Deigh's model. The second strand of that model, as we developed it, had to do with the possibility of conceptually articulated understanding (or explicit notions) infusing this sort of 'primitive' affective responsiveness, so as to give rise to a new and richer affective complex. I do not find any direct counterpart of this idea in Newman or Otto. On Otto's view, the language of religion does not so much infuse our affective experience of the mysterium as simply attempt to represent its content by means of 'ideograms', or analogies drawn from our experience of the world. In fact, rather than infusing an affectively toned sense of the divine, this recourse to language may well have a tendency to dissipate it. Consider, for example, these remarks on animism, where Otto is rejecting the thought that 'primitive' religion has its origins in some theory (or 'notional' account) of the nature of things:

Representations of spirits and similar conceptions are rather one and all early modes of 'rationalizing' a precedent experience, to which they are subsidiary. They are attempts in some way or other – it little matters how – to guess the riddle it propounds, and their effect is at the same time always to weaken and deaden the experience itself . . . Both imaginative 'myth', when developed into a system, and intellectualist scholasticism, when worked out to its completion, are methods by which the fundamental fact of religious experience is, as it were, simply rolled out so thin and flat as to be finally eliminated altogether.[7]

So on Otto's account, the wellspring of religion is not discursive thought, but affectively informed encounter with the transcendent. As he puts it: 'It is through this positive feeling-content that the concepts of the "transcendent" and "supernatural" become forthwith designations for a unique "wholly other" reality and quality, something of whose special character we can *feel*, without being able to give it clear conceptual expression.'[8] So we can speak of the 'transcendent' and the 'supernatural' or 'wholly other', and to this extent we can give discursive form to what is made known in religious experience, but the content of these concepts can be fully apprehended only by reference to religious feeling. Doctrine on this view is a derivative and imperfect attempt to convey the real content

---

7 *Ibid.*, p. 41.   8 *Ibid.*, p. 44, Otto's italics.

of religious understanding, and one that may prove subversive of religion itself, if it becomes detached from the experiences which are the real source of religion – by seeking to 'rationalise' those experiences and substituting discursive thought for 'feeling-content'.

Given his religious allegiances, Newman naturally cannot be quite so dismissive of doctrine. And despite his willingness to suppose that doctrinally uninformed children can have a 'real image' of God, he insists that religious affections should remain answerable to doctrine:

Knowledge must ever precede the exercise of the affections. We feel gratitude and love, we feel indignation and dislike, when we have the informations actually put before us which are to kindle these several emotions. We love our parents, as our parents, when we know them to be our parents; we must know concerning God, before we can feel love, fear, hope, or trust towards Him. Devotion must have its objects; those objects, as being supernatural, when not represented to our senses by material symbols, must be set before the mind in propositions . . . It seems a truism to say, yet it is all that I have been saying, that in religion the imagination and affections should always be under the control of reason.[9]

This account seems closer to Goldie's than to Deigh's, in so far as it postulates an initial doctrinally or discursively conveyed picture of things, which can then be taken up in feeling. I take it that feeling at this point, while it depends for its intentionality in part upon the prior work of doctrine, is still capable of deepening a purely discursive, doctrinal understanding, when it involves first-hand experience of God. This is because it is only in feeling that we can achieve a real image of God.[10] So Newman's view is that reliance on doctrine need not detract from the vitality of religion. It is all a matter of how doctrinal propositions are used. As he puts it: 'The propositions may and must be used, and can easily be used, as the expression of facts, not notions.'[11] And they can be used in this way providing that they maintain a connection with an affectively lively sense of the reality of God. In that case, doctrine and feeling can work together, doctrine specifying objects for feeling, and feeling deepening our understanding of those objects, by representing them in a 'real image'. Although

9 *Grammar of Assent*, p. 109.
10 Compare Newman's remark: 'I can understand the *rabbia* of a native of Southern Europe, if I am of a passionate temper myself; and the taste for speculation or betting found in great traders or on the turf, if I am fond of enterprise or games of chance; but on the other hand, not all the possible descriptions of headlong love will make me comprehend the *delirium*, if I never have had a fit of it . . . ' (*ibid.*, p.43). In other words, a real image of love requires relevant first-hand experience, which yields a content that cannot be conveyed in verbal terms alone; in the same way, a real image of God requires an affectively toned apprehension of God.
11 *Ibid.*, p. 108.

Newman does not address the issue, it is possible to include within this general scheme his suggestion that a child may achieve, independently of doctrine, a real image of God. We could say that there is a 'primitive' responsiveness to God which itself can lend impetus to the formulation of doctrine (for example, the child may reflect upon the implicit notional content of their experience). In turn, the results of doctrinal reflection may make possible new kinds of feeling, where these further feelings are embedded in complexes which owe their character in part to conceptualisation. This account conforms to the models both of Deigh (given its use of the idea of a 'primitive' affective responsiveness) and of Goldie (given the thought that feeling can extend the understanding achieved in discursive thought).

Jonathan Edwards is another doctrinally serious theologian who seeks to accord a cognitive significance to feeling, and we might wonder whether he (like Newman) thinks that there is an understanding of God that is available, in full, only in affectively toned religious experience. Edwards sets himself the problem of how to distinguish authentic religious feeling, and his answer, in brief, is that genuine religious experience is distinct phenomenologically and in terms of its cognitive content from any experience of a merely natural object:

a saint's love to God has a great many things appertaining to it, which are common with a man's natural love to a near relation . . . But yet that idea which the saint has of the loveliness of God, and that sensation, and that kind of delight he has in that view, which is as it were the marrow and quintessence of his love, is peculiar, and entirely diverse from any thing that a natural man has, or can have any notion of.[12]

So the saint takes a kind of delight in God that is different (in respect both of 'idea' and of 'sensation') from that which is elicited, or could be elicited, by any natural object. (Compare Otto on the experience of the *mysterium*.) Indeed, Edwards thinks that 'the spiritual perceptions which a sanctified and spiritual person has, are not only diverse from all that natural men have after the manner that the ideas or perceptions of the same sense may differ from one another, but rather as the ideas and sensations of different senses do differ'.[13] In other words, in 'spiritual perception' we have as it were another sensory modality, and not simply a different object falling under one of the familiar sensory modalities. This

---

12 Jonathan Edwards, 'Religious Affections', in C. H. Faust and T. H. Johnson (eds.), *Jonathan Edwards: Representative Selections* (New York: Hill & Wang, 1962), p. 239.
13 *Ibid.*, p. 236.

gives us a test in principle, Edwards thinks, whereby we may establish the trustworthiness of religious experience. If the experience involves a distinctive phenomenology (a distinctive 'sensation') and a distinctive content (a distinctive 'idea' of God's 'loveliness'), neither of which can be compounded from the experience of any merely natural thing, then we may suppose that the source of the experience is God. (Contrast, for example, apparent visions of Christ – such visions are not sufficiently different in content from experiences of natural objects to satisfy the test).[14]

I am not sure about the usefulness of Edwards's approach as a way of discriminating authentic religious experiences. (I take it that the approach is intended to establish only whether an experience is genuinely of God, which leaves open the possibility that a non-God-directed experience might still be truthful and spiritually important.) Might I be deceived in practice (and relatively easily deceived) about whether an experience is sufficiently distinct phenomenologically, or in terms of content, from other (natural) experiences I have had? And even if an experience is distinct in the requisite way, and I know this, how sure could I be that only a supernatural reality could stand as the proximate cause of such an experience? And anyway, how useful would this sort of test be as a public criterion for the authenticity of religious experience, enabling one person to assess the validity of another's experiences? No doubt there are replies which can be made on Edwards's behalf to these questions; however, these matters are rather peripheral to our concerns, so let us return instead to his account of feeling and its intentionality.

The talk of 'delight' and 'sensation' in the extract above indicates that Edwards is concerned here with emotional feelings. Moreover, it seems that these feelings have God as their primary object (and not a state of the body, for example). Hence Edwards talks of 'that idea which the saint has of the loveliness of God' and of the delight which the saint has 'in that view'. This suggests that what is involved is some kind of affectively toned reckoning with an intellectual content (namely, the loveliness of God). But doesn't this formulation also suggest that what comes first is the idea of God's loveliness, and that the delight is a response to that idea; and if not exactly the 'add-on' view of feeling (because the delight does seem to be targeted at the idea, and not just caused by it), doesn't this account suggest that the intentionality of feeling is at any rate derivative? This does seem to be Edwards's view. For example, he remarks that:

14 Edwards discusses this case *ibid.*, pp. 243–4.

As it is the soul only that has ideas, so it is the soul only that is pleased or displeased with its ideas. As it is the soul only that thinks, so it is the soul only that loves or hates, rejoices or is grieved at what it thinks of.[15]

On this account, ideas appear to be held in the mind independently of love and hate, or pleasure and displeasure, and these states are then directed towards them or what they represent. So Edwards seems to be committed to the thought that when compared with the 'natural man', the saint has, first of all, distinctive ideas and, following on from those ideas, distinctive feelings. But the distinctiveness of the saint's ideas cannot be a matter of their having a different discursive understanding of God: the credal understanding of the natural man may extend as far as that of the saint. So to account for the distinctiveness of the saint's ideas, it seems we need to postulate some non-discursive, non-affective apprehension of God, which yields, as Edwards says, 'a new simple idea'.[16] However, if we adopt the intrinsic intentionality of feeling hypothesis, as I have expounded it, we can simplify this picture. On this hypothesis, the distinctiveness of the saint need not be a matter of their having both different ideas and thereby different feelings: the difference of idea may be realised in the difference of feeling. So while we do not find in Edwards the version of the intrinsic intentionality of feeling hypothesis that we have been discussing (the version that is implied in Newman's 'real image' doctrine, for example), that version of the hypothesis does enable his central claim (that the saint is distinguished from the natural person in respect of both their feelings and their ideas) to be formulated with greater economy, and arguably therefore with greater cogency.

As we have seen, Edwards thinks that saintly experience is in principle inexplicable in naturalistic terms. So it is God who is directly the source of such experience. More exactly, Edwards maintains that God is conferring a new nature upon the saint. Hence he speaks of God 'dwelling' in the saints 'as an abiding principle of action'.[17] As a consequence, the transformation that is effected in the saints is not simply a matter of their having qualitatively new experiences or ideas. Their behaviour is also changed, corresponding to their new principle of activity.[18] This

---

15 *Ibid.*, p. 212.
16 *Ibid.*, p. 235. The reference to 'simplicity' here indicates that the idea is not compounded from others.
17 *Ibid.*, p. 234.
18 As he says: 'False discoveries and affections do not go deep enough to reach and govern the springs of men's actions and practice' (*ibid.*, p. 251). See also his comment: 'if the old nature be indeed mortified, and a new and heavenly nature be infused, then may it will [*sic*] be expected, that men will walk in newness of life, and continue to do so to the end of their days' (p. 254).

suggestion provides a more obviously public criterion for distinguishing saintly affective experience from that of the 'natural person'. It also conforms to the thought we explored in Chapter 4 about how variations in emotional feeling correspond to variations in the body's readiness for action (see the discussion of Pickard and Solomon). We spelt out this thought by supposing that the intentionality of an emotional feeling may be realised in an awareness of the body's readiness for action. I don't find precisely this idea in Edwards, but he certainly thinks that if the saint's emotional feelings have a distinctive content (are directed at a new idea of God's loveliness, for example), then they should also be associated with a distinctive pattern of activity. So on this point too we can see some convergence between Edwards's approach and the models we have been developing. And again, it is arguable that the account we have adopted enables his position to be stated with greater elegance: on that account, the correspondence between emotional feeling and readiness for action is a direct consequence of the kind of intentionality that is characteristic of emotional feelings – whereas on Edwards's view, we have to suppose that variations in emotional feeling correspond to differences in conduct because certain emotional feelings can only be produced by God, and therefore they require God to be at work in the person who has them in a special way, and in particular in such a way as to confer a new nature (this is, I suggest, a more complicated story).

It might be wondered whether it makes sense to suppose that the intentionality of a God-directed emotional feeling can be mediated by an awareness of the body's readiness to act; after all, God is not present to us in the fashion of a material object, and therefore the body cannot literally incline towards, or withdraw from, or in some other such way point towards God. However, Edwards at least is clear that proper responsiveness to God implies a way of life that is quite distinct from anything that the natural person can achieve. (We might compare here Gaita's account of the nun, and the implied thought that saintliness involves a quite distinctive demeanour and pattern of conduct.) And if that is so, then the body's readiness to act in certain ways may indeed suggest (in so far as it is a necessary and sufficient condition for) a saintly kind of directedness towards God, and not just a directedness towards certain natural objects. Moreover, there are evidently certain gestures that are typical of prayer or other forms of attentiveness to God; it is no coincidence that slouching on a couch, for example, is not a posture associated with mental directedness to God. So in this way too, we could make sense of the thought that, even in religious contexts, emotional feelings achieve their intentionality, at least in part, by reference to a disposition of the body: they have the subject matter they do because of their connection to patterns of behaviour which befit our relationship to God.

Alvin Plantinga has recently offered this account of Edwards's understanding of the relationship between emotion and understanding:

> I think he thinks that one first perceives the beauty and loveliness of the Lord, first comes to this experiential knowledge, and then comes to develop the right loves and hates . . . It is the perceiving that comes first; in this respect, therefore, intellect is prior to will.[19]

This interpretation of Edwards is similar to the one I have just propounded – ideas comes first, grounded in a non-affective perception, and affects then follow on. Again, we might wonder whether we can simplify this sort of view by supposing that, in some cases anyway, the beauty of the Lord is grasped in an affectively toned perception. In that case, it would not be so much that understanding engenders love; rather, we ought to speak of understanding being realised in love, or of a loving understanding. And it is just because it is affectively toned that this sort of understanding surpasses anything of which the 'natural man' is capable – given the intrinsic intentionality of feeling hypothesis, it is easy to connect the thought that the natural man's affections do not run so true as those of the saint with the thought that neither do his ideas run so true. Plantinga himself suggests, against Edwards (as he interprets him), that neither cognition nor affection is prior; but this is not because Edwards's distinction between the two needs to be questioned, but because:

> The structure of will and intellect here is perhaps a spiral, dialectical process: heightened affections enable us to see more of God's beauty and glory; being able to see more of God's beauty and glory and majesty in turn leads to heightened affections. There are certain things you won't know unless you love, have the right affections; there are certain affections you won't have without perceiving some of God's moral qualities.[20]

This is the sort of model towards which we were moving before, in our discussion of Newman. Perhaps a (relatively) primitive affective responsiveness can help to give rise to new kinds of discursive understanding, and perhaps those new forms of understanding will in turn lead on to new kinds of feeling, and so on. However, the model that we were considering,

19 Alvin Plantinga, *Warranted Christian Belief* (New York: Oxford University Press, 2000), p. 301.
20 *Ibid.*, p. 303.

unlike Plantinga's, makes explicit appeal to the thought that feelings can be themselves the bearers of intellectual content (and a content that cannot be specified in full in purely discursive terms).[21] So it is not just that a new thought 'leads to' a new feeling, or that a new feeling leads to a new thought. Rather, a new feeling may of itself constitute a new thought, and verbalised or doctrinal thought and feeling may together produce a unified state of mind whose intentionality reflects in part the contribution of doctrine, and in part that of emotional feeling.

To take stock, drawing upon Deigh and Goldie, I have been arguing that the relationship between emotional feeling and religious understanding is one of reciprocal influence. In the style of Otto, we can say that a certain kind of religious understanding (a religiously deep understanding of the 'mysterium') is available only in affective experience. (I bracket the question of whether he is right about the phenomenology of such experience.) However, we do not have to follow Otto in supposing that religious language and doctrine are only an imperfect stammering out of what is revealed most fully in such experience, or that they are apt to undermine the liveliness of religious feeling. Rather, a primitive affective responsiveness (understood in broadly the terms of Newman or Otto, or otherwise) can help to generate new doctrinal reflections, which in turn can help to produce new possibilities for religious feeling, and so on (here with Plantinga's 'spiral' account). Moreover, we do not need to see 'feeling' and 'thought' as mutually exclusive categories in this process. The spiral may also involve feeling, which has its own content, being penetrated by discursive thought (following Deigh's model) and feeling taking further (while remaining infused with) the understanding achieved in discursive or doctrinal thought (as Goldie proposes, and Newman implies). The affective complexes which arise in this way will be unified states of mind, and will owe their intentionality in part to feeling. In turn, this helps to explain why the person of saintly feeling will also have a distinctive 'idea' of God (here expanding on Edwards). Lastly, we should suppose that the saint's emotional feelings contribute not only to their 'ideas', but also to their conduct, in so far as such feelings owe their intentionality, at least in

---

21 Plantinga does not take affections to be simply devoid of intellectual content. He comments in a footnote: 'I don't mean to suggest for a moment that an affection is simply a *feeling* of some sort, as if it had no intentional component' (*ibid.*, p. 297). Nonetheless, Plantinga still supposes that heightened affections 'lead to' new understanding and vice versa, rather than supposing that new understanding may be realised in the heightened affection. This is like the account I have attributed to Edwards, whereby feelings are targeted at ideas which are held in the mind independently of them.

part, to an awareness of the body's readiness to act (here with Pickard and Solomon, and in the spirit of Edwards and Newman).[22]

In Chapter 1, we considered the idea that religious experience can be understood as affectively toned experience of God. In this section, we have been building on that discussion. Newman, Otto, and Edwards all suppose that something like perception of God or the 'mysterium' is possible, and they all find a place for feeling in this connection. And by reference to Deigh and Goldie, Pickard and Solomon, we can see how their accounts of the relationship between affectively toned experience and religious understanding can be stated with new nuance and placed in a larger theoretical context. We have also examined the possibility of an affectively toned, value-rich perception of human beings (Chapter 2) or of the world as a whole (Chapter 3). In principle, I suggest, the Deigh–Goldie model can also be applied here. But since much the same moves can be made here, I suggest that we press on, and consider the implications of our remaining two models for the relationship of emotional feeling and religious understanding. Here we move beyond the account of affectively toned value perception that was in play in Chapters 1–3.

APPLYING THE MODELS OF DE SOUSA AND MADDELL

Let us begin by looking at some examples of how de Sousa's model might be applied in a religious context, and how it might be further developed for this purpose. I shall start by examining some remarks of Pierre Hadot on the origins of metaphysical thought in the ancient world.

Hadot has argued that the philosophical systems of ancient Greece and Rome were grounded in a prior non-discursive apprehension of the kind of life that befits a human being:

One too often represents Stoicism or Epicureanism as a set of abstract theories about the world invented by Zeno or Chrysippus or Epicurus. From these theories would spring, as if by accident one could say, a morality. But it is the reverse that is true. It is the abstract theories that are intended to justify the existential attitude. One could say, to express it otherwise, that every existential attitude implies a representation of the world that must necessarily be expressed in a discourse. But this discourse alone is not the philosophy, it is only an element of it, for the philosophy is first of all the existential attitude itself, accompanied by inner and outer discourses: the latter have as their role to express

---

22 I include Newman here because he thinks that a real image of God is in some fashion embedded in an affectively toned awareness of the voice of the conscience, which is to say that having such an image is bound up with an attitude of moral seriousness, which in turn implies a disposition to act in certain ways.

the representation of the world that is implied in such and such an existential attitude, and these discourses allow one at the same time to rationally justify the attitude and to communicate it to others.[23]

Here Hadot distinguishes between philosophical discourse (a verbal, theoretical account of the nature of things) and a prior 'existential attitude', to which the discourse is answerable. More exactly, he has characterised the 'attitudes' which are typical of Stoicism as 'tension', 'duty', and 'vigilance', and those typical of Epicureanism as 'serenity' and the 'joy of existing'.[24] On Hadot's view, this sort of pre-theoretical grasp of the meaning of things can help to generate a discursive, metaphysical account of the world, such as those elaborated by the ancient Stoics and Epicureans. The role of the worldview is, as he says, to help communicate the attitude and to justify it. Hadot is explicit that the metaphysics here is dispensable, and indeed needs to be radically overhauled periodically to accommodate changing intellectual circumstances.[25] But 'existential attitudes' such as those favoured by the Epicureans and Stoics represent, he thinks, enduring possibilities for the human spirit: their sense and importance are not tied to the particular metaphysical worldview in which they were cast in ancient times.[26] For our purposes, it is important to note that such attitudes are (in some cases at least) affectively toned states of mind. They involve, for example, 'tension' and 'serenity'. If all of this is so, then Hadot seems to be proposing that we can have a pre-theoretical, intuitive, affectively toned appreciation of the kind of life that befits a human being, and that such an understanding may then be articulated, in some degree, in the form of a worldview.

This account suggests a further way in which emotional feeling and religious understanding may be related. While Hadot starts from what appears to be a relatively 'primitive' affective state (here with Deigh), he does not speak of such states being infused by developments in discursive thought (here his approach is unlike Deigh's).[27] Rather, the existential

---

23 The passage is cited by Arnold Davidson in his Introduction to Pierre Hadot, *Philosophy as a Way of Life: Spiritual Exercises from Socrates to Foucault,* tr. Michael Chase (Oxford: Blackwell, 1995), pp. 30–1.

24 Cited by Davidson in his Introduction, *ibid.,* p. 35.   25 *Ibid.,* pp. 282–3.

26 Davidson quotes Hadot's view that Stoicism and Epicureanism identify 'two opposite but inseparable poles of our inner life: tension and relaxation, duty and serenity, moral consciousness and the joy of existing' (*ibid.,* p. 35).

27 The non-conceptual or 'primitive' character of this sort of insight is evident in remarks such as this: 'everything that touches the domain of the existential – which is what is most important for human beings – for instance, our feeling of existence, our impressions when faced by death, our perception of nature, our sensations, and a fortiori the mystical experience, is not directly communicable. The phrases we use to describe them are conventional and banal' (*ibid.,* p. 285).

attitude persists through changes in theoretical understanding. Again, the role of theory is to provide a picture of the world which will help to inculcate the attitude, by showing how it is rationally appropriate. For instance, the Epicurean doctrine that the gods are indifferent to human beings suggests the appropriateness of the ideal of serenity (since it implies that we need not fear, or be anxious about, the judgement of the gods).

This model seems to be broadly of the kind that we have associated with de Sousa: an initial affectively toned state helps to shape the development of our theoretical enquiries. And in terms of de Sousa's account, we can understand why such a connection may be rationally appropriate. For instance, if a person is anxious about the possibility of punishment in the afterlife (or equally, if a person has an affectively toned sense of the inappropriateness of such concerns), then questions about the nature of the gods, and their interest in human life, will be lit up as deserving attention. And in this way, an affective state may propel a person quite properly to think about certain issues, and to examine those issues in the light of certain concerns, and thereby to arrive at one kind of worldview rather than another. To this extent, Hadot's proposal can be understood fairly straightforwardly in the terms provided by de Sousa's model. I want now to see whether we can extend de Sousa's model a little, and thereby throw further light on Hadot's account.

I suggested in Chapter 4 that there is an analogy between de Sousa's account of the emotions as paradigms and Teasdale and Barnard's discussion of implicational meanings (where such meanings may be grasped in feeling, but not in purely 'propositional' terms). As we have seen, implicational meanings offer a kind of template in terms of which current experience may be construed (and in this way they may themselves contribute to the character of current experience: in this case as more generally, the relationship between interpretation and experience is not a purely external one.) Moreover, some such templates may be particularly deep-seated, so that they are applied to our experience in a relatively pervasive way. For example, a depressive person might read their current experience in terms of the implicational code 'myself as a failure'. Now, as we have seen, such pervasive interpretive strategies are not easily dislodged by counter-evidence, because they have a tendency to construe the data in their own terms. (For example, a depressive person might do quite well at some activity, but attribute their success to forces for which they can claim no credit.) This suggests that implicational meanings may not just direct our attention to a certain subject matter, and lead us to put certain questions to that subject matter (here with de Sousa's model) –

they may also control our reading of the world in this more fundamental kind of way.

Of course, sometimes, a pervasive interpretive strategy of this kind may leave a person locked in an illusory world, unable to see the force of genuine counter-evidence, because of their predisposition to read the evidence in ways that conform to their prior assumptions. It is tempting to conclude: let us then set aside implicational meanings, and approach the world free from any overarching preconception of its sense. But it is doubtful that this strategy is available to us psychologically – our favoured implicational readings of the world tend to be too deeply ingrained for that, and are anyway not readily accessible to consciousness. More importantly, even if this were an option, it would not, I suggest, be rational to take it up. For we would then be in something like the position of Damasio's patient (recall that he was unable to decide on which day of the week to hold a meeting). We would approach situations without any preconception of their likely import; and that would imply that in each new circumstance, we would have no initial sense of what is at stake and what in particular deserves attention, and we would therefore need to work though an indefinitely extended review of the situation before reaching any conclusion about its overall character and what it may require of us by way of action. As the example of Damasio's patient suggests, this is surely not a practically rational stance, however much it may privilege 'rational', discursive reflection. I suggest, then, that it is practically rational to allow ourselves to be governed by affectively toned, implicational readings of experience in the first instance. Of course, this is not to say that such readings are infallible, but they provide a way of interpreting the world that is prima facie justified.

This extension of the de Sousa model (one that is implied in de Sousa's own conception of the emotions as 'paradigms') suggests another reading of Hadot's examples. Perhaps the 'existential attitudes' to which he refers can be understood as pervasive 'implicational meanings' which are grasped by means of a non-discursive, affectively toned insight. In that case, such attitudes, and the feelings in which they are embedded, may properly direct the course of our theoretical enquiries not only by picking out a certain subject matter as worthy of attention, and certain questions about that subject matter as deserving of consideration; they may also properly direct our enquiries by providing a 'pre-reading' of the overall force of experience, which is justified until reason can be given for thinking otherwise. For example, in so far as the Epicurean worldview conforms to such a pre-reading, then it is prima facie justified. To suppose otherwise is to invite scepticism about our pre-established tendencies to read the world in terms of certain implicational meanings rather than others; and that sort of scepticism, I suggest again, is not practically rational. In this way, we could take existential attitudes to constitute research programmes of metaphysical dimensions. Naturally, not every such research programme has been successful (and the Epicurean research programme has itself run aground, I suggest, at any rate to the extent that it involves the metaphysical scheme that was favoured by the ancient Epicureans). We could see an analogy between this general picture and Alasdair MacIntyre's much-discussed proposal that our moral enquiries have to be embedded within particular traditions which supply some initial sense of how the subject matter of ethics is to be construed, and what sorts of question are worth asking of that subject matter.[28] Similarly, we could say that our theoretical enquiries into the ultimate character of the world have to be embedded within some prior sense of the existential meaning of experience, where this prior sense is properly taken as prima facie justified.

An objector might say: while it is rational to defer to pre-established implicational meanings which are relevant to everyday, practical decision-making, so as to avoid the predicament of Damasio's patient, why suppose that we are thereby committed to any larger, more metaphysical picture of the world? After all, I can avoid the predicament Damasio describes given simply a sense of the human meaning of such situations – so why think that I also need a metaphysics for purposes of practical rationality? The philosopher who has considered most deeply the connection between metaphysical and practical rationality is, I suggest, somewhat contentiously, William James. Here is one of his examples of the connection:

A philosophy may be unimpeachable in other respects, but either of two defects will be fatal to its universal acceptance. First, its ultimate principle must not be one that essentially baffles and disappoints our dearest desires and our most cherished powers. A pessimistic philosophy like Schopenhauer's . . . or Hartmann's . . . will perpetually call forth essays at other philosophies . . . But a second and worse defect in a philosophy than that of contradicting our active propensities is to give them no object whatever to press against. A philosophy whose principle is so incommensurate with our most intimate powers as to deny them all relevancy in universal affairs . . . will be more unpopular than pessimism. Better face the enemy than the eternal Void![29]

28 See, for example, Alasdair MacIntyre, *Three Rival Versions of Moral Inquiry: Encyclopaedia, Genealogy, and Tradition* (London: Duckworth, 1990).

29 William James, 'The Sentiment of Rationality', in William James, *Essays in Pragmatism* (New York: Hafner Press, 1948), p. 17.

Here James holds out not exactly the predicament of Damasio's patient (who is unable to act because he cannot decide what to do) but a related practical frustration, where we cannot act because our deepest desires are denied relevance or the possibility of constructive expression. And he is surely right to say that if a metaphysical scheme commits us to such frustration, then that is a reason for thinking that it cannot provide a satisfactory stopping point for enquiry. So once again, the way through the frustration is supplied by affect: in this case, it is a matter of allowing the 'bafflement' and 'disappointment' of desire to signal the inadequacy of a worldview, and to move us on to further enquiry. It may be replied: while James is right to suppose that certain metaphysical schemes are disabling, and to that extent contrary to the requirements of practical rationality, he does not show that we positively need a metaphysical scheme of some sort: why should we not simply decline to adopt meta-physical worldviews of the kind he mentions? Of course, James has thoughts on this question too.[30] (And there is indeed an answer implied in the passage just cited, in so far as a rejection of 'the Void' implies a rejection of atheism.) But for a response to this issue, let us turn, once again, to Newman:

One of the most important effects of Natural Religion on the mind, in preparation for Revealed, is the anticipation which it creates, that a Revelation will be given. That earnest desire of it, which religious minds cherish, leads the way to the expectation of it. Those who know nothing of the wounds of the soul, are not led to deal with the question, or to consider its circumstances; but when our attention is roused, then the more steadily we dwell upon it, the more probable does it seem that a revelation has been or will be given to us. This presentiment is founded on our sense, on the one hand, of the infinite goodness of God, and, on the other, of our own extreme misery and need – two doctrines which are the primary constituents of Natural Religion. It is difficult to put a limit to the legitimate force of this antecedent probability. Some minds will feel it to be so powerful, as to recognize in it almost a proof, without direct evidence, of the divinity of a religion claiming to be true, supposing its history and doctrine are free from positive objection, and there be no rival religion with plausible claims of its own.[31]

This account is reminiscent of the extended version of de Sousa's model that we have been considering. The emotions function here to

---

30 See, for example, his essay 'The Will to Believe', where he suggests that the 'religious option' offers benefits of great moment in the present. The essay is reproduced in William James, *The Will to Believe and Other Essays in Popular Philosophy* (Cambridge, MA: Harvard University Press, 1979), pp. 13–33.

31 *Grammar of Assent*, pp. 328–9.

render certain issues salient: a person who experiences 'the wounds of the soul' and the associated 'earnest desire' of revelation has their 'attention roused' by the idea of revelation, and accordingly they 'dwell upon it'. Moreover, this affective state does not just render a certain subject matter salient, or encourage us to raise certain questions in relation to it. It also properly makes a difference to our assessment of the evidence in favour of revelation. The affective state properly makes a difference, we could say, to our 'take' on the evidence (which is to be distinguished from the thought that it is itself part of the evidence)[32] – by shaping our sense of the 'antecedent probability' of revelation. In effect, Newman is saying that a person who knows of 'the wounds of the soul' has good prima facie reason to suppose that a claim to revelation is true: rather than evidence having to be amassed in support of such a claim, it is enough if alleged counter-evidence can be turned aside, by replying to objections which may rebut or undercut the claim (where a 'rebutting' objection poses a difficulty for the 'history and doctrine' of the religion considered in themselves, and an 'undercutting' objection proposes that a 'rival religion' is equally belief-worthy). This picture suggests that Newman's approach is broadly that of the extended de Sousa model, for he is making a judgement about where the onus of proof lies, and maintaining that affective considerations are relevant to this judgement.

But how do Newman's remarks constitute a response to the objection to James that we noted just now, namely, the objection that while certain metaphysical systems may be unsustainable for purposes of practical living, it is still possible to get along well enough practically without any positive metaphysical commitment? Newman's answer is in effect an appeal to individual psychology: some people at least cannot get by in this way. These are people who feel the wounds of the soul, and who depend for their healing, and flourishing, on the availability of a revelation.

Newman is clearly unconcerned that his position leaves him unable to resolve the doubts of those who lack the requisite affectively toned state of mind:

Why am I to begin with taking up a position not my own, and unclothing my mind of that large outfit of existing thoughts, principles, likings, desires, and

---

32 I am borrowing William Wainwright's phrasing of this point. Although he does not discuss this passage in particular, Wainwright defends a similar reading of Newman to the one I propose here. See, for instance, his discussion of Newman's sermon 'Faith Without Sight', and the role here of a felt need of revelation in bringing a person to recognise the truth of revelation: *Reason and the Heart: A Prolegomenon to a Critique of Passional Reason* (Ithaca, NY: Cornell University Press, 1995), pp. 76–7.

hopes, which make me what I am? If I am asked to use Paley's argument for my own conversion, I say plainly I do not want to be converted by a smart syllogism, if I am asked to convert others by it, I say plainly I do not care to overcome their reason without touching their hearts. I wish to deal, not with controversialists, but with inquirers.[33]

Once again, this is a position that can be helpfully understood in the terms supplied by the Teasdale–Barnard–de Sousa model. Newman indicates that he does not wish to divest himself of his 'existing thoughts, principles, likings, desires, and hopes' – and he indicates that he does not wish others to divest themselves of their 'existing thoughts' and the rest. In the language of Teasdale and Barnard, we may see these 'principles' and 'likings' as a person's established patterns of implicational meaning. This identification is warranted, I think, given that Newman is here conjoining 'principles', which presumably direct discursive thought, and 'likings, desires, and hopes', all of which are, in standard cases, affectively toned; for implicational meanings also serve to order our enquiries, and are made known in feeling. If this identification holds, then following Teasdale and Barnard, we may agree with Newman's determination to start from his 'principles' and 'likings' – in as much as implicational meanings have a proper part to play in directing our enquiries and guiding our construal of the evidence. In this passage, Newman also implies that our 'likings' and 'principles' provide a proper starting point for enquiry because they 'make me what I am'. Expanding on this thought, we might say that Newman is proposing that a case for revelation needs to address the person in their psychological integrity, where this includes their 'likings' as much as any theoretical claims to which they subscribe, for only so will the case meet with a 'real' rather than a merely 'notional' assent. So an appeal to implicational meanings, and the feelings in which they are recognised, is relevant for this reason too: not only do such meanings offer a legitimate prereading of experience; they are also integral to our affective-intellectual identity.

Of course, a more ambitious response to James's critique is also possible in principle. For instance, it might be argued that human beings in general *ought* to feel the wounds of the soul to which Newman alludes. There are no doubt genuine considerations which can be cited on either side of this question, and certainly there is more at issue here than simply the working out of differences of psychological orientation. But Newman is religiously right, I think, to say that at any rate we should not aspire to

---

33 *Grammar of Assent*, p. 330.

bypass such differences by moving directly to some 'neutral', Paleyan starting point for enquiry.

I want to note briefly one further way in which de Sousa's model might be extended. Here I shall just sketch a possibility. De Sousa's account as I have developed it involves the claim that prima facie we may take the emotions to pick out matters of importance, matters which are therefore properly the object of attention. Given this picture, we can expound in the ways we have considered the thought that the emotions can rightly help to guide our theoretical enquiries. But we might wonder whether anything else follows from the idea that certain matters are genuinely of importance. For example, Hadot considers that a part of the Stoic 'existential attitude' is a commitment to 'the absolute value of the human person'.[34] And we might ask: what are the conditions of possibility of human beings having this sort of importance?[35] (Of course, it is Kant rather than James who provides the obvious philosophical exemplar for this strategy of argument.) Would a belief in the absolute value of persons commit us, for example, to the falsity of eliminativist accounts of belief and intention (accounts which take notions like belief as the expression of a merely 'folk' understanding, analogous to folk belief in witches, and just as much in need of being superseded by a purely scientific account of the causal structure of the world, which makes no reference to such 'spooky' entities)? I do not wish to explore the cogency of such a case here, but there are examples of such arguments in the recent literature which bear serious examination.[36] For our purposes, it is enough to note the possibility that, in this further way, an affectively toned value perception may provide the basis for a discursive, metaphysically committed account of the nature of things. In brief, here we would not be just reflecting upon

---

34 The phrase is quoted by Davidson in his Introduction to Pierre Hadot, *Philosophy as a Way of Life*, p. 34.

35 The Stoic commitment to the 'brotherhood' of all human beings is reminiscent of Gaita's commitment to the 'humanity' of all human beings, but these approaches are also importantly different. For instance, the Stoic ideal associates the worth of human beings with their rationality, a connection which Gaita challenges; and if the Stoic ideal is rightly seen as part of an 'existential attitude' in Hadot's sense, then it is not dependent upon a particular, culturally specific set of categories, whereas Gaita seems to think that the nun's insight is infused by some such set of categories.

36 See, for example, George Mavrodes's defence of the idea that our notion of moral obligation calls for metaphysical underpinning in his 'Religion and the Queerness of Morality', in Louis Pojman (ed.), *Ethical Theory: Classical and Contemporary Readings*, 3rd edn (Belmont, CA: Wadsworth, 1998), pp. 649–56. Assuming that our recognition of our moral obligations involves, at least onto occasions, an affectively constituted insight, Mavrodes's case could in principle be grafted on to the discussion presented here.

matters which feeling has marked out as important, but asking what must be true if they are to bear that sort of importance.

We have been considering how de Sousa's understanding of the emotions as paradigms may help to illuminate the relationship between emotional feeling and religious understanding. And we have seen that there are various ways of applying his model in this context. Feelings may properly direct the unfolding of our discursive understanding in so far, first, as they render certain topics salient, and suggest the appropriateness of raising certain questions rather than others in regard to those topics; in so far as, secondly, they bring to consciousness pervasive 'implicational' commitments of the kind that properly shape our reading of evidence; and finally, in so far as they (appear to) disclose values whose conditions of possibility include the world's having a certain metaphysical character.

Of the four models of the relationship between emotional experience and understanding that we examined in Chapter 4, there is one that we have yet to apply in the context of religious understanding. This is, of course, Maddell's model. I shall keep my discussion of this model especially brief, in part because related ideas will be in play in the next chapter. Maddell proposes that our affectively toned responses to a piece of music can provide a way of reckoning with its character, and that we can thereby understand in anticipation what is required for the 'resolution' of a particular musical 'tension'. This account is similar to de Sousa's inasmuch as it is concerned with the question of how a disclosure of value (the recognition of 'tension' in the music) may issue in further understanding; but it remains distinct, because the further understanding is non-discursive in character (since the required 'resolution' is identified in non-propositional, affectively toned terms).

There are, of course, any number of cases of religious yearning which lend themselves in principle to interpretation in these terms. In the passage quoted at the beginning of this chapter, James writes of the felt 'need of deliverance', and we have seen Newman speak of the 'earnest desire' for revelation. Perhaps such needs and desires point, at the level of feeling and however inchoately, to the character of whatever it would take to satisfy or 'resolve' them. If so, this provides a further way in which an understanding of God may be embedded in feeling. In bringing this chapter to a close, I shall explore at rather greater length one way of developing this idea.

There is a well-known tradition of spiritual formation, common in Catholic circles until at least the middle years of the twentieth century, which represents the spiritual life as a progression that begins with

discursive forms of thought and culminates in a state of wordless, affectively toned contemplation. In general terms, this transition corresponds
to the movement from the 'purgative' to the 'illuminative' and then to the
'unitive' phase of spiritual development.[37] Expounding this tradition in a
standard spiritual handbook of the early years of the twentieth century,
Adolphe Tanquerey writes that as they develop, 'souls' 'experience great
difficulty in making their mental prayer in a purely *discursive* fashion', and
accordingly 'the Holy Ghost inspires them to give less time to considerations and more to affections and petitions'.[38] On this view, the will or the
heart is accorded an intentionality that is distinct from that of the
intellect. In Tanquerey's words: 'The will attains its object in a manner
different from that of the mind: the latter knows an object only according
to the representation . . . the will or the heart tends towards the *object* as it
is *in itself*'.[39] This formulation is reminiscent, of course, of some of the
central themes of this book. Tanquerey is clearly postulating a state of
mind whose intentionality is achieved in feeling, and not by way of some
discursive thought. And the suggestion that the 'heart' tends towards its
object as it is 'in itself' recalls Newman's teaching that in affectively toned
experience, we can achieve a 'real image' of God, that is, an understanding
that rests on direct acquaintance with God, as distinct from knowledge of
God by description. However, it is worth emphasising that for Tanquerey
(as for Newman, on the whole) the soul is only ready to cultivate a
wordless affective relationship to God once it has mastered a more
discursive, doctrinally informed understanding of God and God's relationship to the world. Given that Tanquerey is representing a large,
historically extended tradition of spiritual formation, it is significant that
his formulation echoes the themes that we have been exploring – this
suggests, at least, that those themes are not merely a matter for philosophical speculation, but capable of informing the 'spiritual life' in practice.

We could understand Tanquerey's account by reference to Goldie's
suggestion that affects can pick up the understanding embedded in some
discursive appreciation of a state of affairs and deepen it, so providing a
further content which may elude formulation in verbal terms. However,
Goldie's model does not provide any direct counterpart to Tanquerey's
thought that feeling in some way brings earlier phases of understanding to
completion, by pointing in a more intimate way to their goal. I take it that

---

37 I shall say a little more about one reading of these phases in Chapter 7.
38 Adolphe Tanquerey, *The Spiritual Life: A Treatise on Ascetical and Mystical Theology*, tr. Herman
   Branderis, 2nd edn (Tournai: Desclée et Cie, 1930), p. 455, Tanquerey's italics.
39 *Ibid.*, p. 654, Tanquerey's italics.

on Tanquerey's account what is achieved in feeling is not just a deepening of an already-acquired discursive understanding, but in some way a bringing of that understanding to fruition; and feeling does this by offering a new mode of relationship to the goal of the spiritual life. Maddell's account of feeling's role in our appreciation of music suggests a more direct parallel with Tanquerey's scheme on this point. On Maddell's view, as a person listens to a piece of music, feeling may direct them towards a 'resolution' which has yet to be consummated in experience, but which is identified by way of their desire and longing in the present. By analogy, we could suppose that instruction in Christian doctrine (of the kind that Tanquerey takes to be required before we can progress to a non-discursive, affectively toned 'tending towards' God) engenders certain desires which are directed at the 'goal' or 'resolution' of the spiritual life. In both these cases, affectively grounded understanding picks out the goal of what has come before, whether that be earlier phases of the music, or doctrinal instruction.

Clearly, Tanquerey takes the kind of intentionality that belongs to feeling or desire as superior to that of 'representational' (or discursive) thought, as befits a later stage of spiritual development. Our models also throw some light on why this should be so. Goldie's model (in conjunction with the Teasdale–Barnard account of implicational meaning) suggests that an affectively toned understanding of God will be superior because it represents a more integrative kind of knowing, one that draws on the content of discursive thought, so as to bring out its deeper existential sense. Or, to persist with Maddell's musical analogy, we might suppose that just as we may be able to identify the character of the music's resolution in abstract musicological terms, and independently of feeling, so we may be able to identify the object of our religious fulfilment in abstract doctrinal terms, and independently of feeling; but in the musical as in the theological case, it may be said, such an apprehension of the consummation is qualitatively inferior to one which consists in an affectively toned apprehension of its character. The person who grasps the musical resolution in purely musiciological terms has not seen 'from the inside' what the music is about; and similarly, someone who grasps the divine nature in purely discursive terms, without engaging the intentionality of emotional feeling, has not seen with their whole being (in ways that implicate the body and its activities) what is involved in the being of God. And, to urge a familiar thought, it is surely a response of the person in their bodily-affective-intellectual integrity that is required if a religious understanding is to run deep.

It might be objected that Tanquerey's account is concerned with the 'unitive' phase of the spiritual life, whereas the analogy with musical experience implies that God is still in some way removed from the believer as an object of longing. However, even in Tanquerey's scheme, our relationship to God in this life falls short, needless to say, of the kind of communion that is reserved for the beatific vision; and accordingly, even on his scheme, there remains a place for longing – indeed, some such state is surely required. So, tentatively, I suggest that the understanding of affect that is found in the tradition represented by Tanquerey can be explicated at least in part in the terms provided by Maddell's model: in the case of musical appreciation, feeling is able to take us beyond a certain sensory input so as to pick out a reality that has yet to be fully revealed in sensory terms; and analogously, in the case of God, feeling is able to take us beyond a certain doxastic input, so as to relate us to a reality that has yet to be fully understood in doxastic terms. This model has the further advantage of enabling us to speak of affectively toned theistic experience without offending against the religious sense that God qua transcendent reality cannot be an object of direct experience in this life.[40] The account we have been exploring accommodates this concern by supposing that God is experienced precisely through longing, that is, through a sense that the divine is not fully possessed in the present.

CONCLUSION

At the beginning of this chapter I quoted William James's claim that doctrinal and philosophical understandings of God should be 'classed as over-beliefs, buildings-out performed by the intellect into directions of which feeling originally supplied the hint'. In the course of our discussion, we have seen some respects in which this claim appears to be true, and some points at which it seems to invite qualification. Here are some respects in which it is true that feelings come first: primitive, religiously informed affects (of the kind postulated by Otto and Newman, for example) can help to guide our discursive enquiries, in so far as such enquiries seek to spell out the content of such experience (in the way Otto describes); or again, feelings may render a certain religiously significant subject matter salient, and encourage the posing of certain questions in relation to that subject matter; and they may properly constitute a

---

40 See again the reservations I noted when setting out the Newman–Alston model of religious experience in Chapter 1.

'paradigm' which shapes the reading of evidence pertaining to these questions. Feelings may also give shape to theological reflection by grounding value claims which invite completion in metaphysical terms. In all of these ways, feeling can enjoy a kind of priority vis-à-vis doctrine, as James supposes. But the relationship is, more fundamentally, one of reciprocal influence, and sometimes it is doctrine which comes first. Doctrine may sponsor new forms of feeling; and doctrine and feeling may join together to constitute unified states of mind which depend for their intentionality upon the contribution of both, and in such a way that neither can claim temporal or any other kind of precedence.

Someone might think this picture too messy: surely we need to come down on one side or the other ('doctrine' or 'feeling'), if only as a generalisation? I would resist this thought. With James, I am inclined to think that but for religious feeling, we would not have religious movements and the bodies of doctrine that they have developed. In this sense, feeling has a certain explanatory priority when we consider religion as a sociological phenomenon: the doctrines only get going because of the feelings. And it is this fact (supposing it is a fact) that makes the subject matter of this book worthy of attention: if the doxastic commitments of religious believers are profoundly shaped by feeling, then the epistemic standing of those commitments may well depend upon the capacity of feeling to bear a positive cognitive significance. However, even if feeling has priority in this sense, there is no reason to suppose that religion would have persisted but for the ability of discursive thought to articulate doctrines which possess at least a measure of theoretical plausibility, and which in turn are able to engage and give shape to feeling. And in practice, no doubt there are bits of doctrine which cannot be traced to any particular precedent feeling, but which engender religious feeling, just as there are feelings which do not owe their origin (in their most basic form) to conceptualisation and which help to stimulate discursive thought about religious questions. In short, the messiness is to some extent intrinsic to the subject matter: to speak in general terms, religion depends on discursive thought and also on feeling; and to speak of particular cases, it is sometimes thought which comes first, sometimes feeling, and sometimes neither.

If there is a figure who emerges as the hero of this discussion, it is Newman. His thought anticipates (and sometimes simply articulates) each of the four models that we have considered, and I have been able to draw upon the *Grammar of Assent* to provide illustrations of what is at stake in each case. He admits (at least in passing) the possibility of a 'primitive' affectively toned sense of God; he allows for the possibility that feeling may be infused by prior doctrinal commitments while building upon and deepening those commitments (this is his favoured view, which we examined in Chapter 1); he grants that feelings may properly shape our reading of evidence; and he speaks eloquently of the 'wounds of the soul' and the 'earnest desire' for revelation, and at least by implication he takes these states to provide a proleptic, affectively toned sense of the goal of human life. If not a messy, this is at any rate a somewhat complicated picture, but at least we know that nothing less complicated will do if we are to understand the workings of religious belief with proper epistemic and psychological nuance – allowing that in this context epistemic and psychological considerations are not to be sharply distinguished, because of the various ways in which religious content, and its cognitive significance, may be grounded in feeling.

CHAPTER 6

Representation in art and religion

> I entered the little Portuguese village . . . It was evening and there
> was a full moon. It was by the sea. The wives of the fishermen were
> going in procession to make a tour of all the ships, carrying candles
> and singing what must certainly be very ancient hymns of a heart-
> rending sadness . . . There the conviction was suddenly borne in
> upon me that Christianity is the religion of slaves, that slaves cannot
> help belonging to it, and I among others.[1]

Here Simone Weil writes of how she came to an appreciation of the real
import of Christian teaching – and her own Christian identity – in an
affectively toned experience of music. At the time of this episode, Weil
was of course already familiar with the credal claims of Christianity; so in
the terms I have been using, this seems to be a case of feeling building
upon a prior doctrinal understanding, so as to provide a deeper, more
integrative, more self-involving understanding of what was previously
grasped in purely verbal or 'notional' terms. Weil makes no reference to
the meaning of the words of the hymns. So the revelatory force of the
music does not depend, it seems, upon any verbal mediation. Nor is its
religious suggestiveness evidently the product of a religious context: the
sense that the women's behaviour bears a religious meaning is presumably
given, at least in large part, in the music itself. In these respects, Weil's
comments point towards what is for many an obvious datum of experience, namely, that music in particular and the arts in general are religiously potent, even when (and sometimes especially when) they lack any
explicitly religious subject matter. In this chapter, I want to explore a little
how this might be. The discussion will have three phases. I begin
by setting out Mikel Dufrenne's theory of representation in the arts,
and I then apply this theory to the question of how the gods may be

---

1 Simone Weil, *Waiting on God*, tr. Emma Craufurd (London: Routledge & Kegan Paul, 1979),
pp. 19–20.

represented. Finally, I shall draw some implications for the nature and working of religious language. So this chapter will extend the discussion of earlier chapters, by detailing a further way in which our affectively toned responses may provide a basis for religious understanding. Here it will not be an affectively toned understanding of God, the human person, or the world that is the focus of attention (as in Chapters 1–3), but our experience of art, and its role in helping us to represent 'the gods'. The chapter could be read as supplying a further, fifth model of the relationship of emotional experience and religious understanding, or it could also be read as an extension of the aesthetic model of Maddell that we discussed in Chapters 4 and 5.

MIKEL DUFRENNE'S THEORY OF AESTHETIC EXPERIENCE

The French phenomenologist Mikel Dufrenne has argued that aesthetic representation is rooted in the capacity of an artwork to evoke an affective response. He gives this summary statement of the theory:

When a poet invokes the sea, we genuinely feel the sea's presence . . . It is present . . . with a presence we must call affective and with a truth of its own which can be discovered only through art. Thus art truly represents only in . . . communicating through . . . the sensuous a certain feeling by means of which the represented object can appear as present.[2]

On this account, an artwork represents an object by engendering a set of feelings of the kind that befit the object, so allowing the object to 'appear as present'. To take another example concerning the sea, Dufrenne suggests that Debussy's *La Mer* succeeds in representing the sea in this way: 'Something like the essence of the sea is revealed to me, with respect to which every image is gross and vain. We are concerned with what I experience when I am before the sea, of what there is of the truly "marine" in it – with its affective essence.'[3] We could put this point by saying that *La Mer* communicates not the 'real essence' of the sea (its nature considered scientifically), but its 'nominal essence' (its defining qualities from the point of view of human subjective experience). More exactly, *La Mer* expresses the 'affective essence' of the sea (its defining qualities from the point of view of human affective experience). So in brief, Dufrenne's proposal is that an artwork can represent an object by

---

2 Mikel Dufrenne, *The Phenomenology of Aesthetic Experience*, tr. Edward S. Casey et al. (Evanston, IL: Northwestern University Press, 1973; first published in French 1953), p. 137.
3 *Ibid.* p. 520.

engendering a set of feelings that befit the object; in this way the artwork communicates the object's 'affective essence' and enables it to 'appear as present'. So like many theories of representation, Dufrenne's account appeals to an isomorphism of what represents and what is represented, but here the isomorphism has to do with the quality of affective response that is elicited by each, and not with, say, simple physical resemblance.

In the passage just cited, there is an echo of Newman's account of the superiority of an affectively toned over a merely notional representation of God. Dufrenne thinks that mere 'images' of the sea (which we could take to mean any affectively neutral representation of the sea, however detailed and faithful) are 'gross' when compared with the kind of representation that is made available in feeling. This is, I suggest, because any affectively neutral or merely 'notional' representation does not of itself disclose the human significance of the object (how it bears on our concerns, for good or ill). Such a representation may, of course, provide the basis for an assessment of an object's human significance; but by contrast with *La Mer*, the object is not represented by way of a recollection or revelation of its 'affective essence' (its felt significance for human life). So this account of representation has immediately some affinity with the kind of representation which arises in religious contexts, when that sort of representation is affectively toned and not merely 'notional'.

If this model is to work, the represented object should not share its affective essence with (too many) other things – for then the representation will be ambiguous, and too much ambiguity will interfere with the ability of the artwork to represent the object at all. But in the case of the sea (Dufrenne's example), and even more of God, there is good reason to think that this condition is satisfied. (Compare again Jonathan Edwards's thought that the saintly life, the life lived in proper responsiveness to God, has a thoroughly distinctive character, affectively and practically.[4])

To understand Dufrenne's proposal more exactly, it is worth noting the somewhat technical sense in which he is using the terms 'feeling' and 'emotion':

the emotion of fear is not to be confused with the feeling of the horrible. It is, rather, a certain way of reacting in the face of the horrible when the horrible is taken as a characteristic of the world as it appears at the time, that is, as a means of struggling within the world of the horrible.[5]

---

4 Edwards's account does pose a question which will be addressed below: if the saintly feelings which befit God can only be brought about directly by God, and not by any natural object, how might an artwork elicit feelings of the kind that befit God? See n. 6 below.
5 *Phenomenology*, p. 378.

Similarly, Dufrenne distinguishes the feelings of the comic and the tragic, and the emotions of merriment and terror or pity, considered as responses to those feelings. This sort of perspective is broadly compatible with the account that we have been developing in this book, since it assigns a cognitive role to feeling: on Dufrenne's view, our felt responses reveal the human significance of situations (as horrible or tragic, for example). One important point that follows from Dufrenne's distinction is that *La Mer*, for example, is able to represent the sea by summoning up feelings of the kind that befit the sea without thereby summoning up 'emotions' that befit the sea. Evidently, something of this kind needs to be said: after all, even if *La Mer* engenders feelings which befit the sea, we are hardly disposed to behave towards it in the way that we would behave towards the sea. This suggests a need for some elaboration of our earlier analysis of the intentionality of feelings: there it was suggested that feelings achieve their intentionality at least in part by registering the body's readiness to act in certain ways. If Dufrenne is right, then our feelings can be about the sea (we can 'feel the sea's presence') without our being disposed to act as we would if we were in fact before the sea. One way of understanding this possibility is by supposing that the readiness to act that arises in this case is of a make-believe variety: I 'feel the sea's presence', but the readiness to act that I thereby register is qualified by my knowledge that I am not in fact before the sea, and is therefore an imaginative or make-believe readiness to act. In this way, we can keep the connection between the intentionality of feeling and registering the body's readiness to act, while further specifying what is involved in the latter.

It might be said: in that case, it is a mistake to suppose that *La Mer* engenders even the same 'feelings' as the sea, since feelings (in Dufrenne's sense) have to do with the human significance of an object (as horrible, tragic, or whatever), and the sea and the artwork surely do not have the same human significance. I don't see any need to offer a judgement on this point. What matters is that through the feelings elicited by the artwork we can 'feel the presence' of the represented object. Most simply, this is possible because the artwork may elicit feelings which phenomenologically are like those elicited by, say, the sea, but shorn of their implications for action. In this way, we can keep hold of the thought that the affective responses elicited by the representing and the represented objects are related isomorphically, even if they are not strictly 'of the same kind'. To mark this possibility, I shall continue to speak of artworks eliciting feelings which 'befit' the represented object, bracketing the question of whether the feelings which arise in each case are of 'the same kind'.[6]

Along with the suggestion that artworks can represent an object by engendering feelings of the kind that befit the object, Dufrenne also proposes that an artwork can generate a kind of 'atmosphere' which envelops and shapes our appreciation of a whole region of experience. Consider these remarks, for instance:

> Versailles speaks to us through the rigor of its lay-out, the elegant equilibrium of its proportions, the discreet pomp of its embellishment . . . Its pure and measured voice expresses order and clarity and sovereign urbanity in the very countenance of stone . . . And the surroundings – the park, the sky, and even the town – which the palace annexes and aestheticizes speak the same language. The setting is like a bass accompaniment to the clear voice of the monument.[7]

Following this example, we may suppose that the feelings engendered by an aesthetic object can constitute a kind of atmosphere which extends beyond the object to embrace various things in its environment (in this case, 'the park, the sky, and even the town'). Hence the artwork and its surroundings may come to be experienced in terms of a single overarching pattern of affective response. The idea that a work of art can subsume a number of things within a single order whose unity is defined in affective terms leads Dufrenne to speak of artworks as 'expressing a world'. The same sort of idea is evident in his comment that: 'The soft delicate tranquillity which is expressed by the interiors of Vermeer is not contained between the walls which the painting encloses. It radiates upon an infinity of absent objects and constitutes the visage of a world of which it is the potentiality.'[8] Let us consider this thought a little further, to bring out its relevance for our concerns.

An affectively toned appreciation of a work of art may help to structure our experience more generally, as other objects are drawn into the 'affective world' constituted by the artwork. For instance, an affectively toned recognition of the 'soft delicate tranquillity' of a Vermeer interior might lead us to experience an indeterminate range of other objects in terms of 'tranquillity'. Here the artwork provides a kind of interpretive key in terms of which we may experience the world more generally – a key which does not just provide a way of reading an already constituted set of

---

6 This terminology provides the beginnings of a response to the objection noted above in n. 4: the model is not committed to the idea that the artwork engenders feelings 'of the same kind' as are fitting in relation to God, or that the phenomenology of these feelings is exactly the same. For a lengthier response, see the discussion of 'Platonic' and 'incommensurable' traditions below.

7 *Phenomenology*, pp. 179–80.   8 *Ibid.*, p. 181.

experiential data, but shapes the phenomenology of experience, by giving it new meaning and structure. Accordingly, an artwork can provide the 'visage of a world', that is, a way of reading our experience in general so that it comes to have a 'face', or in other words, so that it comes to bear a certain human significance. This thought is religiously suggestive: in a similar way, surely, religious world-views seek to communicate some pervasive sense of what matters in human life, where this sense is embodied in feeling, and thereby rendered motivationally effective. And if that is so, then we may wonder whether religious language may function aesthetically, in the way that Dufrenne describes – a possibility to which I shall return shortly.

This general perspective is not, of course, original to Dufrenne. It is also evident, for example, in the tradition of romantic art appreciation, where the mind's role in experience is said to be akin to that of a lamp – which is to say that the mind does not so much passively receive the data of sense, as actively give them shape and colour by way of its own active, affectively toned engagement with the world. William Hazlitt gives voice to this kind of perspective in his 1818 essay 'On Poetry in General'. He comments: 'The light of poetry is not only a direct but also a reflected light, that while it shews us the object, throws a sparkling radiance on all around it.'[9] In the terms we have been using, we could say that the poem 'shews' us the object in the sense of revealing its human significance (this is the first of the themes we have taken from Dufrenne). And thereby it also throws 'a sparkling radiance' upon surrounding objects, as they are absorbed into its 'affective world' (here is the second theme we have taken from Dufrenne). In his poem 'Dejection', Coleridge offers a similar assessment of the role of feeling in lighting up the world. Here he writes of the contribution of joy in particular:

> Joy, Lady! is the spirit and the power,
> Which, wedding nature to us, gives in dower
> A new earth and new Heaven,
> Undreamt of by the sensual and the proud –
> Joy is the sweet voice, Joy the luminous cloud –
> We in ourselves rejoice!
> And thence flows all that charms or ear or sight
> All melodies the echoes of that voice,
> All colours a suffusion from that light.[10]

9 The passage is cited in M. H. Abrams, *The Mirror and the Lamp: Romantic Theory and the Critical Tradition* (Oxford: Oxford University Press, 1953), p. 52. I am grateful to Peter Byrne for drawing this book to my attention.
10 The passage is from the fifth stanza and is cited *ibid.*, p. 67. See also this comment from the fourth stanza: 'Ah! From the soul itself must issue forth/A light, a glory, a fair luminous cloud/

Here again we find the thought that an affective state can shape our experience of the sensory world, and thereby stand as the source of a 'new earth and new Heaven'. As M. H. Abrams remarks, in this poem Coleridge is offering a vision of 'the perceptual mind as projecting life and passion into the world it apprehends'; and as a consequence there is 'a ceaseless and circular interchange of life between soul and nature in which it is impossible to distinguish what is given from what received'.[11] This view is reminiscent of Gaita's suggestion that the quality in the patients that is revealed by the nun cannot be identified independently of her affectively toned response to them: the quality is, as it were, lit up by that response and not otherwise visible. Again, this is not to say that the property in question is a 'mere projection'; the thought is, rather, that in some cases, the projection–discovery distinction does not really apply, since it is only through our active, affectively toned, lamp-like engagement with the sensory world that certain qualities can be apprehended at all.[12]

In a somewhat similar vein, Merleau-Ponty describes how the embodied, affectively toned responsiveness that is characteristic of sexual awareness can make for a new kind of perception of the sensory world. Here he is talking of a sexually impotent man by the name of Schneider:

Perception has lost its erotic structure, both spatially and temporally. What has disappeared from the patient is his power of projecting before himself a sexual world, of putting himself in an erotic situation, or, once such a situation is stumbled upon, of maintaining it or following it through to complete satisfaction . . . At this stage one begins to suspect a mode of perception that is distinct from objective perception, a kind of significance distinct from intellectual significance, an intentionality which is not pure 'awareness of something'. Erotic perception is not a *cogitatio* which aims at a *cogitatum*; through one body it aims at another body, and takes place in the world, not in a consciousness.[13]

Analogously, Dufrenne is suggesting that in our experience of art, we may enter into an affective world (as distinct from a 'sexual world'). And

---

Enveloping the Earth.' See 'Dejection: An Ode', reproduced in H. J. Jackson (ed.), *Samuel Taylor Coleridge* (Oxford: Oxford University Press, 1985), pp. 113–17.
11 *The Mirror and the Lamp*, p. 68.
12 Compare McDowell's position as expounded in Chapter 1. A nice illustration of this sort of phenomenon is given by Janet Sockice when she writes of 'the scanning, native to parents of toddlers, of any new surroundings for steep steps, sharp, breakable or swallowable objects': here again, the mind imposes a certain order or pattern on its experience, one which is correlative to its concerns, but without thereby simply 'inventing' the order: 'Love and Attention', reprinted in P. Anderson and B. Clack (eds.), *Feminist Philosophy of Religion* (London: Routledge, 2003), p. 207.
13 M. Merleau-Ponty, *Phenomenology of Perception*, tr. Colin Smith (London: Routledge & Kegan Paul, 1962), pp. 156–7.

the world of the artwork, like the world which Merleau-Ponty describes here, is one we come to inhabit by taking on a correlative affectively toned 'mode of perception', which in turn will shape the experienced character of the sensory world. I noted above that in apprehending the affective essence of the sea by way of an affectively toned appreciation of *La Mer*, our bodily response may be of a purely make-believe variety. However, as the example of a 'sexual world' makes particularly clear, once we have transferred a particular pattern of affectively toned perception from a purely aesthetic context, so that it comes to inform our dealings with the world, a correlative pattern of bodily response ('real' response, not make-believe) is likely to be implied. Merleau-Ponty's comments also recall Deigh's suggestion that there is a distinctive kind of intentionality that belongs to 'primitive' affective responses – this sort of intentionality is non-'conceptual' (or as Merleau-Ponty puts it, non-'intellectual'), but can also come to infuse more sophisticated, conceptually articulate kinds of awareness. Similarly, Merleau-Ponty remarks that 'sexuality is not an autonomous cycle. It has internal links with the whole active and cognitive being.'[14]

I suggest that we can carry two ideas forward from this discussion: an artwork may represent an object by engendering feelings of the kind that befit the object; and it may project a 'world' which we may come to inhabit by taking on a correlative propensity for affectively toned perception and bodily responsiveness. It is worth noting that these two themes are connected, for it is by adopting the requisite affectively toned mode of perception that I can come to understand the artwork in the first place. As Nelson Goodman puts the point:

in aesthetic experience the *emotions function cognitively*. The work of art is apprehended through the feelings as well as through the senses. Emotional numbness disables here as definitely if not more completely as blindness or deafness. Nor are the feelings used exclusively for exploring the emotional content of a work. To some extent, we may feel how a painting looks as we may see how it feels. The actor or dancer – or the spectator – sometimes notes and remembers the feeling of a movement rather than its pattern, in so far as the two can be distinguished at all. Emotion in aesthetic experience is a means of discerning what properties a work has and expresses.[15]

14 *Ibid.*, p. 157.
15 Nelson Goodman, *Languages of Art: An Approach to a Theory of Symbols* (London: Oxford University Press, 1969), p. 248, Goodman's italics.

This thought recalls Maddell's point about feeling as a mode of perception of qualities of 'tension' and 'resolution' in music. And accordingly we should say that the artwork does not elicit a set of feelings just by virtue of its brute impact on the senses; rather, the feelings it draws out are those required for a proper perception of the character of the work. And the mode of perception that is called forth by the work can then be transferred, at least in principle, to our experience more generally, so that we come to inhabit a correlative 'world'. Following Goodman (and with him, Merleau-Ponty, Deigh, Goldie, and Gaita), we may say that within such a world, 'Perception, conception, and feeling interact; and an alloy often resists analysis into emotive and nonemotive components.'[16] In other words, here feeling, conceptually articulate thought, and perception are not just component parts of an experience (as though they were simply juxtaposed); instead they constitute an integrated state, in which the character of each element is transformed through its contribution to the whole. (Compare again the example of romantic love in Chapter 4, pp. 95–6 above.)

So the themes that we have identified in Dufrenne prove to be related in this way: an artwork may represent an object by engendering feelings of the kind that befit the object (the first theme); these feelings are engendered at least in part because they are required for an understanding of the work; and they may then be transferred to other contexts, and thereby help to constitute a 'world' (the second theme). For example, understanding the 'soft delicate tranquillity' of a Vermeer may require taking on a correlative affectively toned mode of perception (so that our experience is tinged with softness or tranquillity as we contemplate the work). This kind of sensibility may then inform our perception of the sensory world more generally, so that we perceive objects in general in the same terms – and thereby inhabit a correlative 'affective world'.

APPLYING DUFRENNE'S MODEL

It is commonly suggested that coming to understand the religious import of the world is not fundamentally a matter of getting hold of new data (through religious experience, say), or a matter of working through some deduction from existing data (of the kind implied in the cosmological argument, say); it is rather a question of 'seeing' a particular pattern, or a particular meaning, in the data. John Wisdom sets out such a proposal in

16 *Ibid.*, p. 249.

his essay 'Gods', where he distinguishes religious understanding from the kind of understanding that is the goal of the sciences and logic.[17] He offers this analogy. Suppose that two people are trying to determine whether a particular patch of ground has been tended by a gardener. And suppose that they have carefully assembled whatever empirical evidence is relevant to this question (and in this sense exhausted the resources of a scientific understanding). Suppose too that there is no purely deductive (no purely logical) route from the evidence to the claim that 'this is a garden'. In that case, what they need to do is to establish what pattern is presented by the data; in particular, they need to ask whether their data present a pattern which is sufficiently similar to the pattern evident in situations where indisputably a gardener was present. So analogously, when we consider the world, we need to ask: does the overall pattern presented by events suggest that the world is tended by someone? This is also a question which cannot be settled by empirical investigation (by amassing further evidence), but even so it is, Wisdom avers, a factually meaningful issue. Interestingly, in this essay Wisdom also argues that this same sort of understanding is required for the appreciation of works of art: here again, what is needed is a sensitivity to pattern.

Wisdom's essay suggests a number of parallels with the position we have been exploring in this book. What is the nature of the additional understanding that sets someone who has a 'real image' of God apart from someone who has simply a 'notion' of God, or that sets the nun apart from the psychiatrists, to revert to Gaita's example? It is not that the person who has a 'real image' or who believes something 'in their heart' has gained a bit of additional information; nor is it that they have managed by way of discursive argument to establish some new conse-quence of the information that is already known; rather, they 'see' in depth what is involved in the facts that are already before us. And we could say that this is a matter of recognising the 'pattern' that is presented by these facts; or to put the point in terms of another vocabulary that we have used, it is a matter of seeing the facts with proper 'salience'. And in keeping with our discussion in earlier chapters, we might suppose that if we are to recognise such patterns, then we need to adopt the relevant affectively toned mode of perception (where, once more, such perception is not a matter of 'merely projecting' some quality onto the data).

If we can sustain this thought that religious understanding involves a kind of sensitivity to pattern, then (in conjunction with Dufrenne's theory) we have in outline an account of how artworks can bear a religious significance. The story could go, in part, like this: through an affectively toned perception of a work of art, I may come to inhabit a correlative 'affective world', and thereby come to experience the sensory world in new ways, so that new 'patterns' or new structures of salience come into view. And in the spirit of Wisdom's discussion, we may then add that some such cases of pattern recognition may be constitutive of religious understanding. By reference to Newman, Gaita, and others, we have already considered a number of ways in which religious understanding may be taken to involve a kind of pattern recognition (since both these authors suppose that we need to understand the phenomena in depth, or 'really' and not just 'notionally'). But Wisdom's comments suggest a rather different sense in which religious understanding may involve pattern recognition. On his account, religious understanding is a matter of picking out the pattern presented by whole regions of sense-experience, rather than a matter of apprehending the character of any individual entity. (On this point he differs from Newman and Gaita, I take it, in so far as they are concerned with the possibility of an affectively toned encounter with God or individual human beings.) As Rowan Williams has observed, on this sort of view, God-talk 'is structurally more like talking about some "grid" for the understanding of particular objects than talking about particular objects in themselves'.[18] I want next to see whether this particular account of the sense in which religious under- standing involves pattern recognition can be married up with Dufrenne's theory of representation in the arts. I shall begin with the case of 'primal' religions.

The gods of ancient Greece and Rome are naturally taken as personifi- cations of various regions of experience – Poseidon of the sea, Aphrodite of love, and so on. In this sense, the stories of the gods do not so much describe individuals as present 'grids' or 'patterns' in terms of which we can assess the significance of a whole field of human experience. Dufrenne's model of aesthetic representation offers a way of understand- ing how figures like Poseidon are able to function in this way. On this model, an artwork such as *La Mer* can represent the sea by engendering affects of the kind that befit the sea; and analogously, we might suppose, the figure of Poseidon is also able to represent the sea by summoning up feelings which befit the sea, so revealing the sea's 'affective essence'. Let's explore this question further by reference to a more contemporary

18 Rowan Williams, '"Religious Realism": On Not Quite Agreeing with Don Cupitt', *Modern Theology* 1 (1984), p. 15. In this remark, he is expounding a comment of Wittgenstein.

example, one which concerns once more the sea. Keith Ward offers these reflections on the Inuit stories of a sea-dwelling power known as Sedna:

Perhaps there may be those who take literally the story of the girl who began to eat her giant parents and was cast by them beneath the sea – the fundamentalists of Inuit religion . . . [but] What is here represented in an image is the character of the sea itself, as a power for good and harm. What the shaman meets in the dream-quest is this internalised image of the powers which bound Inuit life.[19]

On this reading, the Sedna stories do not gain their religious significance by picking out a particular individual who inhabits the bottom of the sea. (That is the 'fundamentalist' reading.) Rather, the stories provide 'an image' of 'the character of the sea itself, as a power for good and harm'. In other words, the stories represent the human significance of the sea (its capacity to bear on human life for good and ill). And how might they do that? Dufrenne's account offers a direct and, I think, a persuasive response to this question. The stories have this capacity by functioning aesthetically: by eliciting feelings of the kind that befit the sea, they succeed in representing the sea. So they represent the sea not neutrally or in a spirit of detachment, but by way of an affectively toned engagement with Sedna and the sea: when the Sedna stories are understood by means of an appropriate affectively toned mode of perception, they engender feelings of the kind that befit the sea, and thereby 'the represented object can appear as present' (to borrow Dufrenne's phrasing of the point). It is worth noting that in so far as the Sedna stories are treated realistically (to the extent that they are taken to be about some principle which really is at work in the sea), an affectively toned apprehension of the figure recorded in the stories may elicit patterns of bodily response which are not simply of the make-believe variety. (However, if the stories are treated as, say, records of Sedna's past activities, then, of course, they need not call for the bodily response that would have been appropriate at the time with which the narrative is concerned.)

Let us pause briefly to consider an objection. It might be said: in expounding this model you have made appeal at various times to the 'human significance' of the sea. Thus Sedna (or Poseidon, or some such figure) is said to represent the sea by virtue of disclosing its human significance. But does this way of putting the matter open the possibility

---

19 Keith Ward, *Religion and Revelation: A Theology of Revelation in the World's Religions* (Oxford: Clarendon Press, 1994), p. 65. Ward's interpretation of Inuit religion is borne out by Daniel Merkur's detailed study of the same theme in his *Powers which we Do Not Know: The Gods and Spirits of the Inuit* (Moscow, DE: University of Idaho Press, 1991).

that feeling's role is dispensable or at any rate derivative? Perhaps what really matters for representation of this kind is that the artwork should communicate the human significance of the represented object, and perhaps feeling need have no part in this, or at most, a secondary part? However, that the sea has a certain human significance is, I suggest (to revert to a familiar theme), most clearly recognised in our felt responses to the sea (compare Gaita's thought that the 'human significance' of other human beings is most clearly revealed in our felt responses to them). And in that case, we should expect feeling to play an important role when an artwork communicates the human significance of the sea, in rather the way that Dufrenne describes. Justin D'Arms and Daniel Jacobson's account of the pride which a football supporter may take in his team suggests a way of developing this point. Let's take my brother Rob and his support of Liverpool Football Club as an example. A theory of emotion which gives priority to discursive thoughts might suppose that Rob's taking pride in X is fundamentally a matter of his judging that X in some way belongs to him, where the notion of belonging can be elucidated in some standard way. But this analysis can sound strained when we consider Rob's pride in Liverpool's achievements. (How might those achievements 'belong' to him when he is not causally implicated in them?) And even the thought that his pride is a matter of his taking Liverpool's achievements *as though* they belonged to him seems strained, if that implies that at any rate he entertains the idea that they belong to him, where the notion of belonging is again accorded some relatively standard sense. It is better, D'Arms and Jacobson affirm, to put things the other way about: in this case, anyway, it is not that the notion of Rob's being proud of X is to be elucidated by reference to some logically prior notion of what it is for X to belong to him; it is, rather, that what it is for X to belong to Rob is to be elucidated by reference to the pride he feels: here 'belonging' bears a sense that is affectively conditioned, that is, that cannot be fully articulated without reference to feeling. As D'Arms and Jacobson put the point: 'We contend that by claiming thoughts of possession to be a necessary constituent of pride, the judgmentalist tradition has things backwards. The sense in which the club's accomplishments belong to the fan is simply that he is able to be proud of them. It is, after all, "his team" – but in this sense only.'[20]

20 Justin D'Arms and Daniel Jacobson, 'The Significance of Recalcitrant Emotion (Or Anti-Quasijudgmentalism)', in Anthony Hatzimoysis (ed.), *Philosophy and the Emotions* (Cambridge: Cambridge University Press, 2003), pp. 135–6.

Analogously, we might say that just as the sense in which Liverpool Football Club and its achievements belong to Rob can only be specified by reference to the feelings he has for the team, so what it is for the sea to bear a certain 'human significance' can only be specified by reference to the feelings that it engenders. And this is surely plausible, for the human significance of something is in important part a matter of how it engages our feelings. So for this reason too, the separation of affective response and human significance which is envisaged in the remarks with which we began is mistaken: the second implies the first not only epistemically but also conceptually, since the notion of human significance is affectively conditioned. We have encountered this kind of idea at various points already – for example, when noting how Newman's 'real image' of God's accessibility, or Gaita's concept of 'humanity', may be affectively conditioned, that is, may be fully intelligible only by reference to what is revealed in feeling. The property of 'human significance', like those of 'humanity' and 'divine accessibility' (when grasped in a real image), proves to be affectively conditioned not least because it is constituted, at least in part, by our affective responses: the property is to be specified, in part, by the quality of affective response that it calls forth.[21]

We have been exploring Ward's thought that Sedna offers an 'eidetic representation of the harsh, often arbitrary-seeming and yet life-supporting conditions of the arctic world'[22] – which is to say that she represents a whole region of experience, rather than a particular individual. And I have suggested that we can put this point by saying, in Dufrenne's terms, that the Sedna stories engender feelings of the kind that befit the sea; thereby Sedna records the 'affective essence' of the sea, and hence she represents the sea. This example indicates one thing that needs to be added to Dufrenne's account to make the model applicable to representations of 'the gods'. The figure of Sedna and Debussy's *La Mer* both function as aesthetic representations of the sea; but only the first is of religious

---

21 As I have indicated, I do not think that Gaita's concept of 'humanity' can be specified simply by reference to quality of affective response. As the exchange with Schacht indicates (see Chapter 2), the 'humanity' of the patients is not reducible to the fact that they can elicit a certain kind of affective response; it has also to do with the fact that such responses are more fitting than others. As Schacht puts the point, at this juncture, the revelatory rather than the constitutive theme wears the trousers. In this connection, I noted another reason why 'humanity' is affectively conditioned: not only is this quality in part constituted by our affective responses; it is also only revealed in full in our affective experience, and can therefore only be specified in full by reference to such experience.

22 Ward, *Religion and Revelation*, p. 65.

importance. Why should this be? The answer lies, surely, in the difference in the sea's human significance for the Inuit and a Frenchman of the late nineteenth and early twentieth centuries. The sea is the basic power that bounds the lives of the Inuit, and on its 'moods' they depend for their livelihood and well-being; and it is for this reason that the sea bears a religious significance for them. But of course the sea has a very different and existentially far less serious meaning for Debussy and his public. This suggests that Dufrenne's model will be relevant to the question of how an artwork may represent the gods only on condition that it communicates an 'affective essence' of the requisite existential seriousness.

We have been trying to understand the religious significance of art by reference to the first of the two focal themes that we have taken from Dufrenne, namely, the thought that an artwork can represent a region of experience, such as the sea, by engendering feelings that befit that region. The second of these themes is also relevant to the question of art's religious potency. Following Dufrenne we could say that a figure like Sedna projects an 'affective world', and that the Inuit can inhabit this world by adopting a correlative affectively toned mode of perception of the sensory world, and of the sea in particular. So Sedna does not just passively record the felt significance of the sea in Inuit life; she also helps to shape that significance, by providing an 'atmosphere' within which the sea is encountered and understood. So in this way too, Sedna is religiously important, by helping to form the Inuit understanding of the basic power that bounds their lives. To put the point in the terms I used above, Sedna makes it possible for the Inuit to recognise particular 'patterns' in their marine experience, and thereby she brings out the sea's human significance. The second of Dufrenne's themes throws new light on the thought that our felt responses in part constitute the human significance of an object: this is true not simply because when our feelings are (passively) stirred by an object, it thereby acquires a certain significance for us, but also because our feelings can function as modes of perception, actively structuring the sensory world, and in this way giving it significance.

Again, we can take these two themes in Dufrenne to be connected. Grasping the meaning of the Sedna figure requires an affectively toned responsiveness to the stories that record her deeds – it requires, for example, being fearful of Sedna's capriciousness (where such fearfulness can be understood in make-believe terms if Sedna is treated non-realistically). This repertoire of feeling can then inform the Inuit relationship to the sea, by providing an affectively toned mode of perception in terms of which the Inuit can understand the sea's human significance. It may be asked: if Sedna is treated non-realistically (or understood in purely 'mythological' terms), how can the affective repertoire which is relevant in understanding the stories which record her deeds be transferred to the sea, which is emphatically 'real'? I do not see any difficulty of principle with such a transfer. Analogously, a child raised on stories which emphasise, let's say, the precariousness of human life may find that in adult life these stories condition their experience of the sensory world, even when they judge that the stories are simply fiction. For even if they judge that they are fictitious, the stories will still provide them with a way of assigning significance to situations (and a particularly accessible way of assigning such significance if the stories on which they were raised have predominantly this character, and if this reading of the world has become to some extent habitual). (Compare Teasdale and Barnard's comments on how implicational meanings may be laid down in emotional memory and thereby shape the sense that we find in new situations.) And by assumption, the Sedna stories elicit feelings whose phenomenology is in some degree isomorphic with the phenomenology of our experience of the sea; so in this case in particular, it is relatively easy to see how the affective complex that is relevant to the appreciation of the Sedna stories may interact with, and help to shape, the felt sense of the sea's significance.

It might be wondered whether this account of the Sedna figure implies a debunking attitude to Inuit religion. Whatever the Inuit themselves may believe, aren't we saying that the religious significance of the Sedna figure is adequately understood in terms of the thought that she discloses the human significance of the sea? And isn't this to say that talk of Sedna is really (whatever the Inuit may suppose) just a way of talking about the sea and its tendencies? The same kind of question could be put to Wisdom's account of religious understanding. His view assimilates very closely religious understanding and the kind of understanding that is required if we are to label a set of events appropriately. Wisdom points out that there may well be a fact of the matter about which label is appropriate (compare: was he driving with 'due care and attention'?); and preserving the factual meaningfulness of religious claims, in the face of positivist critique, seems to be the main concern in his essay. However, we might wonder whether the implication of Wisdom's discussion is that religion is therefore concerned with the characterisation of sensory appearances (by labelling them appropriately) rather than searching for something deeper than the appearances, some metaphysical source which is manifest in them. Whatever view we reach on this question, Dufrenne's model does not require, I think, a debunking or anti-metaphysical reading of the Sedna stories. Suppose we agree that the Inuit themselves are not 'fundamentalists' about the Sedna figure (see the passage from Ward above). In other words, they do not take the stories about her as literally true of some figure living beneath the sea. Even so, they may still take the stories to reveal the character of a power which is at work in the sea (and which is not to be reductively identified with the sea). This metaphysical reading of the Sedna story is not compromised by the Dufrenne model. If we assign to the Sedna figure this sort of metaphysical significance, then we may suppose that the stories succeed in referring to Sedna so understood by disclosing the human significance of the sea, which in turn discloses the human significance of the power that is at work in the sea. In that case, the stories will represent that power at one remove. In this sense, Dufrenne's model is neutral on the metaphysics of Sedna: it does not depend for its cogency upon a ruling one way or other about whether Sedna refers to anything over and above the sea. But what the model brings out is that Inuit religious language gets its purchase by eliciting feelings of the kind that befit the sea and by summing up in this way the existential significance of the sea, not by characterising in some more abstract way the principle (if any) whose nature is revealed in the sea.

It would be easy to multiply examples of the Sedna type, where a figure sums up the human significance of some existentially important region of experience and thereby carries religious meaning.[23] But the Sedna example is enough to show how Dufrenne's model can in principle be applied to cases of this kind. What, however, of other, more 'sophisticated' religious traditions? These traditions are likely to differ from primal religions in two respects. First of all, they may reject heno- or polytheism, preferring to think of reality as underpinned by a single religious principle. And they may differ, secondly, in their sense that God or the sacred otherwise understood is radically transcendent, so that the human significance of various regions of experience, or even the world itself, is not to be identified with the human significance of God. Given these two points of difference, we might wonder whether Dufrenne's model can be applied to representations of God or the sacred that are found in more 'sophisticated' traditions. The first point invites the

23 To name just one example, see Godfrey Lienhardt's description of the religion of the Dinka: *Divinity and Experience: The Religion of the Dinka* (Oxford: Clarendon Press, 1961), especially pp. 159–60.

question: is it possible for a figure of the Sedna type to sum up the significance not only of some particular region of experience, such as the sea, but of the sensory world in general? If not, then Dufrenne's model may not be applicable to traditions which posit a religious principle which is manifest in the world as a whole, and not just in relation to some particular field of human thought and activity. The second point invites the question: if God is transcendent, then even if a figure of the Sedna type elicits feelings of the kind that befit the sensory world in general, it will not thereby represent God, because the feelings which befit God are different again – and does that show that Dufrenne's model cannot be extended to cover this sort of case? Let us take these two questions in turn.

It has often been thought that a particular individual can in some way body forth the character of the world as a whole, and thereby carry religious significance. As Mircea Eliade comments: 'The great paradox common to all religions is that God in showing Himself to mankind is free to take any form whatsoever but that, by this very assertion of His freedom, He "limits Himself" and reduces Himself to a mere fragment of the whole which He represents.'[24] Here it is suggested that God 'represents' the whole, but also that God can assume a particular form, and that implies, I take it, that the particular can in some way point towards the character of the whole, and thereby the character of God. Similarly David Tracy remarks that: 'To enter the conversation of the religious classics through real interpretation . . . is to enter a discourse of a world of meaning and truth offering no certainty but promising some realized experience of the whole by the power of the whole.'[25] The implication of this remark is that the stories of particular individuals that fill the pages of sacred texts in some way body forth the meaning of human experience in general. So here again we find the idea that an individual can in some fashion stand for the whole, and thereby bear a religious significance. Of course, in the Christian context, this idea is expressed with particular clarity in the doctrine of the incarnation, and the thought that the Logos (God's agent in making the world, who is the meaning of the created order) is embodied in a particular historical figure. As John Paul II writes: 'In the incarnation of the Son of God . . . the Eternal enters time, the

---

24 Mircea Eliade, 'Divinities: Art and the Divine', first published in English in 1961, and reprinted in Diane Apostolos-Cappadona (ed.), *Mircea Eliade: Symbolism, the Sacred and the Arts* (New York: Crossroad, 1985), p. 56.

25 David Tracy, 'The Religious Classic and the Classic of Art', in Diane Apostolos-Cappadona (ed.), *Art, Creativity and the Sacred* (New York: Crossroad, 1984), p. 248.

Whole lies hidden in the part.'[26] And as we have seen, Schleiermacher propounds a related idea when he supposes that it is possible to have an 'intuition' of the universe by way of our encounter with particular things. As he comments: 'To accept everything individual as a part of the whole and everything limited as a representation of the infinite is religion.'[27] Here Schleiermacher allows (rather as Eliade allows) that in principle anything can function as a 'representation' of the infinite; but in practice he supposes, as we might expect, that some things are more powerfully revelatory of the universe's character than others.[28]

If a particular thing can body forth 'the whole' in this sort of way, and if it can thereby represent God (as these authors in different ways suppose), then in principle we can apply Dufrenne's model to monotheistic traditions, providing they share this sort of understanding of the relationship of God and world, and not just to a figure like Sedna who bodies forth the character of a particular region of experience. In brief, this model will run as follows: an individual entity or religious symbol may represent the world in so far as it elicits feelings of the kind that befit the world; thereby the symbol will also elicit feelings of the kind that befit 'the whole' (even if the world and 'the whole' are not simply to be identified, I take it that, in the usage of the authors cited above, the two are closely enough related to ensure that the feelings which befit one also befit the other); in that case, the symbol will also represent 'the whole' and in turn therefore it will (given the usage of these authors) represent God. As we have seen, the thought that individual things can bear this larger significance can easily be supported by reference to a range of authoritative sources, but it is helpful, I think, to consider a particular case by way of illustration. Here is Holmes Rolston writing about a native North American plant, the pasqueflower:

The brilliance of this pasqueflower has its simplest explanation in mechanisms for flowering so soon at the winter's end. It must have petals (or, as the botanists prefer, petallike sepals) large enough to attract the few insects that are out so early. The downy surface of transparent hairs on its palmate leaves and stem insulates and also, as do those of pussy willows, allows a radiation heating to temperatures high enough for development, providing a miniature greenhouse effect.

This is, of course, a scientifically informed appraisal of the pasqueflower's character, cast in the terms of an affectively neutral, analytically

---

26 John Paul II, *Fides et Ratio* (Sydney: St Paul's Publications, 1998), Section 12.
27 Friedrich Schleiermacher, *On Religion: Speeches to its Cultured Despisers*, tr. Richard Crouter (Cambridge: Cambridge University Press, 1976; first published 1799), p. 25 (see Chapter 3 above, n. 22).
28 See, for example, his comments on the special place of other human beings, *ibid.*, pp. 37–8.

precise vocabulary. Rolston continues in this vein for a few lines, and then comments:

but the pasqueflower helps me to glimpse something more, the skill of art superimposed on the science of survival. This is exuberance in the fundamental, etymological sense of being more than expectedly luxuriant. Does not such an encouraging beauty speak of that face of nature that overleaps the merest hanging on to life to bear the winds of the storm with vigorous, adorning beauty? Nor is it just the grand petals of delicate purple whorled about the yellow stamens and pistils, for the fingered involucre frames the flower so well, and the villous coat has a sheen that, seen backlighted by the sun, gives a lustrous aura to complement the gentle leafy green.[29]

Here Rolston describes the pasqueflower in a rather different vocabulary, as 'grand', 'delicate', and 'lustrous'. This is, of course, the language of aesthetic appraisal, and we might suppose that these qualities of the pasqueflower are picked out, in part, by way of an affectively toned appreciation of its character (compare Rolston's reference to its 'encouraging beauty'). Although the flower is now being described in affectively resonant terms, the scientific style of description has not been simply set aside: to capture the flower's appearance we still need to distinguish petals, stamens, and pistils, for example. So Rolston's appreciation of the flower could be seen as a further illustration of how conceptual understanding and affective response may unite, to produce an affectively toned complex or 'alloy' whose intentionality cannot be traced simply to feeling or simply to discursive understanding.

Moreover, when appreciated in affectively informed terms, the flower can carry a larger significance: as Rolston says, its 'encouraging beauty speak[s] of that face of nature that overleaps the merest hanging on to life to bear the winds of the storm with vigorous, adorning beauty'. So the flower represents an existentially profound feature of the world, namely, nature's resilience, its capacity to bring forth flourishing in the face of hardship, and accordingly the flower can bear a religious significance. (Compare the way in which Sedna is religiously significant for the Inuit, given her role in communicating the character of an existentially significant region of experience.) Again, we can apply Dufrenne's model to understand how it is possible for an individual item to carry this larger meaning.[30] Rolston comments: 'We are born to die, but it is life rather

---

29 Holmes Rolston III, *Philosophy Gone Wild* (Buffalo, NY: Prometheus Books, 1989), p. 257.

30 I do not say that this is the only way of understanding how the pasqueflower can bear this significance: for our purpose, it is enough if it is one such way.

than death which is the principal mystery that comes out of nature, and our emotions are stirred proportionately.'[31] So by virtue of its 'encouraging beauty', the flower engenders a felt response of the kind that befits 'the principal mystery' of nature; and thereby, given Dufrenne's model, it can represent that mystery, and in turn therefore the natural order in general. Moreover, because the flower participates in the regenerative power that it represents, the encouragement which it arouses need not be of a make-believe variety – the encouragement that we feel in the face of the flower can be one and the same as that we feel (if we are Rolstonians) in our encounter with the natural order as a whole.

The pasqueflower's name is a reference to the time of its flowering, but in the light of Rolston's reflections, it can also be assigned a more precise significance: we could see the flower's name as evoking the Christian theme of resurrection, and the flower as symbolising both the annual resurrection of the natural order that is presaged by its own growth at winter's end and the wider pattern of death and renewal which is, from a Christian point of view, folded into the rhythm of human life more generally. Rolston himself picks up this Christian reading of the flower's significance when he comments that 'The way of nature is, in this deep though earthen sense, the Way of the cross. Light shines in the darkness that does not overcome it. This noble flower is a poignant sacrament of this.'[32] Here the flower's meaning is understood in terms of a specific theological motif of cross and resurrection, but affects retain their role in this sort of interpretation for at least two reasons. First of all, the meaning of the cross and resurrection motif itself needs to be apprehended in depth (or 'really' rather than 'notionally') and therefore at least in part by means of an affectively constituted insight (to follow Newman once more). And secondly, seeing the applicability of the cross and resurrection motif to our experience of the world will depend on an affectively toned apprehension of the meaning of that experience. Again, these themes are connected: the cross and resurrection theme, when apprehended in depth, can itself contribute to an affectively toned mode of perception of the world. And in other ways too, ways not dependent upon the cross and resurrection theme, discerning the meaning of our experience will depend upon an affectively informed, 'lamp-like' engagement with the sensory

---

31 *Philosophy Gone Wild*, p. 255.
32 *Ibid.*, p. 261. Rolston develops the theme that our natural history is cruciform at greater length in his essay 'Does Nature Need to be Redeemed?', *Zygon: Journal of Religion and Science* 29 (1994), pp. 205–29.

world (compare again the comments of Hazlitt and Coleridge). Here, then, is another instance of how 'doctrine' and feeling can interpenetrate to produce an affective complex of which both are inextricably a part.

To sum up, the pasqueflower can represent the regenerative power of the natural order by eliciting feelings of the kind that befit that order. Thereby the flower can also represent God, for (on Rolston's assumptions) the divine nature is revealed in the life-affirming tendencies of nature, and the feeling of encouragement which befits the regenerative power of nature is therefore also appropriate to God. The pasqueflower can play this role both on account of its place in the natural order and in so far as its life cycle can be assimilated to the specifically Christian story of cross and resurrection. Affects play a part at various points in this story: they help us to see the flower's encouraging beauty; thereby they induct us into the affective world of the flower, and enable us to find encouragement in nature more generally; thereby they help to ensure that the feelings engendered by the flower also befit the natural order as a whole. Affects may also help us to grasp the Christian story's significance, which may lead us to find new significance in the natural order, and so on. If all of this is so, then Dufrenne's model of aesthetic representation can be extended from the Sedna kind of example to encompass at least certain kinds of monotheism. It is worth noticing that here as in the Sedna case, the representation works not by offering some abstract characterisation of the divine nature, and not necessarily by appeal to any explicitly religious subject matter, but by summing up the felt significance of some region of experience. On this point, the model remains true to Wisdom's account of the nature of religious understanding.

It may be thought that even if this example works well enough, it is rather exceptional: not many objects in the natural world will be quite so rich in potential theological meaning as a plant which bears the name of pasqueflower! But in fact, it is a common enough experience that individual items can come to epitomise the meaning of the 'whole' in this sort of way. Indeed, flowers of all kinds can play such a role, in as much as they speak of an 'encouraging beauty'. Rolston picks up this theme when speaking of the Shanidar Cave, where a Neanderthal corpse was found strewn with the remains of flowers:

If the flower has for fifty thousand years served as an emblem of resolution in the face of death, then my thoughts run steady in a natural track as perennial as the springs since Neanderthal times. The flower is a very powerful symbol, it has had a psychologically uplifting effect in every culture, and if anyone cares to say that this is not scientific, but romantic, that does not make it any less real. Our recent 'flower children' knew this impact when they hung flowers in protest in the guns of destruction.[33]

This example suggests that there may be a kind of primitive affective responsiveness (of the kind postulated by Deigh) that leads us to take encouragement from the beauty of flowers in general. That sort of responsiveness can then be deepened by conceptual reflection (and deepened in the thoroughly tradition-specific ways suggested by the example of the pasqueflower), but without thereby depriving the primitive response of its energy, or its importance in shaping the character of the larger affective complex of which it forms part – where, once again, this complex is not to be understood reductively as simply the sum of its parts.

Using Dufrenne's model of aesthetic representation, we have been considering how individual things may bear a sacramental significance, by representing the basic conditions of human life, and in turn thereby the nature of God, whose creative will is revealed in those conditions. This sort of account presupposes a relatively sanguine assessment of the natural order: it implies that the feelings which befit this order, or at least certain items within it, are also appropriate in relation to God. But of course not all monotheistic traditions have taken this view: some have wanted to insist that God is 'transcendent' in a sense which implies that attitudes towards the world, even when it is understood as a theatre of divine activity, are not straightforwardly transferable to God. Here we turn to the second of the two difficulties that I noted earlier for the project of extending Dufrenne's model from the Sedna kind of case to other kinds of religious tradition. What should we say on this question?

Even if we take God to be transcendent in the sense that God's 'real essence' is beyond the reach of human concepts, because the worldly things picked out by those concepts fail to image God, the kind of model we have just been sketching may still have some relevance. Maimonides famously thought that we cannot speak affirmatively of God's real essence. So he interprets talk of God either as a matter of negation (when applied to God's real essence) or as a way of characterising God's relationship to the world (as a reference to God's 'nominal essence'). Expounding the second of these themes, he writes:

We see, e.g., how well He provides for the life of the embryo of living beings; how He endows with certain faculties both the embryo itself and those who have to rear it after its birth, in order that it may be protected from death and destruction, guarded against all harm, and assisted in the performance of all that is required [for

33 *Philosophy Gone Wild*, p. 260.

its development]. Similar acts, when performed by us, are due to a certain emotion and tenderness called mercy and pity. God is, therefore, said to be merciful.[34]

On this view, God's mercy is realised in the tendency of the natural order to preserve embryos (and to uphold human well being in other respects). If that is so, then Dufrenne's model appears to be relevant once more to an understanding of how we are able to represent at least certain divine attributes. For on this account of the divine mercy, the feelings which befit the natural order in respect of its tendency to promote human well being will also befit God considered as merciful. (For instance, if it is appropriate to have confidence in the natural order's tendency to uphold human well being, then it will also be appropriate to have confidence in the divine mercy, and vice versa.) And accordingly, given Dufrenne's model, an entity which engenders feelings which befit the world in respect of its tendency to preserve human well being will be able thereby to represent the divine mercy. And as we have seen, individual mundane items can bear this sort of significance in principle. So even if we adopt a view of God's real essence as radically beyond the reach of any positive, literal characterisation, the model that we have derived from Dufrenne can still shed light on how it is possible to talk of 'the gods'. Indeed, the model may have a special importance in this sort of case. If we cannot represent literally and positively God's real essence, then religious language will have to be anchored (as Maimonides saw), at least in large part, in facts concerning God's activity in the world, and in particular, in facts concerning how that activity impinges upon human lives. And this sort of conception of the working of religious language is exactly suited to Dufrenne's account, given its interest in how to represent the human significance of various regions of experience.

But what of other cases – where it is the representation of a transcendent God's *real* essence that is at issue, and where mundane things do not adequately image that essence? We can distinguish two cases here. First of all, there is the case where worldly entities are said to echo in some relatively imperfect fashion the reality of God. For instance, human wisdom may be said to point imperfectly not just to God's nominal essence, but to the divine wisdom considered as a quality inhering in the divine nature itself. For ease of reference, let us call this the 'Platonic' picture. Then there is the case where the world is taken to be radically other than God, so that the world cannot echo the divine nature. Let us

34 Moses Maimonides, *The Guide for the Perplexed*, tr. M. Friedlander, 2nd edn (New York: Dover Publications, 1956), Chapter liv, p. 76.

call this the 'incommensurability' view. How, if at all, might Dufrenne's model be extended to these cases? Let us take them in turn.

On the 'Platonic' view, God's reality outstrips that of the world, without being entirely discontinuous with it. If Dufrenne's model is to apply here, we shall need, naturally, to translate this understanding of the relationship of God and the world into affective terms. This can be done, I suggest, by allowing that just as God's reality is richer than that of the world, so the feelings which befit that reality are richer and more elevated than those which befit the world. There is a passage in Dufrenne which provides an intimation of how the account might proceed from here:

Suppose that a captive in his prison, delivered to hatred and seeing the sky only 'beyond the rooftop', hears a Bach fugue . . . He cannot doubt that this world of Bach exists, even if it is reserved for enjoyment by others. There is joy, and it is of little importance which particular objects manifest it.[35]

The fugue expresses 'joy', whereas the captive's surroundings are suggestive rather of confinement and 'hatred'; so, clearly, there is a mismatch between the quality of feeling engendered by the artwork and that which befits the world, or at least that portion of the world to which the captive has access. This contrasts, of course, with the case of Sedna and the pasqueflower, where an aesthetic symbol elicits a feeling which befits the world or some region of experience. So the Bach fugue will not be able to represent the divine after the fashion of Sedna and the pasqueflower, that is, by virtue of representing the world. But on the 'Platonic' view, it still seems religiously suggestive. The fugue expresses joy, and this is a feeling richer than any which is elicited by the captive's surroundings. And on the Platonic view, joy of some sort is a feeling which befits God, for God (to continue the Platonic theme) is our true homeland, rather than our embodied state, which constitutes a kind of 'prison' (on the view expounded in the *Phaedo*, for example). This suggests a sense in which the Bach fugue can be taken to represent God – not by eliciting feelings which befit the world, but rather by engendering an affective state which transcends what is appropriate in relation to 'the world' (what we encounter in ordinary mundane experience).

This is not to say that the joy that is elicited by the music bears a very close resemblance phenomenologically to the joy that is fitting in relation to God. That would be to revert to something like the first view again

---

35 *Phenomenology*, p. 519. The quotation is from Verlaine.

(where a mundane object elicits feelings that befit God). Rather, this joy points towards God by training our attention away from the world, by moving us on from the affective condition that goes along with immersion in the world – so providing a new, God-directed orientation. So perhaps it would be better to say not that the music represents God, but that it points towards God, by turning the self's gaze away from the world. (In the terms of the allegory of the cave, in Plato's *Republic*, the fugue is perhaps the fire, if not the sun.) Of course, Plato himself was sceptical about the ability of art to play such a role, but there is a long-established tradition of taking aesthetic experience to imply a contemplative absorption in the artwork for its own sake, and a turning away from the world understood simply as a resource for feeding the cravings of the ego.[36] Moreover, in keeping with this tradition of aesthetic theory, art is commonly experienced as offering a kind of liberation from everyday reality and everyday concerns; and to this extent, the fugue example is by no means unrepresentative of aesthetic experience more generally. It might even be thought that the raison d'être of art is to provide human beings with an object that is proportioned to their deepest and truest powers of perception, and accordingly an object that is richer (and potentially, more divinely suggestive) than anything that is encountered within ordinary mundane experience. In art, it might be said, 'One escapes from natural and social worlds to which we are at best satisficingly adapted into worlds designed to challenge and satisfy, from which all extraneous noise has been extracted.'[37] If that is so, then in art, or at least in the best art, we should find expressed a quality of feeling that outstrips the 'affective essence' of the everyday world, and projects us towards a richer, more expansive sense of human possibilities.

On this view, while the affective essence of the world does not match the divine affective essence, individual mundane things can still lift the mind in the direction of God, by engendering feelings which outstrip the affective essence of the world as a whole. But what of a tradition which is committed to the 'incommensurability' of God and world, by accentuating the discontinuity between the objects of mundane experience and the transcendent God? On this view, our condition in general is one of radical difference from God, and there are not even isolated mundane experiences, such as that afforded by the fugue, which can orient us

36 The most famous exposition of this view is perhaps Arthur Schopenhauer's *The World as Will and Representation*, tr. E. F. Payne (New York: Dover Publications, 1969), Vol. 1, Book 3.
37 Alan Goldman, *Aesthetic Value* (Boulder, CO: Westview Press, 1995), p. 155.

towards God by engendering feelings of the kind that in some way prefigure the affective essence of God. How might Dufrenne's kind of model be applied here?

When it is embodied in its life setting, a conception of God of this kind will still imply some understanding of the affective essence of the world. The world may be experienced, for example, in terms of abandonment or restlessness or longing of some sort. Or again, the sense of difference from God could be registered as a kind of liberation: mundane objects are free to be themselves, and do not need to be in some fashion absorbed into God, or seen as gods manqués. In any event, on this sort of view, just as much as on the primal and 'Platonic' views, a certain view of God's reality is correlated with a view of the world's affective essence. This suggests that Dufrenne's model has some purchase in this case too. Suppose, for example, that the feelings which are elicited by an aesthetic symbol befit the world, so that the symbol represents the world. So far we have the pattern of the Sedna kind of model again. But suppose also that these feelings are, say, of restlessness or longing (compare Maddell's example of anticipating the resolution of a musical composition): in that case, given the perspective of incommensurability, they may point towards God, by representing not so much God as God's absence or difference.[38]

The passage from Weil quoted at the beginning of this chapter could be read as an illustration of something like this possibility. The hymns she hears express 'heart-rending sadness', and she takes her own condition to be that of a 'slave'. In our terms, we could say that the feelings elicited by the artwork befit the world considered as a place of enslavement, and therefore they befit God's absence, in so far as our enslavement is bound up with the 'distance' of God from the world; and therefore (to follow Dufrenne) they represent the divine absence, and in this sense allude to God. I do not want to say that Weil's experience in fact carried this sort of significance for her.[39] But this interpretation provides one example of how aesthetic experience may in principle permit a reference to God within the framework of a tradition that is committed to the incommensurability of world and God.

38 Whether Maddell's example will serve as an illustration depends on how it is developed. If the 'resolution' constitutes a kind of enrichment and extension of what has come before, then it is more naturally assimilated to the 'Platonic' model.
39 Indeed, if we read Weil's references to being a slave in the light of the second chapter of St Paul's letter to the Philippians, then her experience could be taken to involve not a sense of difference or distance from God, but an identification with the condition of the incarnate God. I am grateful to Tim Gorringe for drawing my attention to the potential relevance of Paul's text in this connection.

The three models I have outlined (illustrated by Sedna, the fugue, and Weil's experience) are not intended to be absolutely exhaustive. But they do seem to me to pick out the central forms of religious sensibility in practice, corresponding to the sense that God's nature is fully disclosed in the general tendencies of the sensory world, that this nature is at any rate anticipated in certain, perhaps isolated, experiences of transcendence, and that the divine nature is radically distinct from anything that we can encounter in the world. And Dufrenne's model can be applied in each case, I suggest, to understand how an aesthetic object may represent, or at least to allude to, the sacred. Having considered how Dufrenne's account of representation might be extended to the religious case, I want to conclude by offering some general remarks on the implications of all of this for our understanding of religious language.

SOME IMPLICATIONS OF DUFRENNE'S MODEL

Clearly, not all representations of the divine work in the way that I have been describing. God can be characterised in purely abstract terms, as the first cause, for example, and in this sort of case, the representation surely does not require any aesthetic or affective mediation. (And following Newman, we may suppose that a characterisation of God whose content is rightly understood in part by way of affective response may in fact be apprehended in purely notional terms.) However, there is good reason to think that in practice, religious traditions make quite extensive use of the sort of representation that we have been discussing. Certainly they have an abundant supply of the requisite means: in the course of human history, most art has had a religious provenance, and even traditions which prohibit any figurative representation of the divine have been a prolific source of abstractly decorative and other kinds of art. Moreover, religious traditions also have the requisite motive. For they are interested in inculcating a 'real image' of God or, more generally, a motivationally effective sense of the sacred – and aesthetic representation of the sacred achieves just this, by offering a symbol of the divine whose content can be grasped only by way of an affectively engaged response to the symbol and the world. If all of this is true, then there is good reason to suppose that the kind of representation that we have been exploring is quite commonly exemplified in religious traditions.

To put the point in the terms of Dufrenne's model, as I have developed it, the art of a particular tradition may engender feelings that befit the world, or outstrip the feelings that are properly elicited by the world; and thereby a particular work may represent, or at least allude to, God in the various ways I have been describing. Moreover, artworks may themselves help to shape our sense of which feelings befit the world, by constituting an affective world and making possible a correlative affectively toned mode of perception. (These are respectively the two central themes we have taken from Dufrenne, of course.) The possibility of this sort of representation is beautifully illustrated in the passage from Weil at the beginning of this chapter. On hearing the women's singing, she is reminded of, or perhaps discovers with the aid of the 'artwork', the meaning of the world (she comprehends its heart-rending 'affective essence'). And thereby she comes to a new understanding of the Christian God (as the God of slaves) and of her own Christian identity. It is worth emphasising once more that the affective-aesthetic dimension of Weil's state of mind is not to be viewed in isolation. It may be true that Weil grasps the religious meaning of the women's behaviour without understanding the words of the hymns they sing; but her sense that Christianity is the religion of slaves is, surely, doctrinally informed, so that feeling's role here is to provide a more integrative, self-involving way of apprehending what has been grasped in notional terms, rather than a purely non-discursive route to religious insight. But at the same time, Weil's example suggests (along with our discussion of the pasqueflower, for instance) that religiously suggestive art need not be religiously explicit in content. Other kinds of art, including non-representational art, are also capable of bearing a religious meaning, providing that they elicit feelings which can be mapped onto those befitting the world in the various ways described above.

If this is the right way to think about how religious representation (and accordingly, religious understanding) works in at least many cases, then it follows that philosophy of religion may need an expanded sense of the kinds of epistemic 'failure' which lie at the root of non-belief. Philosophers have, naturally, wondered about the kind of non-belief that is grounded in an inability to see the evidential force of certain arguments (or, even, an inability to grasp the reasons for thinking that religious belief need not be evidence-dependent). The account of religious representation that we have been considering suggests that the inability to participate in a religious tradition may have other sources, also epistemic in their way, but at the same time profoundly related to questions of sentiment and personality. First of all, I may be unable to participate in a religious tradition if its art fails to engender in me the right kind of affective response. Moreover, even if I understand the art of a religious tradition in this sense, I may still be unable to participate in the tradition if I cannot share in its affectively toned sense of the world's human significance. Remember that religious representation on Dufrenne's model depends upon an appropriate mapping of the feelings elicited by the artwork onto those elicited by the world; and accordingly, a representation may fail to work in either of these ways – that is, either because it does not elicit the requisite feelings, or because the world does not. (Again, these achievements are related, in as much as understanding an artwork may enable me to inhabit a correlative affective world that will in turn provide a new, affectively toned mode of perception of the sensory world.) In both of these ways, then, a person may find themselves unable to participate in a religious tradition, for cognitive-cum-affective reasons. So Dufrenne's model, as applied to representations of the gods, invites us to revisit some familiar issues concerning the working of religious language, and the kind of epistemic achievement that is implied in religious commitment.[40]

In these first six chapters, we have considered various models of the relationship between emotional experience and religious understanding. Emotional experience may function as a mode of value perception, and thereby carry religious import, in the ways described in Chapters 1–3 (and set out in the first two models of Chapters 4–5). Or again, emotional feelings may serve to direct the development of discursive understanding, including religious understanding, or they may point towards God as an object of longing (in the ways set out in the third and fourth models of Chapters 4–5). Or, to revert to the theme of this chapter, religious language and symbolism may function aesthetically, and secure their reference by engaging our feelings. Throughout this discussion we have been concerned with the positive contribution that may be made by emotional feeling to religious understanding. But of course there is also a case for supposing that emotional feeling can obstruct understanding. In the closing chapter, I want to consider how this theme might be developed – and understood within the framework of our discussion so far.

---

40 There are a number of issues arising from this discussion that deserve further attention. Notably, it is important to attend to the different significance carried by different art forms, and to the person-relative character of felt responses to art. These issues are addressed in my paper 'Musical Affects and the Life of Faith: Some Reflections on the Religious Potency of Music', *Faith and Philosophy* 21 (2004), pp. 25–44.

CHAPTER 7

The religious critique of feeling

When all is said and done, the long line of saints and spiritual writers who insist on 'experience', who speak of sanctity in terms of ever-deepening 'experience', who maintain that to have none of it is to be spiritually dead, are absolutely right provided we understand 'experience' in the proper sense, not as a transient emotional impact but as living wisdom, living involvement. All the truths of faith there in our minds will be translated into practical terms, all we believe becoming principles of action. Thus spiritual 'experience' is as necessary a mark of a loving soul, of a holy person, as medical 'experience' is of a doctor. So often, however, what the less instructed seek is mere emotion. They are not concerned with the slow demanding generosity of genuine experience.[1]

These are the words of Ruth Burrows, a Carmelite nun, and she stands, of course, within a larger tradition which has at times and for religious reasons taken a rather severe view of the value of emotional experience. In this chapter I want to consider some of the ways in which Burrows and others have thought that emotional experience may prove disruptive of religious understanding. This exercise will also provide an opportunity to formulate some of the central themes of this book with new nuance.

TWO OBJECTIONS TO THE EMOTIONS

In the passage above, Burrows identifies two kinds of difficulty for the emotions in the 'spiritual life'. She is concerned both with the transiency of their impact and also with the tendency of the spiritually immature to 'seek' 'mere emotion'. Let's begin by considering these objections in turn. We have already encountered the thought that one test of the authenticity of a religious emotion is its tendency to give rise to enduring behavioural change. Jonathan Edwards notes that the Holy Spirit's action in the saints

---

1 Ruth Burrows, *Guidelines for Mystical Prayer* (London: Sheed and Ward, 1976), p. 55.

does not just produce new 'religious affections', but confers upon them a new, 'abiding principle of action'.[2] On this account, 'religious affections' are most evidently trustworthy when they are embedded within some larger and enduring change in a person's practice. To this extent, Edwards and Burrows are of one mind in looking for a 'living wisdom', rather than a passing state of emotional exaltation that makes no continuing difference to a person's concerns and commitments. I have been arguing, in addition, that this sort of 'living wisdom' may be realised in an affectively toned apprehension of the import of 'doctrine'. On this view, it is not that authentic religious affections are merely associated with a change of behavioural orientation, or even that they simply cause such a change by having some mysterious, not further specifiable impact on the springs of action. Rather, emotional feelings can shape the personality, and its activities, in fundamental ways, by virtue of their status as forms of understanding. We have explored various ways of giving further content to this proposal. For instance, by taking on a new, affectively toned understanding of some religious teaching, I may come to inhabit a correlative 'affective world', and thereby I may come to recognise new patterns of salience in the sensory world; and thereby I may take on a new motivational state, so that what is believed serves, as Burrows says, as a 'principle of action'.

Gaita's description of the nun offers an illustration of some of these connections. Because of what she believes 'in her heart', she sees the humanity of the patients on the ward 'in depth', or with proper salience, and thereby she is able to act towards them in the ways that Gaita finds so remarkable. Once more, we can understand the possibility of this sort of cognitive-affective-behavioural gestalt by supposing that genuine emotional feelings (as distinct from what Burrows calls 'mere emotions') are tied to action because their intentionality involves an awareness of the directedness of the whole body towards its surroundings. Moreover, the kind of affectively toned sensitivity that the nun displays is, I take it, the hard-won fruit of experience: this sort of understanding cannot be communicated in merely verbal or 'notional' terms, but requires instead continuing engagement with the phenomena, of the kind that will enable the formation of appropriate habits of seeing. In all of these ways, the emotional feelings with which we have been centrally concerned in this book amount to ways of being in the world: they are not just transient states of consciousness, but integral to the enacted identity of the person.

---

2 Jonathan Edwards, 'Religious Affections', in C. H. Faust and T. H. Johnson (eds.), *Jonathan Edwards: Representative Selections* (New York: Hill & Wang, 1962), p. 234.

Burrows's second concern is that the spiritually uninitiated sometimes 'seek' 'mere emotion'. Part of the problem here is, I take it, that the emotions are being sought for themselves, perhaps because they have a pleasant 'feel', or because they are thought to signify spiritual advancement of some sort. The first approach seems narcissistic, and the second to imply an interest in spiritual security of the kind that Burrows, along with many other spiritual writers, considers irreligious – because it can appear to involve the idea that I 'deserve' God's favour, or at any rate to invite a kind of pride in the self's spiritual achievements, or the thought that my standing with God is in some way guaranteed by the experience. As Rowan Williams comments, summarising the view of St John of the Cross (and the Carmelite tradition within which Ruth Burrows stands): '*no* "spiritual" experience whatsoever can provide a clear security, an unambiguous sign of God's favour'.[3]

David Pugmire notes how motives of both these kinds may be at work when affects are artificially produced in other, non-religious contexts. There are, he says, 'attractions of mode as well as of content: the fervent, the intense, the gripping, the consuming, the jarring, the delicate, the fleeting, the glowing, the strange, the sweet, the dark'.[4] So for these various reasons a person may seek to experience a certain emotion for the sake of its phenomenological feel. As Pugmire's references to states of 'fervour' and 'intensity' suggest, it is not difficult to imagine someone being drawn to certain kinds of religious experience for this sort of reason. (Compare too the interest in transcendental meditation techniques in cases in which a particular state of mind is cultivated for the sake of its phenomenological feel.) This first kind of possibility Pugmire labels 'narcissistic'. He describes a second reason for manufacturing emotions in these terms:

The character of my emotion can place me at an advantage, morally or socially, or it can console me or reassure me about the kind of person I am. Where a particular emotion is wanted out of a concern for one's lodgment in the world or for self-regard, the motive could be termed Dramaturgical.[5]

---

3 Rowan Williams, *The Wound of Knowledge: Christian Spirituality from the New Testament to St John of the Cross* (London: Darton, Longman and Todd, 1979), p. 173, Williams's italics. Burrows herself allows for a kind of certainty concerning God's favour in the final phase of the spiritual life, but here too it is not a matter of 'spiritual experience' serving as a simple, self-verifying condition of such certainty. She comments: 'though there is no seeing or feeling of God and his love and that he is pleased with me, there is a profound certainty': *Guidelines*, p. 124.
4 David Pugmire, *Rediscovering Emotion* (Edinburgh: Edinburgh University Press, 1998), p. 119.
5 *Ibid.*, p. 119.

Transferring these remarks to a religious context, a person might seek out the kind of emotional experience that is taken to signify closeness to God, as a way of buttressing their self-esteem, or with a view to securing their standing with God. Burrows notes a related phenomenon in Teresa of Avila's association of the emotional intensity of an experience with spiritual advancement: 'Teresa sees here a gradation: the more intense the emotional experience the deeper the prayer. It is this assessment of prayer by emotional intensity that we reject.'[6] Burrows is surely right on this point; and again the same perspective is set out clearly by Jonathan Edwards: 'It is', he says, 'no sign [of authenticity] one way or the other, that religious affections are very great, or raised very high.'[7] However, given the belief that there is a positive correlation between the affective charge of an experience and its claim to be accorded religious significance, it is to be expected that the dramaturgical motive will also be at work in religious contexts. As Burrows remarks: 'One of the main reasons why so few attain union with God is because people want these things [exalted emotional experiences] and seek them and take a secret pride in them.'[8] This second sort of reason for manufacturing religious emotions is particularly subversive of genuine piety because it involves pride, the emotion which Burrows, in common with a long theological tradition, sees as lying at the root of the various conditions which obstruct a person's relationship to God.[9]

The various forms of affective awareness with which we have been concerned in this book are not, I trust, of a narcissistic or dramaturgical kind: above all, we have been interested in the role of the emotions as modes of value perception, whether in relationship to God, other human beings, or the world as a whole (in Chapters 1, 2, and 3 respectively). This sort of affectively toned experience involves by its nature an other-centredness and a correlative humility, because it requires attentiveness to the goodness of realities external to the self, and a willingness therefore to allow those realities to become constitutive of the self's well being and determinative of its action. To this extent, the kind of experience with which we have been concerned seems to be free from the corrupting influence of both narcissistic and dramaturgical motives.

It might be objected: but aren't the people who cultivate emotions for dramaturgical and narcissistic kinds of reason often deceived about the

---

6 *Guidelines*, p. 52.   7 'Religious Affections', p. 227.
8 *Guidelines*, p. 52.
9 She comments: 'Pride and sloth together form the tap root from which the other sins branch out' (*ibid.*, p. 82).

real character of their experience? Indeed, in a religious context, don't narcissistic and dramaturgical emotions require their real origins to be disguised? After all, if I come to realise that my exalted, religiously informed affective state is the product of my desire for it, whether for narcissistic or dramaturgical reasons, then that state can hardly confer any religious consolation. On the contrary, in that case, I might well think that my spiritual life is pretty worthless, since it turns out to involve a kind of wish fulfilment rather than any genuine encounter with God. But can't we then press this difficulty: while it is true that the focus of this book has been with affective states which function as modes of value perception, how can we be sure that a particular candidate for this title is free from the influence of dramaturgical or narcissistic motives? And if we can't be sure, doesn't that suggest that we can't after all rely very much upon affectively constituted kinds of insight in the way that this book has proposed?

Burrows's scepticism about emotional experience is also fuelled, I think, by this sort of concern. She notes, for example, how easy it is for a self-deceiving 'autosuggestion' to take hold in religious communities once it is accepted that elevated emotional states are the marks of spiritual progress: 'You see this in communities, especially enclosed communities. If an influential person within it – a prioress or some other with a personal ascendancy – goes in for "experiences in prayer", esteems them and communicates her esteem, inevitably you will get an outbreak of them. Quite innocently others will produce them. They will become the "thing", the sign of an authentic mystical life.'[10] In such cases, people are in the grip of unconscious motivation: they do not grasp the fabricated nature of their experiences, or their reasons for wanting them. A similar sort of objection might be pressed in relation to Newman's account of affectively toned experience of God. Newman is talking of how, in our moral experience, we take ourselves to be accountable to a non-mundane judge whose presence is felt to be inescapable. But post-Freud, why should we not suppose that Newman has not grasped the real meaning of his experience – why should we not see it as really an experience of the voice of an introjected parental authority figure? This is not directly a case of a dramaturgical or narcissistic motive shaping the character of the emotions (though such motives may be involved); but here again the real source of the experience remains unrecognised.

10 *Ibid.*, p. 51.

Burrows goes so far as to suppose that even Saint Teresa's experiences of mystical rapture are to be understood in such terms:

She does not seem to have been of a contemplative temperament, one who could be walled up in her cell and find in God all she needed. She was not naturally passive. Her psychic pressures forced her, wholly unconsciously, to manufacture 'experience'.[11]

What are we to make of the objection that our affective experience may be the product of unconscious forces, especially, perhaps, in matters of religion, where the pull of narcissistic and even more dramaturgical motivations may be particularly strong?[12]

THE PROBLEM OF UNCONSCIOUSLY MOTIVATED

EMOTIONAL EXPERIENCE

Clearly, the problem of unconscious motivation is not peculiar to religiously informed value commitments. The same issues also arise in connection with our discernment of ethical values, and our ability to grasp the real meaning of everyday choices. In this spirit, John Cottingham has argued powerfully that the whole tradition of western ratiocentric ethical reflection is vulnerable to critique on account of its failure to reckon seriously with the kinds of blindness and insight that are the concern of psychoanalytic therapies:

in the key areas of human passion and emotion, when it comes to anger, jealousy, fear, ambition and sexual desire, linear rationality seems to fail us. What is amiss is not just that we imperfectly understand the past causes and future consequences of what we are 'choosing' to do and why. For if the structure of our deepest feelings and desires is conditioned by the influences of the dormant past, to the extent that the significance of our actions and choices will often be opaque to us, then the very notion of rational deliberation as a guide to action seems shaky. Unless and until the past is reclaimed, unless we come to appreciate the significance of our past, and the role it plays in shaping our emotional lives, then the very idea of an ordered plan for the good life will have to be put on hold.[13]

11 *Ibid.*, p. 98. She does add directly: 'It does not diminish Teresa, it makes her all the greater as a torn and suffering woman.'
12 J. Kellenberger has suggested that religious understanding may involve a new perception of the meaning of things, which in turn may arise when certain unconscious motivations (having to do, for example, with shoring up a favoured sense of self-identity) are set aside. See Kellenberger, *The Cognitivity of Religion: Three Perspectives* (Basingstoke: Macmillan, 1985), Chapter 2. Clearly, this perspective is animated by the same kinds of questions that I am seeking to address here.
13 John Cottingham, *Philosophy and the Good Life: Reason and the Passions in Greek, Cartesian and Psychoanalytic Ethics* (Cambridge: Cambridge University Press, 1998), p. 135.

We are considering the problem of unconsciously motivated emotional experience, and the objection that such motivation may render the emotions unreliable as sources of understanding. But as Cottingham's remarks make clear, the solution to this difficulty can hardly lie with giving up on our 'deepest feelings and desires', and retreating to an ideal of 'pure' practical reason, unadulterated by emotional feeling. For reason itself is put at risk by the same phenomenon: as he says, these considerations mean that 'the very notion of rational deliberation as a guide to action seems shaky'. This is because however much reason may try to weigh the various issues which seem relevant in choices of love, friendship, career, or any other life commitment, it may not see the real import of the information with which it is presented. As Cottingham points out, even Kant's supremely 'rational' approach to ethical decision-making may be vulnerable to this sort of objection. Speaking of the categorical imperative, he comments: 'the nagging suspicion begins to surface that the very rigidity of its authority, its very harshness, may turn out to be a complex outgrowth from infantile reactions to parental power, operating in a way that is inherently inimical to the possibility of true rational autonomy'.[14] (Here we might compare again Newman's treatment of conscience.)

If all of this is so, then the objection to the cognitive status of emotional feeling that we are considering can be turned aside to this extent: if emotional feelings are subject to unconscious motivation in this fashion, then that will have a pervasive influence upon our ability to engage in practical reasoning; and the only solution, therefore, is not to give up on emotional feelings, or 'our deepest feelings and desires', but to examine them with renewed urgency, as a precondition of getting our lives in good practical order. Cottingham has his own views about how we might attain a larger awareness of this sort, one that embraces the emotions and will prevent 'reason' from becoming the prisoner of meanings which it does not properly apprehend. He proposes that we need a 'Full self-awareness', which 'must involve more than widening the scope of deliberative reason; it requires a new *kind* of understanding, one mediated not by the grasp of the controlling intellect, but by a responsiveness to the rhythms of the whole self.'[15] Or again, he comments:

There is an intense *anxiousness* that such [ratiocentric] models betray – the fear that unless reason remains fussily and tensely at the helm, our lives will lose direction. Yet even a moment's reflection should reveal that what most gives our lives direction – the springs of human creativity, inventiveness and imagination –

14 *Ibid.*, p. 137.   15 *Ibid.*, p. 163, Cottingham's italics.

are in an important sense beyond reason's power wholly to encompass and regulate . . . Yet for all that, many try to cling to the image of themselves as thinking beings who are always 'in charge', who are somehow *directing* their thought-processes from beginning to end.[16]

These two passages suggest in turn that we need to do two things if we are to free the deliberations of the conscious, logical mind from unwholesome, unacknowledged conditioning by our feelings and desires. First of all, we need a mode of understanding that is responsive to 'the rhythms of the whole self'; and secondly, we need at some level to 'let go', to give up the fiction that we 'direct' the working of our imagination and other thought processes 'from beginning to end'. Let's consider these recommendations in turn. I am not suggesting that Cottingham's comments offer a full response to the problem of unconscious motivation (or that he intends them to do so), but they provide the beginnings of a response, by noting how we can become more fully aware of the ways in which ordinary processes of ratiocination may be conditioned by factors whose nature and operation may elude the perspective of the analytical intelligence.

Attending to emotional feelings offers one way of becoming aware of Cottingham's 'whole self', because by means of such feelings we apprehend not just a state of the discursive intellect, but the attitude that is struck by the whole body in its dealings with the world. Robert Roberts offers a helpful way of developing this kind of perspective. Emotional feelings are, he suggests, forms of self-perception, where again the self with which we are here concerned is not just the ratiocentric self, but Cottingham's 'whole self' – that is, the self considered as a bundle of emotional and other commitments, with their own history and significance:

If emotions are states of the self, and indeed states quite directly related to the self's core, and the feeling of an emotion is a conscious, quasi-perceptual awareness of being in such a state, it would seem that emotional feelings are a very special and important form of self-knowledge. To the extent that we are 'out of touch with our feelings' (for 'feelings' read 'emotions'; for 'be in touch with' read 'feel') – to the extent that we do not feel the resentment, envy, anxiety, and fear that characterize us or do feel a compassion, joy and gratitude that do not characterize us; to the extent that the objects of the emotions we feel are not quite the objects of our real emotions – to that extent we are blind to ourselves.[17]

16 *Ibid.*, p. 164, Cottingham's italics.
17 Robert Roberts, *Emotions: An Essay in Aid of Moral Psychology* (Cambridge: Cambridge University Press, 2003), p. 325.

This understanding of emotional feelings coheres closely with the account that we have been developing in this book. It acknowledges the intentional content of emotional feelings (they are genuinely about something), and it recognises in particular that they involve an awareness of the 'core' self and its embodied (or emotional) stance in relation to the world. And this is a reason for thinking that attending to emotional feeling offers a route to the larger self-knowledge to which Cottingham refers. Moreover, as we have seen in other connections, the kind of understanding that is achieved in emotional feeling is akin to pattern recognition: feelings provide not so much an additional bit of information as a way of setting that information in proper order, and grasping what it signifies. And the fact that one sees a certain significance in a body of information can be deeply revelatory of the self. This is because the pattern we see is more obviously something we contribute (but without being, as we have seen, a 'mere projection'). How you read the facts about your fellow human beings, for example, tells us a lot not just about what you know, but who you are. So for this reason too, attention to emotional feelings seems important for the wider self-understanding to which Cottingham refers.

We have been discussing the first of Cottingham's strategies for dealing with the fact that the operations of the conscious, logical mind are hedged about by other kinds of meaning. I turn now to Cottingham's second recommendation. Here he suggests that it is important not just to understand the 'whole self' but in a way to surrender to it, by ceasing to try to 'direct' our 'thought-processes from beginning to end'. There is a sense in which we have no choice about not directing the process of conscious reflection 'from beginning to end'. When I think through even the simplest train of thought I am dependent upon ideas coming to me in due order, where their coming is not, and cannot be, simply at the bidding of the conscious, ratiocentric self. After all, as I work through the train of thought, I do not keep all the various steps before my conscious mind, and then place them more centrally in my awareness at the point required for the unfolding of the argument. Even if I could do this, I would still be dependent upon the non-conscious mind supplying me with all the elements to hold in awareness in the first place. But of course this is not the way in which we typically think: we actually show more trust than that, allowing each further thought to enter consciousness in turn.

While we do not in fact control our processes of thought from beginning to end, nonetheless we cling, Cottingham suggests, to an image of ourselves as capable of exercising this sort of control. We need then to give up the 'intense anxiousness' of ratiocentric approaches. One way of doing this is by acknowledging the role of emotional feelings as 'paradigms', which provide a supralogical guidance of our enquiries (see again de Sousa's discussion of this point). In acknowledging the paradigmatic character of emotional feeings, we are not just subject to them unwittingly (the condition, perhaps, of those who cling to the ratiocentric image of the mind); instead, we allow ourselves to become conscious of their influence, and thereby recognise the ways in which they set the agenda for our thinking, and predispose us to reach certain conclusions rather than others. In so far as giving up the attempt to direct our thought processes from beginning to end takes this form, Cottingham's two projects will turn out to be related – because in heeding emotional feelings in this sort of way, we will also come to a better understanding of the 'whole self', since emotional feelings offer (I have argued) a mode of perception of the whole self. So, to summarise, both of Cottingham's proposed ways of saving 'reason' from the unwholesome unacknowledged influence of our 'deepest feelings and desires' suggest a need to attend to emotional feelings, and the importance of according such feelings epistemic significance.

THE THEOLOGICAL RESONANCES OF COTTINGHAM'S 'WIDER SELF'

The thought that we need to surrender to a 'larger self' which is not to be identified with the conscious, logical, directing mind has obvious theological analogues. William James writes that 'whatever it may be on its *farther* side, the "more" with which in religious experience we feel ourselves connected is on its *hither* side the subconscious continuation of our conscious life'.[18] And more generally, it has been, of course, a central theme of Christian reflection across the centuries that growth in the life of faith requires the progressive taking on of an identity that is not of our own making, but is given to us by a reality that lies beyond the conscious mind – but whose effects can be registered in the data of conscious experience. In thinking further about the theological resonances of Cottingham's project, we can take Ruth Burrows as our conversation partner once more. Her reflections on the spiritual life suggest one way of

---

18 William James, *The Varieties of Religious Experience: A Study in Human Nature* (London: Longmans, Green and Co., 1902), p. 512, James's italics.

enacting Cottingham's invitation to entrust ourselves to a more extensive self than the ratiocentric, controlling self of everyday experience. In the following passage, she is talking of the centrality of trust for faith:

> If we consider deeply what faith in God or faith in Jesus means we sense, though perhaps dimly, that it involves a total dying to self. St Paul points this out. By faith we 'die'. It means renouncing myself as my own base, my own centre, my own end. It means so casting myself on another, so making that other my raison d'être that it is, in truth, a death to the ego. The whole of the spiritual journey can be seen in terms of trust, growing in trust until one has lost oneself in God. But we are mistaken if we think that we can do this for ourselves. Not only can we not do it, we cannot even dream of what is meant by it, what it is like. True, we grasp the words: trust, giving, no confidence in self, poverty, humility . . . but they are words to us, though we think we really do grasp the concepts. What we are talking about is so much a part of our fabric that we cannot stand out of it and look on. It is our way of being to be our own centre, and we do not realise it until God begins to shift us. It is only one in whom God has worked profoundly who can see the difference. The rest have no yardstick.[19]

So the life of faith is a life of self-surrender: it means giving up 'being our own centre'. This project is potentially convergent, I suggest, with Cottingham's attempt to escape the ratiocentric perspective. The ideal of ratiocentric living, as Cottingham characterises it, involves both an attempt to direct our lives by reference to the conscious, logically ordered reflections of the analytical intelligence, and a sense that our real self is to be found there. Both of these assumptions are challenged in Burrows's remarks. Let's take them in turn. The logical intellect is so limited, Burrows says, that from this perspective, we cannot even grasp the meaning of notions like 'trust' and 'giving' in ways that are relevant to the achievement of true selfhood. This is to set a pretty radical restriction on the role of the intellect in shaping our understanding of how we are to live. Burrows does not say that the deeper, supralogical understanding of these concepts needs to be affectively toned; but in the ways that are indicated by Newman (along with many of the other authors discussed in this book), this seems to be one particularly fruitful way of spelling out what is required.

Secondly, Burrows is challenging the assumption that the real self is to be identified with the will of ordinary experience, or what she calls here the 'ego'. These two themes are connected, of course. If we cannot recognise our own good by means of the discursive intellect, then we need to find another centre of activity that can move us towards personal

---

19 *Guidelines*, p. 59, Burrows's italics.

wholeness, and in moving us serve as the real centre of the self. Burrows sometimes associates this new centre with the unconscious regions of the self. For instance, quoting from a letter written to someone in the 'illuminative' or middle phase of the spiritual journey, she writes: 'He [Jesus] is showing himself to you at a depth within you that your consciousness – your senses, your emotions, your mind – simply cannot register. It is your deepest self that is seeing him . . . You can't forget him morning, noon or night and yet, poor little you, none of this is experienced "up above".'[20] Here the 'real me' seems to be (some part of) the unconscious mind. But as a person is led more deeply into the spiritual life, it is God, rather than some region of the self conceived in distinction from God, who is increasingly our real centre. Consider, for example, this remark made by one of Burrows's fellow Carmelites in conversation with her: 'Jesus has always been my music, but the music was all I noticed. I wasn't aware, before, that it was in some way "I" who played, or "I" who was the organ. But after he brought me to the third island [the final, 'unitive' phase of the spiritual life], I found this difference. He was now all. The music played of itself – there was *only* the music . . . Now myself had become him.' Or as another sister observes: 'I saw or realised in a mysterious way that *I* was not there. There was no "I".'[21] So here too Cottingham's proposals are reminiscent of Burrows's position, in as much as both challenge the identification of the real self with the conscious, logical, controlling mind.

Plainly Cottingham's project does not, as a matter of simple logic, issue in this theological vision. But the spiritual path which Burrows is describing, which can sound so far removed from any conventional understanding of the nature of human flourishing, comes into new focus when it is seen as broadly continuous with the kind of commitment that each of us needs to make, whether we are people of faith or not, if we are to address

---

20 *Ibid.*, p. 88.
21 *Ibid.*, pp. 120–1, Burrows's italics. Burrows notes with approval de Caussade's correlative distinction between the time when 'the soul lives in God' and the time when 'God lives in the soul' (*Guidelines*, p. 119). The passage appears in Jean-Pierre de Caussade, *Self Abandonment to Divine Providence*, tr. Algar Thorwold (Springfield, IL: Templegate, 1962), p. 41. The thought that the real centre of the self lies beyond the reach of conscious experience may seem to call into question the role I assigned to emotional feelings just now, when I suggested that they could function as modes of perception of Cottingham's 'whole self'. But even on Burrows's account, emotional feelings can still be seen as a kind of self-perception, where the self that is perceived is not God but a relatively deep region of the person, concerned with fundamental life commitments, and correlative ways of seeing things. This sort of self-knowledge seems essential for the spiritual journey she describes.

the predicament that Cottingham has identified.[22] Moreover, the theological rendering of this commitment may be particularly powerful for two reasons. First of all, in the theological context, the 'real centre' in which we are being invited to trust is characterised in terms which ensure that our trust is merited. Trust in something less than God (the workings of the self considered simply as a biological organism, for instance) may be merited too, but in the nature of the case, the object of this sort of confidence cannot be quite so trustworthy. And secondly, the theological tradition contains a rich repository of materials for living out the kind of recentring of the self that Cottingham takes to be necessary. Again, this is no easy matter: what is needed is not simply the comprehension of some discursive thought, but the taking on of an appropriate pattern of life and associated mental discipline – and an individual is unlikely to have the moral or intellectual resources to contrive such a life for themselves. One example of the sort of thing that is required is provided by Ignatius' *Spiritual Exercises*. Here the self is recentred, and its affections reordered, by way of a succession of exercises involving imagination and repetition: it is not fundamentally the ratiocentric self that is being addressed in this process, but the deeper self, what we might call (following Barnard and Teasdale) the implicational self, whose meanings are not stored up in propositional form, but are accessible to feeling.[23]

CONCLUDING THOUGHTS

Drawing on some remarks of John Cottingham, I have been exploring the thought that emotional feelings are properly part of the spiritual life, notwithstanding the reservations voiced by Burrows and others. In general, while Burrows's rhetoric is often hostile to feeling, I suspect that this

---

22 This thought is perhaps relevant to Martha Nussbaum's objections to Christian (and especially Augustinian) versions of the Platonic ascent (to which Burrows's scheme is clearly an heir). She argues that on this approach, there remains a 'profound shame' of 'a very fundamental element of our humanity – our independence . . . ': Nussbaum, *Upheavals of Thought: The Intelligence of Emotions* (Cambridge: Cambridge University Press, 2001), p. 556. The kind of surrendering of independence that Burrows is discussing is arguably one that must be undertaken by anyone if they are to flourish as a human being, whether or not they take this exercise to be a matter of surrendering the will to God. From this perspective, we need to give up our 'independence' not so much because it is 'shameful' as because it involves no true freedom, but a sort of illusion. Moreover, I do not find in Burrows's text any trace of the disparagement of mundane experience, especially sexual experience, that Nussbaum associates with the Augustinian 'ascent'.
23 See *The Spiritual Exercises of Saint Ignatius of Loyola*, tr. W. H. Longridge, 2nd edn (London: Robert Scott, 1922). Ignatius is explicit that the exercises are designed to enable the retreatant to 'feel an interior knowledge' of religious truth (see, for example, p. 64), and to this end each of the senses in turn is invoked to place oneself imaginatively in various gospel and other scenes.

is partly because she is engaged in a polemic against a particular reading of the significance of feelings for the spiritual life – the reading that would leave the emotions open to narcissistic and dramaturgical kinds of abuse. Although she does not articulate the thought, perhaps for these reasons, I think that her position requires a central and enduring role for feeling in at least two respects. First of all, while she is emphatic that no emotional experience is a sure mark of spiritual standing, of itself this view implies the adoption of an affectively toned stance. For instance, she writes that: 'God's touch always produces humility, always, automatically. But all too often these overflows [of exalted feeling] are a source of secret complacency and self-esteem. In reality, they have no positive value.'[24] Similarly, she remarks of prayertime: 'What I feel afterwards is relatively unimportant, but whatever is important in it flows from this time of humble, empty waiting on God.'[25] Once again, the real target of her objection is feeling of a certain kind read a certain way: namely, intense feeling, taken as a source of self-satisfaction. But the states to which she opposes such high-flown feeling are themselves dispositions of character the living out of which surely implies a certain kind of affective responsiveness. What is it to wait on God in emptiness, or to live humbly, if not to relate oneself to other people in the sort of open-handed way that is modelled by the nun in Gaita's example? More generally, the perspective of 'lived nothingness' to which Burrows refers implies, certainly, the renunciation of various emotions (pride, for example), and the renunciation of various interpretations of states of feeling (for instance, the view that a certain intense experience signals spiritual achievement), but thereby it signals a radical reordering of affect, rather than its negation.[26] On Burrows's kind of view, our basic construal of the world, and of our own selves, should be that all of this comes from a centre not our own, and is therefore to be read as gift: and the enactment of such a construal will surely require a correlative affectively toned responsiveness, one which will enable us to see things with proper salience. Moreover, the process of coming to adopt this perspective will also have, surely, a strongly affective dimension, because it implies a profound un-selfing, a giving up of familiar sources of security and identity.

Secondly, as we have seen, Burrows thinks that even notions such as 'trust', as they apply in the spiritual life, cannot be properly understood in discursive terms alone. And the same is presumably true of the term 'God'

---

24 *Guidelines*, p. 52.   25 *Ibid.*, p. 43.
26 The quoted expression appears *ibid.*, p. 122.

– just as grasping the nature of the trust that is implied in drawing close to God requires relevant first-hand experience, so presumably understanding the God who is revealed in such trust requires relevant first-hand experience. And since this is, once more, a matter of vulnerable self-surrender, we may add that the kind of experience that is at issue here is affectively conditioned.[27] And besides, since God is the magnetic, all-consuming centre around which Burrows's life is organised, it seems that 'God' for her must signify more than 'first cause', or in general, more than can be communicated in purely discursive terms. So we have good reason to think that the concept of God, as it figures in Burrows's reflections, is affectively conditioned. The importance of such conditioning has been a central theme of this book, but let me offer a final illustration of what is being proposed. Exploring the foundations of our moral scheme, Leon Kass remarks that: 'In crucial cases . . . *repugnance* is the emotional expression of deep *wisdom*, beyond reason's power fully to articulate it. Can anyone really give an argument fully adequate to the horror which is father–daughter incest (even with consent), or . . . mutilating a corpse, or eating human flesh, or even just (just!) raping or murdering another human being?'[28] In other words, the full value significance of these various activities is not discernible from the standpoint of discursive reason alone; the real meaning of such activities (the 'pattern' that is presented by the 'facts') is evident in, and only in, the affectively toned perception that is afforded in the response of repugnance. Similarly, I suggest that, for Burrows, the real meaning of the reality we call God is given in certain affectively toned responses to that reality, and not otherwise fully communicable. This is because, as with murder or corpse mutilation, only more so, we are dealing here with a deep, encompassing value, the full recognition of which calls for an appropriate alignment of the whole self, in its bodily-intellectual-affective integrity.

In this chapter, I have been trying to respond to a certain theological critique of the religious significance of feeling. It is a critique whose central claims are well worth hearing. They apply with full force against

---

27 Notice, however, that Burrows is sceptical of the idea of experience of God: 'it must be emphasised that what is experienced is not God, for God cannot be held within the limits of humanity' (*ibid.*, p. 142). And she continues: 'All the feelings and effects are on our side.' However, this perspective seems consistent with the thought that our experience, while not of God's real essence (because 'God cannot be held within the limits of humanity'), is nonetheless of God (compare our everyday experience of water, which does not involve seeing its atomic structure).

28 Leon Kass, 'The Wisdom of Repugnance', *New Republic* 216 (Issue 22, 6 February 1997), accessed online, Kass's italics.

the position taken by a figure like Richard Rolle, whose conception of the relationship between feeling and faith has been summarised in these terms:

Because of Rolle's straightforward identification between the sensation of loving God and the reality, he cannot help but make the sensation something to be deliberately aimed at and cultivated: we are to 'try to feel his love'. And the feeling in turn becomes our guide: we are 'led by sweetness', and this guidance is taken to be infallible. It is easy to see why his critics thought that Rolle was simply abandoning people to their own subjective opinions about life. And Rolle himself certainly acted on his own criterion: he opted for a solitary life, for instance, because he found that the presence of other people interfered with his 'joy'.[29]

While this book has tried to identify various ways in which emotional feeling may contribute positively to religious understanding, it is not committed to Rolle's vision. On the contrary, his approach seems to imply the kind of narcissistic and perhaps dramaturgical use of the emotions which I have taken to be corruptions of genuine religious feeling. I have been arguing that, contrary to Rolle's example, we can take emotional feelings to be cognitively important without supposing that they are important in proportion to the degree of their felt intensity, or that they are to be cultivated for their own sake, or that they invite the kind of self-absorption that is reflected in his decision to withdraw from the world. Nor need they imply mere 'subjectivism' and the forsaking of 'doctrine'.[30] The burden of this book has been that, on the contrary, emotional feelings can provide tradition-grounded ways of reading doctrines in depth, so that they acquire action-guiding force, and take root in a larger self 'of which our intellectualizing is only the thinnest of surfaces'.[31] In these ways, emotional feelings are indispensable to the life of faith both cognitively and practically. Indeed, they point to a mode of understanding which is at once both cognitive and practical – one in which perception, conception, and feeling are bound together inseparably.

29 Simon Tugwell, O. P., *Ways of Imperfection: An Exploration of Christian Spirituality* (London: Darton, Longman and Todd, 1984), p. 164.
30 Like Tugwell, Denys Turner has objected to an 'experientialist', subjectivist, emotionally focused reading of the medieval 'mystical' tradition. While not addressing all his concerns, the position we have been exploring does suggest that a more judicious appeal to the emotions need not imply the privatisation of religion, or a severing of its connections with doctrinal and liturgical context. See Turner, *The Darkness of God: Negativity in Christian Mysticism* (Cambridge: Cambridge University Press, 1995).
31 Cottingham, *Philosophy and the Good Life*, p. 165.

Bibliography

Abraham, W. *An Introduction to the Philosophy of Religion* (Englewood Cliffs, NJ: Prentice-Hall, 1985).

Abrams, M. H. *The Mirror and the Lamp: Romantic Theory and the Critical Tradition* (Oxford: Oxford University Press, 1953).

Adams, R. M. 'Pure Love', in *The Virtue of Faith and Other Essays in Philosophical Theology* (New York: Oxford University Press, 1987), pp. 9–24.

Alston, W. *Perceiving God: The Epistemology of Religious Experience* (Ithaca, NY: Cornell University Press, 1991).

Anselm, St. *Proslogion*, in *The Prayers and Meditations of St Anselm with the Proslogion*, tr. B. Ward (Harmondsworth: Penguin, 1973), pp. 238–67.

Blackburn, S. 'Reply: Rule-Following and Moral Realism', in Holtzmann and Leich (eds.), *Wittgenstein: To Follow a Rule*, pp. 163–87.

Ruling Passions: A Theory of Practical Reasoning (Oxford: Clarendon Press, 1998).

Blum, L. *Moral Perception and Particularity* (Cambridge: Cambridge University Press, 1994).

Blumenfeld, D. 'On the Compossibility of the Divine Attributes', in T. V. Morris (ed.), *The Concept of God* (Oxford: Oxford University Press, 1987), pp. 201–16.

Bonaventure, St. *The Soul's Journey into God*, in *Bonaventure, The Soul's Journey into God; The Tree of Life; The Life of St. Francis*, tr. E. Cousins (Mahwah, NJ: Paulist Press, 1978).

Brandt, R. B. *The Philosophy of Schleiermacher: The Development of his Theory of Scientific and Religious Knowledge* (Westport, CT: Greenwood Press, 1941).

Budd, M. *Music and the Emotions: The Philosophical Theories* (London: Routledge & Kegan Paul, 1985).

Burrows, R. *Guidelines for Mystical Prayer* (London: Sheed and Ward, 1976).

Byrne, P. *Philosophical and Ethical Problems in Mental Handicap* (Basingstoke: Macmillan, 2000).

The Philosophical and Theological Foundations of Ethics: An Introduction to Moral Theory and its Relation to Religious Belief (Basingstoke: Macmillan, 1992).

Capra, F. *The Tao of Physics: An Exploration of the Parallels between Modern Physics and Eastern Mysticism*, 3rd edn (London: Flamingo, 1992).

Caussade, J.-P. De *Self Abandonment to Divine Providence*, tr. A. Thorwold (Springfield, IL: Templegate, 1962).

Coleridge, S. T. 'Dejection: An Ode', in H. J. Jackson (ed.), *Samuel Taylor Coleridge* (Oxford: Oxford University Press, 1985), pp. 113–17.

Cottingham, J. *Philosophy and the Good Life: Reason and the Passions in Greek, Cartesian and Psychoanalytic Ethics* (Cambridge: Cambridge University Press, 1998).

Damasio, A. *Descartes' Error: Emotion, Reason and the Human Brain* (Basingstoke: Picador, 1995).

D'Arms, J. and Jacobson, D. 'The Significance of Recalcitrant Emotion (Or Anti-Quasijudgmentalism)', in Hatzimoysis (ed.), *Philosophy and the Emotions*, pp. 127–45.

Deigh, J. 'Cognitivism in the Theory of Emotions', *Ethics* 104 (1994), pp. 824–54.

De Sousa, R. 'The Rationality of Emotions', in A. Rorty (ed.), *Explaining Emotions* (Berkeley, CA: University of California Press, 1980), pp. 127–52.

Dufrenne, M. *The Phenomenology of Aesthetic Experience*, tr. E. S. Casey *et al.* (Evanston, IL: Northwestern University Press, 1973; first published in French 1953).

Edwards, J. 'Religious Affections', in C. H. Faust and T. H. Johnson (eds.), *Jonathan Edwards: Representative Selections* (New York: Hill & Wang, 1962), pp. 206–54.

Eliade, M. 'Divinities: Art and the Divine', in D. Apostolos-Cappadona (ed.), *Mircea Eliade: Symbolism, the Sacred and the Arts* (New York: Crossroad, 1985), pp. 55–63.

Fox, M. A. 'The Moral Community', in La Follette (ed.), *Ethics in Practice*, pp. 127–38.

Gaita, R. *A Common Humanity: Thinking about Love and Truth and Justice* (Melbourne: The Text Publishing Company, 2000).

Good and Evil: An Absolute Conception (Basingstoke: Macmillan, 1991).

'Is Religion an Infantile Morality?', in Phillips (ed.), *Religion and Morality*, pp. 3–38.

Romulus, My Father (Melbourne: Text Publishing, 1998).

Goldie, P. *The Emotions: A Philosophical Exploration* (Oxford: Oxford University Press, 2000).

Goldman, A. *Aesthetic Value* (Boulder, CO: Westview Press, 1995).

Goodman, N. *Languages of Art: An Approach to a Theory of Symbols* (London: Oxford University Press, 1969).

Greenspan, P. 'Emotions, Rationality, and Mind/Body', in Hatzimoysis (ed.), *Philosophy and the Emotions*, pp. 113–25.

Hadot, P. *Philosophy as a Way of Life: Spiritual Exercises from Socrates to Foucault*, tr. M. Chase (Oxford: Blackwell, 1995).

Hatzimoysis, A. 'Emotional Feelings and Intentionalism', in Hatzimoysis (ed.), *Philosophy and the Emotions*, pp. 105–11.

Philosophy and the Emotions (Cambridge: Cambridge University Press, 2003).

Holtzmann, S. and Leich, C. (eds.). *Wittgenstein: To Follow a Rule* (London: Routledge & Kegan Paul, 1981).

Homer. *Odyssey*, tr. W. Shewring (Oxford: Oxford University Press, 1980).

Hume, D. *Enquiries Concerning Human Understanding and Concerning the Principles of Morals*, ed. L. A. Selby-Bigge, 3rd edn revised by P. H. Nidditch (Oxford: Clarendon Press, 1975).

A Treatise of Human Nature, ed. L. A. Selby-Bigge, 2nd edn revised by P. H. Nidditch (Oxford: Clarendon Press, 1978).

Ignatius of Loyola. *The Spiritual Exercises of Saint Ignatius of Loyola*, tr. W. H. Longridge, 2nd edn (London: Robert Scott, 1922).

James, W. 'The Sentiment of Rationality', in William James, *Essays in Pragmatism* (New York: Hafner Press, 1948), pp. 3–36.

The Varieties of Religious Experience: A Study in Human Nature (London: Longmans, Green and Co., 1902).

'The Will to Believe', in *The Will to Believe and Other Essays in Popular Philosophy* (Cambridge, MA: Harvard University Press, 1979), pp. 13–33.

Järveläinen, P. *A Study on Religious Emotions* (Helsinki: Luther-Agricola-Society, 2000).

John Paul II. *Fides et Ratio* (Sydney: St Paul's Publications, 1998).

Kant, I. *Foundations of the Metaphysics of Morals*, tr. L. W. Beck, 2nd edn (Indianapolis, IN: Bobbs-Merrill, 1959).

Kass, L. 'The Wisdom of Repugnance', *New Republic* 216 (Issue 22, 6 February 1997).

Kellenberger, J. *The Cognitivity of Religion: Three Perspectives* (Basingstoke: Macmillan, 1985).

Kierkegaard, S. *Kierkegaard's Concluding Unscientific Postscript*, tr. D. Swenson and W. Lowrie (Princeton, NJ: Princeton University Press, 1968).

LaFollette, H. (ed.). *Ethics in Practice* (Oxford: Blackwell, 1997).

Lazarus, R. S. *Emotion and Adaptation* (New York: Oxford University Press, 1991).

LeDoux, J. *The Emotional Brain: The Mysterious Underpinnings of Emotional Life* (London: Phoenix, 1998).

Lienhardt, G. *Divinity and Experience. The Religion of the Dinka* (Oxford: Clarendon Press, 1961).

McDowell, J. 'Non-Cognitivism and Rule-Following', in Holtzmann and Leich (eds.), *Wittgenstein: To Follow a Rule*, pp. 141–62.

'Values and Secondary Qualities', in J. Rachels (ed.), *Ethical Theory* (Oxford: Oxford University Press, 1998), pp. 228–44.

MacIntyre, A. *Three Rival Versions of Moral Inquiry: Encyclopaedia, Genealogy, and Tradition* (London: Duckworth, 1990).

Macquarrie, J. Review of Ralph McInerny, *The Very Rich Hours of Jacques Maritain: A Spiritual Life* (University of Notre Dame Press), *Times Literary Supplement*, 27 February 2004 (No. 5265), p. 28.

Maddell, G. 'What Music Teaches about Emotion', *Philosophy* 71 (1996), pp. 63–82.

Maimonides, M. *The Guide for the Perplexed*, tr. M. Friedlander, 2nd edn (New York: Dover Publications, 1956).

Mavrodes, G. 'Religion and the Queerness of Morality', in L. Pojman (ed.), *Ethical Theory: Classical and Contemporary Readings*, 3rd edn (Belmont, CA: Wadsworth, 1998), pp. 649–56.

Merkur, D. *Powers which we Do Not Know: The Gods and Spirits of the Inuit* (Moscow, DE: University of Idaho Press, 1991).

Merleau-Ponty, M. *Phenomenology of Perception*, tr. C. Smith (London: Routledge & Kegan Paul, 1962).

Murdoch, I. *The Sovereignty of Good* (London: Ark, 1985).

Nerlich, G. *Values and Valuing: Speculations on the Ethical Lives of Persons* (Oxford: Clarendon Press, 1989).

Newman, J. H. *An Essay in Aid of a Grammar of Assent* (Notre Dame, IN: University of Notre Dame Press, 1979).

Nielsen, K. *Naturalism and Religion* (New York: Prometheus Books, 2001).

Nussbaum, M. *Love's Knowledge: Essays on Philosophy and Literature* (New York: Oxford University Press, 1990).

  Upheavals of Thought: The Intelligence of Emotions (Cambridge: Cambridge University Press, 2001).

Oatley, K. and Jenkins, J. *Understanding Emotions* (Oxford: Blackwell, 1996).

O'Hear, A. *Experience, Explanation and Faith* (London: Routledge & Kegan Paul, 1984).

Otto, R. *The Idea of the Holy: An Inquiry into the Non-Rational Factor in the Idea of the Divine and its Relation to the Rational*, tr. J. W. Harvey (Harmondsworth: Penguin Books, 1959).

Phillips, D. Z. (ed.). *Religion and Morality* (Basingstoke: Macmillan, 1996).

Pickard, H. 'Emotions and the Problem of Other Minds', in Hatzimoysis (ed.), *Philosophy and the Emotions*, pp. 87–103.

Plantinga, A. *Warranted Christian Belief* (New York: Oxford University Press, 2000).

Plato. *Phaedo*, tr. D. Gallop (Oxford: Oxford University Press, 1993).

Prinz, J. 'Emotion, Psychosemantics, and Embodied Appraisals', in Hatzimoysis (ed.), *Philosophy and the Emotions*, pp. 69–86.

Proust, M. *Remembrance of Things Past*, tr. C. K. Scott Moncreiff (2 vols., New York: Random House, 1934).

Pugmire, D. *Rediscovering Emotion* (Edinburgh: Edinburgh University Press, 1998).

Roberts, R. *Emotions: An Essay in Aid of Moral Psychology* (Cambridge: Cambridge University Press, 2003).

Rolston III, H. 'Does Nature Need to be Redeemed?', *Zygon: Journal of Religion and Science* 29 (1994), pp. 205–29.

  Philosophy Gone Wild (Buffalo, NY: Prometheus Books, 1989).

Ryle, G. 'Feelings', in *Collected Papers*, Vol. II (London: Hutchinson, 1971), pp. 272–86.

Schacht, R. 'Reply: Morality, Humanity, and Historicality: Remorse and Religion Revisited', in Phillips (ed.), *Religion and Morality*, pp. 39–55.

Schleiermacher, F. *On Religion: Speeches to its Cultured Despisers*, tr. Richard Crouter (Cambridge: Cambridge University Press, 1976).

Schopenhauer, A. *The World as Will and Representation*, tr. E. F. Payne (New York: Dover Publications, 1969).

Sherman, N. *The Fabric of Character: Aristotle's Theory of Virtue* (Oxford: Clarendon Press, 1989).

Sibley, F. 'Aesthetic Concepts', reprinted in J. Benson, B. Redfern, and J. Roxbee Cox (eds.), *Approach to Aesthetics: Collected Papers on Philosophical Aesthetics of Frank Sibley* (Oxford: Clarendon Press, 2001), pp. 1–23.

Singer, P. 'All Animals are Equal', in LaFollette (ed.), *Ethics in Practice*, pp. 116–26.

Smith, Q. *The Felt Meanings of the World: A Metaphysics of Feeling* (West Lafayette, IN: Purdue University Press, 1986).

Solomon, R. 'Emotions, Thoughts and Feelings: What is a "Cognitive Theory" of the Emotions, and Does it Neglect Affectivity?', in Hatzimoysis (ed.), *Philosophy and the Emotions*, pp. 1–18.

Soskice, J. M. 'Love and Attention', reprinted in P. Anderson and B. Clack (eds.), *Feminist Philosophy of Religion* (London: Routledge, 2003), pp. 199–209.

Stocker, R. with Hegeman, E. *Valuing Emotion* (Cambridge: Cambridge University Press, 1996).

Tanquerey, A. *The Spiritual Life: A Treatise on Ascetical and Mystical Theology*, tr. H. Branderis, 2nd edn (Tournai: Desclée et Cie, 1930).

Teasdale, J. D. and Barnard, P. J. *Affect, Cognition and Change: Re-Modelling Depressive Thought* (Hove: Lawrence Erlbaum Associates, 1993).

Tracy, D. 'The Religious Classic and the Classic of Art', in D. Apostolos-Cappadona (ed.), *Art, Creativity and the Sacred* (New York: Crossroad, 1984), pp. 236–49.

Tugwell, S. *Ways of Imperfection: An Exploration of Christian Spirituality* (London: Darton, Longman and Todd, 1984).

Turner, D. *The Darkness of God: Negativity in Christian Mysticism* (Cambridge: Cambridge University Press, 1995).

Wainwright, W. *Reason and the Heart: A Prolegomenon to a Critique of Passional Reason* (Ithaca, NY: Cornell University Press, 1995).

Ward, K. *Religion and Revelation: A Theology of Revelation in the World's Religions* (Oxford: Clarendon Press, 1994).

Weil, S. *Waiting on God*, tr. E. Craufurd (London: Routledge & Kegan Paul, 1979).

Wiggins, D. 'A Sensible Subjectivism', in S. Darwall, A. Gibbard, and P. Railton (eds.), *Moral Discourse and Practice: Some Philosophical Approaches* (Oxford: Oxford University Press, 1997), pp. 227–46.

Williams, B. and Smart, J. J. *Utilitarianism: For and Against* (London: Cambridge University Press, 1973).

Williams, R. '"Religious Realism": On Not Quite Agreeing with Don Cupitt', *Modern Theology* 1 (1984), pp. 3–24.

The Wound of Knowledge: Christian Spirituality from the New Testament to St John of the Cross (London: Darton, Longman and Todd, 1979).

Wisdom, J. 'Gods', in J. Wisdom, *Philosophy and Psychoanalysis* (Oxford: Blackwell, 1953), pp. 149–68.

Wynn, M. 'Musical Affects and the Life of Faith: Some Reflections on the Religious Potency of Music', *Faith and Philosophy* 21 (2004), pp. 25–44.

Index